D0240981

The Women and International Development Annual

VOLUME 3

WITHDRAWN
FROM

The Women and International Development Annual
Editorial Board

Bina Agarwal
Institute of Economic Growth, Delhi

Lourdes Arizpe
Centro Regional de Investigaciones
Multidisciplarias, Cuernavaca

Lourdes Beneria
Cornell University, Ithaca

Robert J. Berg
International Development Conference,
Washington

Judith Bruce
Population Council, New York

Mayra Buvinic
International Center for
Research on Women
(ICRW), Washington

Elsa Chaney
University of Iowa, Iowa City

Hemalata Dandekar
The University of Michigan, Ann Arbor

Carmen Diana Deere
University of Massachusetts, Amherst

Billie DeWalt
University of Kentucky, Lexington

Shelley Feldman
Cornell University, Ithaca

Cornelia Butler Flora
Virginia Poly-Technical Institute,
Blacksburg

Louise Fortmann
University of California, Berkeley

Jane I. Guyer
Boston University, Boston

Jane Jaquette
Occidental College, Los Angeles

Elizabeth Jelin
Buenos Aires

Eileen Kennedy
Cornell University, Ithaca

Joan Mencher
City University of New York, New York

Soheir Morsy
University of California, Berkeley

Christine Oppong
International Labour Office, Geneva

Hanna Papanek
Boston University, Boston

Pauline Peters
Harvard Institute of International
Development, Cambridge

Alejandro Portes
Johns Hopkins University, Baltimore

Helen Safa
University of Florida, Gainesville

Gita Sen
Centre for Development Studies,
Trivandarum

Marianne Schmink
University of Florida, Gainesville

Anita Spring
University of Florida, Gainesville

Kathleen Staudt
University of Texas, El Paso

Irene Tinker
University of California, Berkeley

Kathryn Ward
Southern Illinois University, Carbondale

The Women and International Development Annual
Rita S. Gallin and Anne Ferguson
Series Editors

This annual series uses a multidisciplinary approach to explore women's experiences across a wide range of geographical areas, economic sectors, and social institutions. The articles presented in each volume synthesize a growing body of literature on key issues, suggest priorities for research, and propose changes in development policy and programming. Each volume is divided into three major sections. In the first, contributors distill and interpret research in review articles; in the second—a trend report—they provide original analyses of existing data sets; and in the final section, they analyze a specific research concern from varying perspectives.

Rita S. Gallin is director of the Women and International Development Program and associate professor of sociology at Michigan State University. **Anne Ferguson,** an anthropologist, is the women and development specialist with the Bean/Cowpea Collaborative Research Support Program, an international agricultural program with projects in Africa and Latin America. **Janice Harper,** coeditor of Volume 3, is a graduate student of anthropology at Michigan State University.

Published in cooperation with the
Women and International Development Program
Michigan State University

The Women and International Development Annual

VOLUME 3

EDITED BY

Rita S. Gallin,
Anne Ferguson,
and Janice Harper

Westview Press

BOULDER · SAN FRANCISCO · OXFORD

This Westview softcover edition is printed on acid-free paper and bound in library-quality, coated covers that carry the highest rating of the National Association of State Textbook Administrators, in consultation with the Association of American Publishers and the Book Manufacturers' Institute.

All rights reserved. No part of this publication may be reproduced or transmitted in any form or by any means, electronic or mechanical, including photocopy, recording, or any information storage and retrieval system, without permission in writing from the publisher.

Copyright © 1993 by Westview Press, Inc.

Published in 1993 in the United States of America by Westview Press, Inc., 5500 Central Avenue, Boulder, Colorado 80301-2877, and in the United Kingdom by Westview Press, 36 Lonsdale Road, Summertown, Oxford OX2 7EW

ISSN 1045-893X
ISBN 0-8133-8512-1

Printed and bound in the United States of America

The paper used in this publication meets the requirements of the American National Standard for Permanence of Paper for Printed Library Materials Z39.48-1984.

10   9   8   7   6   5   4   3   2   1

Contents

PART III
FORUM: WOMEN IN THE CARIBBEAN

Acknowledgments

As in any collaboration, this volume would not have been completed without the efforts of many people. We wish to thank Rebecca Ritke of Westview Press for her thoughtful comments and the contributors, who produced fine original essays and willingly responded to suggestions for revisions. We are especially grateful to our colleagues in the Women and International Development Program at Michigan State University. Janet Owens, a latecomer to the project, prepared the index, proofed text, and provided crucial support. Laura Carantza coordinated the administration and preparation of the volume with a dedication hard to repay. Special thanks to her for her consistent good humor in the face of deadlines and continuing requests.

Rita S. Gallin
Anne Ferguson
Janice Harper

Introduction

The Plurality of Feminism:
Rethinking "Difference"

Rita S. Gallin and Anne Ferguson

The Women and International Development Annual

This volume is the third in a series of annual reviews which highlight the multiple approaches within the field of Women and International Development (WID). WID grew out of the recognition that the development process has different effects on women and men and that these effects are more negative for women than for men. On this foundation has grown a diversified field, whose membership includes university faculty and students, development planners in national and international governmental systems, practitioners in program implementing agencies, and activists working at the grassroots level in the developing world.

Women and International Development encompasses a variety of disciplines and theoretical approaches and addresses a range of topics on the diverse countries that make up the Third World. Thus far, the field has maintained its differences without separating into narrow specializations. Like the series, this volume is designed to enhance the existing dialogue and to provide a forum for communication among specialists working inside and outside academia. The goal of this series is to contribute to scholarly developments in the field and to changes in development policy and programming.

Each volume in the series contains an introductory essay which highlights a key issue in the field and provides an overview of the chapters. Individual chapters comprise three different types of essays: review articles, trend reports, and forums. Review essays seek to bridge the gap between theory and practice by surveying recent literature and suggesting proposals for research and for policy and programming alternatives. Trend reports address selected issues by assessing both the progress made in effecting changes in women's situation and the work still to be done. Forums examine single issues from a variety of perspectives to highlight different ways of thinking and doing.

In this third volume, the introductory essay includes a discussion of the concept "difference." This discussion is followed by an overview and comparison of the chapters--which deal with women as refugees, AIDS, structural adjustment, the United Nations Convention to End All Forms of Discrimination Against Women, and the diversity of women in Latin America and the Caribbean. In the concluding section of this introductory essay, we briefly consider the implications of the ideas offered in the volume for women's solidarity and action. We invite readers not only to comment on these ideas but also to suggest topics for future volumes.

The Concept of Difference

In Volume 2 of *The Women and International Development Annual*, the introductory essay included a discussion of gender--the nomenclature that recently had been introduced to the WID field. The purpose of that discussion was to highlight different ways of thinking and doing, a theme we had introduced in Volume 1 of this series. In Volume 3 we continue discussion of this theme by considering the notion of difference, a concept currently dominant in feminist thought.

Two disparate understandings of the concept exist. One interpretation emphasizes gender differences and focuses on the contrast between men and women. The other stresses the differences among women, with class, race, ethnicity, nationality, sexual orientation, and age identified as major axes of differentiation (Barrett 1987; Gordon 1991). We highlight these different understandings by exploring the plurality of feminism in the United States and Latin America. While a large body of literature exists on feminism in these areas, here we can explore only a small segment of this work.

United States Feminisms

A variety of separate feminisms exists in the United States. One variant, known as mainstream or "hegemonic" feminist theory (Sandoval 1991:1), consists largely of writings by white, middle-class women. The other version is labeled "third world feminism" (Mohanty 1991a; Sandoval 1991), where the term "third world" is used as "a sociopolitical designation for people of African, Caribbean, Asian, and Latin American descent . . . native peoples of the U.S. [and] 'new immigrants' to the U.S." (Mohanty 1991a:7). The term is often used interchangeably with the term "women of Color" (Mohanty 1991a; Anzaldua 1990; Trinh 1989; hooks 1984).[1]

Mainstream Feminism. Written largely by women working in universities, the literature on mainstream feminist thought approaches the question of difference in a number of nuanced ways. Here we discuss only three of these approaches: liberal, radical, and socialist feminisms.[2] Most feminists identify with one or the other of these three approaches, hence this choice.

(1) Liberal feminists deny that men and women are inherently different. In their view, women are as capable as men and their exclusion from opportunity has no biological reason. Rather, liberal feminists maintain, statutory and customary laws prevent women from realizing their full potential.[3] To improve their position and to allow them to compete with men on an equal basis, liberal feminists thus advocate the reform of political, legal, and social systems.

(2) Radical feminists, in contrast, focus on the differences between men and women and argue that patriarchy is the source of men's power over women and their sexuality.[4] Given this conviction, they insist that the reform of patriarchal legal and political systems will not win equality with men for women. Rather, in their view, women's subordination to men will be abolished only with the elimination of institutions such as the family.

(3) Socialist feminists, like radical feminists, focus on the differences between men and women. They maintain that women's condition is rooted in structures of production, reproduction, and socialization. Although their argument is seldom translated into practice, it implies that the relation of women to men and to capital will change only with the transformation of all systems of oppression.

Although each of these mainstream approaches has strengths, none is without its critics. Sandoval (1991:8), for example, argues that all three fail to incorporate an analysis of power relations--beyond gender relations--into their logic. These approaches also neglect race and class differences among women. (Even socialist feminism, which considers women's relationship to capital, ignores the way class can divide women.) These omissions, according to Baca Zinn and her colleagues (1986), are manifest in three ways. Race and class are considered secondary to women's universal subordination, are acknowledged but not incorporated into analyses, and are described but unexplained (see also Harding 1992).

Third World Feminism. "Third world feminism represents the political alliance made during the 1960s and 1970s between a generation of U.S. feminists of Color who were separated by culture, race, class, or gender identifications but united through similar responses to the experience of race oppression" (Sandoval 1991:17, note 3). They chose the term *third world feminism* for much the same reason that Walker (1983) coined the term *womanism*; they wanted to signal their commitment to egalitarian social relations, a commitment they felt that mainstream feminism had betrayed.

Some mainstream feminists have begun to respond to this critique by acknowledging the centrality of difference to feminist theory (see, for example, Morgen 1989). Nevertheless, in the view of most third world feminists, they continue to ignore two social facts: women of Color experience race, class, and gender subordination simultaneously, and women of Color are oppressed by members of their own groups as well as by whites of both genders (Hurtado 1989). Third world feminists further contend that mainstream feminists have failed to grasp how the simultaneous oppression of women of Color is experienced and resisted (Collins 1986; Wilkinson, Baca Zinn, and Chow 1992).

Hurtado (1989), a Chicana feminist, for example, shows how the intersection of race, class, and gender informs the way third world women come to know their social and political worlds. Commenting on the politics of personal life, she writes:

> Women of Color have not had the benefit of the economic conditions that underlie the public/private distinction. Instead the political consciousness of women of Color stems from an awareness that the public is *personally* political. Welfare programs and policies have discouraged family life, sterilization programs have restricted reproduction rights, government has drafted and armed disproportionate numbers of people of Color to fight its wars overseas, and locally, police forces and the criminal justice system arrest and incarcerate disproportionate numbers of people of Color. There is no such thing as a private sphere for people of Color except that which they manage to create and protect in an otherwise hostile environment (Hurtado 1989:849).

The social fact this excerpt illustrates is integrated into third world feminist thought. For example, Sandoval (1991:11) has created "a topography of consciousness which identifies . . . the modes the subordinated of the United States . . . claim as politicized and oppositional stances in resistance to domination."[5]   She argues that hierarchically-ordered societies create particular positions in which subordinates can function, and that these sites of oppression become sites of resistance with the emergence of consciousness.

According to Sandoval, third world feminism is grounded in a "differential consciousness" which imbues adherents "with the ability to read the current situation of power and to . . . self-consciously change and adopt the ideological form best suited to push against its configurations" (Sandoval 1991:15). She argues that, just as the clutch of a car allows drivers to shift gears, differential consciousness "permits the practitioner to choose tactical positions . . . that permit the achievement of coalition across differences" (Sandoval 1991:15).

In Sandoval's view, the different stances adopted by mainstream feminism "divide the [women's] movement of resistance from within, for each of these sites tends to generate sets of tactics, strategies, and identities which historically have appeared to be mutually exclusive" (Sandoval 1991:13). She thus sees third world feminism, with its grounding in "differential consciousness," as the only feminism with the ability to create grounds for unity across differences (Sandoval 1991:23/note 58).

Latin American Feminisms

The concept of difference is also central to feminism in the Third World. We limit our discussion, however, to Latin America and the Caribbean, the focal area of this volume's Forum. There, in contrast to the United States, discussions of gender differences and differences among women are situated within larger economic and political contexts. As Bunch and Carrillo (1991:73) argue, most women in Latin America see gender issues as a question of women's political participation and empowerment in the context of democracy, militarism, and class. The Forum in this volume, and other works (e.g., Jaquette 1991; Jelin 1990; and Safa 1990), illustrate this concept of difference.

Two recent works in particular (Sternbach et al. 1992 and Vargas 1992) highlight the way difference is manifest in the contemporary women's movement by considering the *Encuentros* (feminist encounters) which have taken place over the past decade in Latin America.[6] Descriptions of these meetings reveal two types of difference within the women's movement over time: those which exist between women and men within male-dominated opposition movements, such as leftist political parties and labor unions, and those which exist among women themselves in the women's movement.

Differences Between Women and Men in Opposition Movements. While some Latin American women were always committed to feminism, others came to it through participation in male-dominated organizations. They began their political careers in leftist movements which denounced broad forms of social, economic, and political oppression. Referred to as *politicas*, many of these women shared, with men in these organizations, the belief that gender subordination was a product of class division, and that it would disappear after the revolution (Sternbach et al. 1992:397).

The strong, early links between women and opposition movements left two legacies. First, although *politicas* theoretically considered broad processes of class formation to inform gender relations, many of them (and most of the feminists) were middle-class, academic women who held elitist views. As such, they considered themselves *the* vanguard of a mass-based, cross-class women's movement. Second, male-dominated opposition movements were sexist in practice. As a result, many *politicas* developed a feminist consciousness that recognized the role of reproduction in women's subordination. Nevertheless, they remained committed to radical change in social relations of production (Sternbach et al. 1992).

Differences Among Women in the Women's Movement. The diversity of the women's movement was evident at the early *Encuentros*, when several different views about women's subordination were debated. While *politicas* advocated the primacy of class as the seat of women's oppression, feminists emphasized women's reproductive role and the need to transform it. Taking a synthetic stand, *doble militancias* (double militants) embraced both goals as their own (Safa 1990, Sternbach et al. 1992, Vargas, 1992).[7]

This debate was widened at later *Encuentros*. For example, Black and indigenous feminists argued that women's lives are shaped by race as much as by class and gender and that, as a result, their lived experience is very different from that of white or *mestiza* women. White, middle-class feminists, they maintain, privilege gender and ignore the fact that women's consciousness emerges at the intersection of race, class, and gender, where it molds unique action.

Economic and political events in the region also sparked the growth of women's organizations, thereby expanding the boundaries of the movement. For example, debt reduction policies (such as structural adjustment) forced increasing numbers of women into poverty.[8] To maintain their domestic units, they organized collective survival strategies and resisted the authorities on a daily basis (Safa 1990). The rise of right-wing military dictatorships, accompanied by ever-growing violations of human rights, also functioned as a catalyst to action. To protest these atrocities, women mobilized and constructed numerous cross-class, oppositional movements.

By the fifth *Encuentro* (1990), the women's movement was politically and socially heterogeneous. Multi-racial and multi-class, it also included "women at different stages of feminist thought" (Sternbach et al. 1992:422) or, put another way, women with a *feminine* consciousness and women with a *feminist* consciousness. Singer explains this distinction by writing:

> The struggles against *carestia* [the rising cost of living] or for schools, day care centers, etc., as well as specific measures to protect women who work interest women closely and it is possible then to consider them *feminine* revindications. But they are not *feminist* to the extent that they do not question the way in which women are inserted into the social context (cited in Alvarez 1991:62, note 9).

These different ways of thinking have implications for praxis, as Molyneux (1985) clarifies. Feminine groups pursue *practical gender interests* that do not challenge gender subordination directly, while feminist groups pursue *strategic gender interests* that analyze women's subordination and develop an "alternative, more satisfactory set of arrangements to those which exist" (Molyneux 1985:232). Although this feminine/feminist contrast suggests that women's different interests are immutable, Safa (1990) intimates otherwise. In her view, women's struggles over practical interests may well be transformed into struggles over strategic gender issues in the process of collective action and politicization.

Summary

In summary, white middle-class feminism in both the United States and Latin America is increasingly being challenged by women of Color, who insist that gender be situated at the intersection of class and race. Their call for the expansion of theory and praxis has created a number of feminisms that mirror women's different realities. We explore the implications of these multiple feminisms, the progeny of difference, in the concluding section of this essay.

Review Articles

Though women make up the largest proportion of the world refugee population, they are under-represented in the refugee literature. Pamela A. DeVoe, an anthropologist, focuses on this problem in her chapter, "The Silent Majority: Women as Refugees." Concentrating on Southeast Asian refugees in the United States, she examines the literature on three phases of the refugee experience: the flight from the homeland, the period spent in refugee camps, and resettlement in the host country.

DeVoe shows that the first two phases are fraught with uncertainty and trauma: in the first instance, pirates often physically and sexually abuse women, while in the second, androcentric programs distribute resources to the benefit of men and at the expense of women.

DeVoe then turns to the large body of literature on the adjustment of Southeast Asian refugees in the United States. Among the topics she considers are women's participation in the labor force and the role of age, ethnicity, family, and gender asymmetry in women's adaptation. DeVoe finds a number of contradictions in this literature and concludes by offering suggestions for additional research that have implications for theory and practice.

In the chapter that follows, "Gender, Development, and AIDS: A Political Economy and Cultural Framework," anthropologist Brooke Grundfest Schoepf argues that AIDS is understandable only in the context of gender relations and development and underdevelopment. Focusing on Africa, she shows how the contemporary economic crisis in a setting marked by pervasive gender inequality has made women particularly vulnerable to the HIV virus. In Schoepf's view, the barriers that deny women control over their own sexual decisions must be eliminated in order to check the spread of AIDS.

Many of these barriers could be overcome, Schoepf maintains, if people were empowered to change their sexual behavior and the social relations in which their actions are embedded. Toward this end, she calls for action-based research in which problem-posing methods are used to fashion more egalitarian behaviors than currently exist. In the absence of such research and in the presence of the refusal by many to see AIDS in the context of gender relations and empowerment, Schoepf concludes that the HIV virus will continue to spread.

Christina H. Gladwin, expanding on Schoepf's discusssion of the current economic crisis in Africa, considers a new strategy to stimulate economic growth in her chapter, "Women and Structural Adjustment in a Global Economy." An agricultural economist, Gladwin examines why Structural Adjustment Programs (SAPs) are necessary, and why women appear to bear a disproportionately large share of the burden of the changes they bring about. In her chapter, she focuses on Africa and Latin America, the areas hardest hit by the debt crisis of the 1980s.

Gladwin's discussion of Africa, where SAPs have mandated higher farm product prices, shows that many women have not benefitted from these policies because they sell little of what they produce. Indeed, she argues, many women have been hurt by SAPs because they are net purchasers of food. Moreover, when fertilizer and other subsidies are removed and the prices of these inputs rise (as they have under SAPs), women farmers who are constrained by lack of cash suffer more than men.

SAPs have also been detrimental to women in Latin America where, according to Gladwin, women have increasingly been drawn into the labor force to counteract the decrease in household incomes caused by SAPs. While working women appear to have gained more control over the family budget and a greater voice in household decision making than they previously had, Gladwin argues that these benefits are offset by decreases in family income, and the skyrocketing costs of food, health care, and education, which together cause immiseration and malnutrition. Gladwin concludes that while SAPs are necessary, alternative adjustment packages with fewer inhuman consequences, especially for women, need to be designed.

Trend Report

The trend report selected for inclusion in this third volume focuses on the United Nations Convention to End All Forms of Discrimination Against Women, the first comprehensive international treaty on women's rights. We chose this topic for several reasons. First, one of the most significant realizations to emerge from the United Nations Decade for Women (1976-1985) was that the majority of women in the world continue to suffer from discrimination. Second, the Convention, in force for more than a decade and ratified by 117 states, has fostered recognition that women's rights are human rights. Third, the field of WID is dedicated to a better future through the empowerment of women. The Convention, therefore, must be of prime concern to the profession.

Margaret E. Galey's contribution, "Women and Human Rights," examines the broad impact of this United Nations instrument, commonly known as the Women's Convention. In the first section of her chapter, she outlines the substance of the instrument, points out that the Preamble affirms men's and women's equal rights; acknowledges that widespread discrimination against women continues to exist; and declares that such discrimination is an obstacle to the development of women, their countries, and the world. Upon ratification of the Convention, states agree to condemn such prejudice and to pursue, by "all appropriate measures" and without delay, a policy to eliminate discrimination against women.

A political scientist, Galey proposes two ways to assess the impact of the Women's Convention. The first and most commonly used way involves an analysis of the extent of the instrument's implementation, a concept defined by legal scholars as the legislative, executive, and judicial measures adopted to secure a convention's provisions. Galey argues, however, that this measure is too narrow and suggests that participation in the processes of treaty making, including negotiation, signature, and ratification, be adopted as a measure of impact.

She illustrates the potential value of this broadened means of assessment by considering the case of the United States, where the Women's Convention has not yet been ratified. Here, many officials and members of non-governmental organizations were involved in discussions about the treaty, a process which by itself transformed their awareness of the position of women. In Galey's view, even though the United States is not a ratifying nation of the Convention, discrimination is not necessarily a part of every woman's experience, and the country has already satisfied several of the standards set forth in the instrument.

Galey then uses Egypt as a case study. Egypt signed the Women's Convention in 1980 and has since maintained that its women have made progress toward equality with men. Nevertheless, Galey notes it is difficult to determine whether this advancement is solely a result of government efforts to implement the provisions of the Women's Convention. In her view, Egyptian women's participation in international conferences and the work of women's organizations as well as Egypt's general drive toward political and economic reform may well have played a part in improving women's position.

Galey's report persuasively argues that involvement in institutional processes and procedures can foster acceptance of treaties and their provisions. This measure of impact thus merits consideration in any evaluation of the Women's Convention. Toward this end, Galey generates a number of propositions to frame future analyses. She concludes by reminding readers that women's experience is a product of gender, class, and ethnicity, and that these social categories must be incorporated into any future investigation of impact of the Women's Convention.

Forum

Women in Latin America and the Caribbean were chosen as the focus of the Forum to draw attention to the diversity of women living in this geographic area. This area was chosen because women there have been an essential labor force in programs of economic liberalization. Their experiences thus can provide insights for women living in other countries undergoing similar political and economic transformations.

In contrast to the latitude given to other authors in this volume to define their topics, we asked the two contributors to the Forum to address the political, economic, and social loci of women's subordination and to explore women's ability to mobilize and effect change in their lives.

The first chapter, "Women's Status in Contemporary Cuba: Contradictions, Diversity and Challenges for the Future," by sociologist Marie Withers Osmond, discusses the world of women living in the only socialist state in the western hemisphere. According to Osmond, Cuban women are more advantaged than women living elsewhere in the region as a result of the 1959 Cuban Revolution. They have gained rights fundamental to the improvement of their status, including free education and health care; they were guaranteed legal equality, access to economic resources, and the right to control their own bodies in the 1976 Constitution. In addition, a powerful state organization, the Federation of Cuban Women (FMC), has worked, with some success, to eradicate female illiteracy, incorporate women into the active labor force, and promote them to political and leadership positions. Nevertheless, Osmond concedes, Cuban women have not achieved equality with men.

To illustrate why this is so, Osmond compares the very different views on women's status held by two groups of Cuban women: factory workers in the garment industry, and professionals whose interests are embodied in the policies of the official Federation of Cuban Women (FMC). While the views of these two groups differ, Osmond argues that traditional gender norms pervade both FMC policies and the aspirations of women factory workers.

For example, the FMC was established to promote social change. According to its directors, however, the FMC is a *feminine* organization which encourages women to emerge from their domestic isolation and become more active in public life. While the organization advocates equality in marriage, it does not address *feminist* concerns such as personal liberation, nor does it speak to relations between men and women or among women themselves. In fact, Osmond contends, the FMC reinforces gender inequality by promoting the myth that women are almost emancipated, by perpetuating the ideology of motherhood, by maintaining gender stereotypes in its training programs, and by encouraging women to work as volunteers rather than as paid employees.

Many of the views and aspirations of women factory workers also perpetuate traditional gender roles and ideology. For example, these women do not define liberation in personal terms. Rather, they see liberation as a release from wage work and as the freedom to focus on their families. Given this definition, Osmond argues, FMC goals, such as the incorporation of women into the paid labor force and gender equality in marriage, hold little appeal for women factory workers. Indeed, she maintains, such goals may actually threaten to their sense of self worth and security.

Osmond concludes that Cuba's economic vulnerability, the FMC's dependent political status, and the tenacity of traditional gender ideology have all contributed to the perpetuation of women's subordination. In her view, women's liberation calls for innovative state policies and the development of autonomous women's movements that reflect the diversity of women and that are willing to translate *women's work* into *people's work* in every institution.

The chapter which follows, "Women and Industrialization in the Caribbean: A Comparison of Puerto Rican and Dominican Women Workers," by anthropologist Helen I. Safa, examines the impact of paid employment in export manufacturing on the status of women. In contrast to Osmond's focus on class differences among women in Cuba, Safa considers differences among working-class women in the Dominican Republic and Puerto Rico. Using quantitative and qualitative data developed in surveys, she concentrates on the locus of gender ideology.

Safa challenges the notion that gender ideology is formed principally within the family through women's dependence on male wages and then propelled outside, where it is maintained and perpetuated by workplace management and the state. Rather, she argues, female subordination has several loci, including the family, the workplace, and the state. To support this argument, Safa examines the relationship between changes in gender relations in the family and alterations in women's status in the eyes of employers and the state, nuancing her analysis by examining the way changes vary among working-class women by stage in the life cycle and civil status.

Her data from the Dominican Republic and Puerto Rico reveal that, as a result of women's paid employment, traditional, patriarchal authority patterns in the family were modified, and relations between men and women became more egalitarian than they had been in the past. These changes, however, were most noticeable in Puerto Rico, where women's more substantial contributions to the household gave them greater leverage in family decisions than women had in the Dominican Republic.

In both cases, however, changes in gender ideology within the family did not affect women's status outside the household. In the eyes of employers and the state, women remained subsidiary workers. The perpetuation of this status, however, was most marked in the Dominican Republic, where women workers are subject to exploitation by management and receive little support from the government in their efforts to achieve improved wages and working conditions.

Safa concludes that management and the state have proven more resistant to change than has the family because they continue to be governed by a traditional gender ideology--one women themselves have begun to abandon. Thus, because working-class women remain vulnerable at the extra-household level, she argues (like Osmond) they may remain reluctant to abandon their primary identities as wives and mothers.

Conclusion

We began this introduction by identifying two approaches to the concept of difference: differences between men and women and differences among women. Outlining the substance of these different approaches, we showed how a variety of feminisms had emerged from this differentiation in the United States and Latin America. As our discussion revealed, the concept of difference incorporates issues of power.

On the one hand, the use of the term to denote differences among women demonstrates that people are created in their relationships with others. Difference is "a series of relationships of power, involving domination and subordination" (Gordon 1991:106, citing Kerber).[9] On the other hand, markers of difference, such as class, race, and gender, are *sites of power* and thus sites of resistance as well (Barrett 1987:35).

These nuanced conceptions of difference are well reflected in our discussion. For example, Hurtado's (1989) description of the politics of personal life shows how the relationship between women of Color and the State shapes their experience. This relationship is also a powerful organizing force in the lives of Latin American women. Further, Sandoval's (1991) concept of "differential consciousness" illustrates how a site of subordination can become a site of resistance, a theme which is echoed in the experience of Black and Indian women in Latin America.

Together, these nuanced conceptions of difference represent a powerful challenge to white, middle-class feminism. First, they highlight the way gender, race, and class converge to produce very different social worlds. Second, they show that dichotomies such as public/private and feminine/feminist have little use as forms of explanation in that they universalize the experiences of women. Third, they demonstrate how class- and race-differentiated experience shape both consciousness and action. Finally, they emphasize how women's different locations in the social fabric generate many different feminisms.

Feminist standpoint theory in fact builds on this insight. Proponents argue that while multiple feminisms are contradictory, this contradiction is the source of feminism's strength (Harding 1991, 1992; Hartsock 1983). In

Harding's view (1991:59), each feminism can achieve only a partial view of reality. None is disinterested, impartial, or detached from its unique social location. Feminists must, in her words:

> scrutinize gender *as it exists* and from the perspective of *all* women's lives. There is no other defensible choice. Refraining from centering multiple subjects in feminist analyses distorts not only the lives of marginalized women, but also of those at the center (Harding 1992:180).

We encourage readers to examine the way they think about paradigms of power and about how class, race, and gender intersect to shape relations among women as well as relations between women and men. For these ways of thinking have implications for action--both for the women in whose behalf we work and for ourselves.

Notes

1.   In using lower case letters for "third world" and upper case letters for "women of Color" we are adopting the convention followed by women of these categories (see Hurtado 1989:833, note 1).

2.   For summaries of First World feminist theory see Donovan (1985) and Tong (1989).

3.   We use the term "customary law" to refer to norms which dictate the roles women occupy and which are enforced through practices such as child socialization.

4.   One variant of radical feminism sees women's biological difference from men as a source of enrichment and considers women superior to them (see, for example, O'Brien 1981). Lesbian feminism is yet another variant of radical feminism, a perspective which is not covered in this essay.

5.   Other modes of consciousness identified include liberal, radical, and socialist feminisms.

6.   The region-wide *Encuentros* have been convened in Columbia (1981), Peru (1983), Brazil (1985), Mexico (1987), and Argentina (1990).

7.   Our use of the term "reproduction" follows that of Edholm et al. 1977 who consider reproduction to encompass: (a) biological reproduction, (b) social reproduction, that is, the maintenance of a social system over time, and (c) the reproduction or maintenance of the labor force.

8.   Debt reduction policies advocated by donor organizations and adopted by national governments diminished the state's involvement in the provision of public transportation, health, education, and other social services, thereby transferring an increasing burden of social reproduction to women. At the same time, employment opportunities for women in the formal sector did not

keep pace with urbanization and population growth. The result was the immiseration of increasing numbers of women. (See Gladwin, this volume.)

9.   This insight is well illustrated in studies of the "other" in which the cross-cultural analysis of "sexual difference" leads to the construction of "third world difference" (Mohanty 1991b:53; see also Trinh 1991).

References

Anzaldua, Gloria
    1990   *Borderlands/La Frontera*. San Francisco: Spinsters/Aunt Lute.

Baca Zinn, Maxine, Lynn Weber Cannon, Elizabeth Higginbotham, and
    Bonnie Thorton Dill
    1986   The Costs of Exclusionary Practices in Women's Studies. *Signs*
           11(2):290-303.

Barrett, Michele
    1987   The Concept of "Difference." *Feminist Review* 26(July):29-42.

Bunch, Charlotte and Roxanna Carillo
    1990   Feminist Perspectives on Women in Development. In: *Persistent
           Inequalities: Women and World Development*, edited by Irene
           Tinker. Pp. 70-82. New York: Oxford University Press.

Collins, Patricia Hill
    1986   Learning From the Outsider Within: The Sociological Significance
           of Black Feminist Thought. *Social Problems* 33(6):14-32.

Donovan, Josephine
    1986   *Feminist Theory*. New York: Ungar.

Edholm, Felicity, Olivia Harris, and Kate Young
    1977   Conceptualizing Women. *Critique of Anthropology* 3:101-131.

Gordon, Linda
    1991   On "Difference." *Genders* 10(Spring):91-111.

Harding, Sandra
    1991   *Whose Science? Whose Knowledge? Thinking from Women's Lives*.
           Ithaca: Cornell University Press.

1992   Subjectivity, Experience and Knowledge: An Epistemology from/for Rainbow Coalition Politics. *Development and Change* 23(3):175-193.

Hartsock, Nancy
1983   The Feminist Standpoint: Developing the Ground for a Specifically Feminist Historical Materialism. In: *Discovering Reality: Feminist Perspectives on Epistemology, Metaphysics, Methodology and Philosophy of Science*, edited by Sandra Harding and Merrill Hintikka. Pp. 283-310. Dordrecht: Reidel Publishing.

hooks, bell
1984   *Feminist Theory: From Margin to Center.* Boston: South End Press.

Hurtado, Aida
1989   Relating to Privilege: Seduction and Rejection in the Subordination of White Women and Women of Color. *Signs* 14(4):833-855.

Jaquette, Jane S. (editor)
1991   *The Women's Movement in Latin America: Feminism and the Transition to Democracy.* Boulder: Westview Press.

Jelin, Elizabeth (editor)
1990   *Women and Social Change in Latin America.* Atlantic Highlands: Zed Press.

Mohanty, Chandra Talpade
1991a Under Western Eyes: Feminist Scholarship and Colonial Discourses. In: *Third World Women and the Politics of Feminism*, edited by Chandra Talpade Mohanty, Ann Russo, and Lourdes Torres. Pp. 51-80. Bloomington: Indiana University Press.

1991b Cartographies of Struggle: Third World Women and the Politics of Feminism. In: *Third World Women and the Politics of Feminism*, edited by Chandra Talpade Mohanty, Ann Russo, and Lourdes Torres. Pp. 1-47. Bloomington: Indiana University Press.

Molyneux, Maxine
1985   Mobilization without Emancipation? Women's Interests, the State, and Revolution in Nicaragua. *Feminist Studies* 11(2):227-254.

Morgen, Sandra (editor)
   1989   Common Grounds and Crossroads: Race, Ethnicity, and Class in
          Women's Lives (Special issue). *Signs* 14(4).

O'Brien, Mary
   1981   *The Politics of Reproduction*. Boston: Routledge and Kegan Paul.

Safa, Helen Icken
   1990   Women's Social Movements in Latin America. *Gender & Society*
          4(3):354-369.

Sandoval, Chela
   1991   U.S. Third World Feminism: The Theory and Method of
          Oppositional Consciousness in the Postmodern World. *Genders*
          10:1-24.

Sternbach, Nancy Saporta, Marysa Navarro-Aranguren, Patricia Chuchryk,
   and Sonia E. Alvarez
   1992   Feminisms in Latin America: From Bogota to San Bernardo.
          Signs 17(2):393-436.

Tong, Rosemarie
   1989   *Feminist Thought*. Boulder: Westview Press.

Trinh, T. Minh-ha
   1991   *Women, Native, Other*. Bloomington: Indiana University Press.

Vargas, Virginia
   1992   The Feminist Movement in Latin America: Between Hope and
          Disenchantment. *Development and Change* 25(3):195-214.

Walker, Alice
   1983   *In Search of Our Mother's Gardens: Womanist Prose*. New York:
          Harcourt, Brace and Jovanovich.

Wilkinson, Doris, Maxine Baca Zinn, and Esther Ngan-Ling Chow (editors)
   1992   Race, Class, and Gender (Special Issue). *Gender & Society*
          6(3):341-502.

Part I

Review Articles

1

The Silent Majority:
Women as Refugees

Pamela A. DeVoe

Defining the characteristics of refugees is problematic; the criteria used to determine who is and who is not "a refugee" are contentious and the subject of considerable debate (Coles 1989; Ferris 1985; Wong 1989; Zolberg, Suhrke, and Aguayo 1989). Scholars, politicians, and practitioners concerned with refugee issues, however, most commonly employ the definition created by the 1951 Convention Relating to the Status of Refugees which defined refugees as individuals who had been persecuted in their home country and subsequently exiled. This definition was modified in the United Nations 1967 Protocol to read:

> any person who, owing to a well-founded fear of being persecuted for reasons of race, religion, nationality, membership of a particular social group or political opinion, is outside the country of his nationality and is unable or, owing to such fear, is unwilling to avail himself of the protection of that country, or who, not having a nationality and being outside the country of his former habitual residence, is unable or, owing to such fear, is unwilling to return to it (Ferris 1985:2-3).

This definition, still used by many governments and organizations, was adopted to meet the needs of World War II refugees and individuals persecuted in association with the Cold War. It does not, however, adequately apply to the many refugees created by the contemporary political environment, in which groups of people are displaced by violence or warfare. First, this definition speaks only to people who are persecuted individually by their own or a foreign government. Many of today's refugees, were members of villages which were destroyed or terrorized as part of a military strategy to create or suppress civil unrest (depending on whether the strategy was devised by insurgents or government agents). Second, this definition emphasizes the concept of exile, such that refugees will never return to their homeland. Any number of the more than 15 million current refugees (USCR 1990:31), however, would return to their homeland if the crisis which expelled them was resolved. Third, this definition stipulates that refugees must live outside the borders of their home countries, ignoring the many refugees who have been displaced within their countries by internal violence. In Guatemala, for example, civil conflict has forced approximately one million people to flee their homes to other regions of the country (Ferris 1985:3). Yet these exiles are not, according to the current Convention definition, political refugees.

Even with this restricted definition, the number of refugees has grown considerably in the last decade. In 1980 the United Nations High Commission for Refugees (UNHCR) assisted 8.2 million refugees, and by 1989 this number had increased to 15 million. Similarly, other international programs have noted a significant escalation in the number of refugees they have assisted; attributing this rise to the terrorization, demoralization, and economic disabling of civilians which is becoming increasingly common in many parts of the world (Minear 1990:13-19).[1] Women are over-represented in these adult refugee populations, with mothers and children disproportionately represented throughout Africa, Asia, and Central America.[2]

The United States and Canada have accepted the largest number of refugees; between 1975 and 1988 the United States resettled 1,249,608 refugees, and Canada resettled 252,225 (USCR 1990:34).[3] While in 1983 600,000 of the 828,000 refugees in the United States were from Southeast Asia, by 1987 Southeast Asian refugees numbered 846,000 with an additional 200,000 children born to them after they had resettled (Haines 1989:2).

The material in this chapter reflects the preponderance of Southeast Asian refugees in the United States, although there are also refugees in the United States from Africa, Asia, Central America, and the former Soviet Union. Most of the published literature focuses on the resettlement and adaptation of Southeast Asian refugees in the United States and Canada, although a few periodicals and reports from organizations such as the United Nations High Commission on Refugees (UNHCR) address the more general refugee population. Moreover, although women are over-represented in the world refugee population, they are generally neglected in the refugee literature.[4] Only a handful of thousands of references concerning refugees deal specifically with women. This dearth may be a factor of time. When the tide of refugees swelled from the late 1970s to the mid-1980s, researchers were concerned with developing an overview of the refugee experience rather than exploring the way individuals experience dislocation. Recent literature is more detailed, although the issue of gender is often ignored in favor of ethnicity, education, or other demographic variables.[5] As the review which follows shows, however, gender critically shapes the refugee experience and the adjustment process.

This chapter deals with three phases of women's refugee experience: (1) the flight from their homeland; (2) the period when they are in refugee camps; and (3) their resettlement (about which there is the most literature). The discussion of resettlement is subdivided into different issues in the adjustment process: economic, aging, health, the family, gender asymmetry, and gender and ethnic identity. In the concluding section, I discuss areas of research which need to be pursued in order to broaden understanding of the relationship between gender and the refugee experience.

Phase One: Fleeing the Homeland

People become refugees when fear compels them to leave their homes. While a few people may carefully plan their escape to another area, most flee with little or no preparation. Unfortunately, the very process of fleeing may subject many women to even greater danger than that which they left. They may be physically abused because, as women, they are particularly vulnerable. In addition, they may be abused because they are considered extensions of their families, not individuals; women embody the family's continuity and pride as wives who will produce a future generation and as chaste daughters who symbolize the family's virtue. An attack on them, therefore, is an attack on the integrity of the family. Attacks on women may also represent an assault on their ethnic group; because they have a reproductive role, women may be viewed as the embodiment of a given ethnic identity's maintenance.

Physical torment, including sexual abuse, is cited as causing the greatest social and psychological damage to refugee women (Golden and McConnell 1986). The enormity of this problem remains difficult to document because a sense of shame leads women and their families to conceal instances of sexual abuse. Nevertheless, women's vulnerability during the flight from their homeland has been well documented among the Vietnamese "boat people," who are victimized by sea pirates (Burrows 1987:13-14; Camus-Jacques 1989; De 1989; Rumbaut 1989:145-146; St. Cartmail 1983:111-117; Winter and Cerquone 1984). Although the UNHCR has tried to alleviate this problem by providing financial support to the Thai government's Anti-Piracy Program, the physical and sexual abuse of women remains a serious problem for those trying to escape from Vietnam by boat (Crisp 1987:21).

Sexual violence against Vietnamese refugee women and girls was likely a systematic attempt by pirates to destroy the morale of the entire group, as women were raped in front of their families and other refugees (Camus-Jacques 1989:146). Victims and other survivors became acutely aware of their vulnerability as a group. Husbands, fathers, brothers, and other men, who were the theoretical protectors of women, were unable to do so, and may even have been forced to accommodate the rapists (Amar 1985:31).[6] Thus, authority figures, who served as protectors of the cultural microcosm on the boat, were exposed as powerless and without real authority.

An unfortunate response of women was their inability to feel anger or rage against their rapists, feeling instead disgust with themselves. Amar (1985:30) reports discussions with such women who said, "I had the feeling that I was dirtying the boat by my mere presence"; and "No matter what my husband says, I don't believe he's ready to forget." In the women's view, they no longer had a right to be a part of the family or the larger social group. According to De (1989), Buddhism, with its concept of Karma, reinforced the belief that the victims caused their own abuse by their behavior in a past life.

Women are not only vulnerable to pirates. If they are not accompanied by male kin, "protectors" chosen by their parents may accompany them, and these protectors often may become their abusers (St. Cartmail 1983:113). The stigma of sexual assault by their own protectors may lead to complete silence and a distrust for all authority figures.

Men in positions of authority have often raped and exploited refugee women, as women from other parts of the world have reported. For example, women crossing the Djibouti border[7] were usually detained and separated from men, thereby becoming targets of sexual violence by border guards (Camus-Jacques 1989:146). The same pattern of abuse from soldiers and immigration officials was reported by Central American refugee women (Golden and McConnel 1986:113-116). Under these conditions, the suppression of the experience is a survival strategy of women who are often held accountable for transgressions over which they have no control.

The severity of the trauma women experienced during their flight is inversely related to their long-term adjustment in the host country (Montgomery 1991:104). Most women retain psychological and emotional scars from their experience, including nightmares, insomnia, phobias, excessive aggressiveness, and apathy (Amar 1985). Some may also have to cope with a pregnancy that resulted from their abuse. While others must contend with the reaction of their families and ethnic communities to their experiences. In sum, the initial phase of the refugee experience, fleeing one's homeland, is fraught with great personal tragedy.

Phase Two: Women in Refugee Camps

Most studies of women within refugee camps treat them as both individuals and members of family units, as the following discussion demonstrates. Women-headed households constitute the majority of families living in refugee camps throughout the world. During the 1980s, for example, 80 percent of Cambodian families in refugee camps (Williams 1990:102), more than 75 percent of Somalian refugee families, and 60 percent of Sudanese refugee families were headed by women (Adepoju 1982). In general, such families are disproportionately represented among encamped refugees in Africa, the Near East, Southeast Asia, and Central America (Parker 1988; Stevens 1988; Williams 1990). Moreover, they are confronted with any number of problems: inequitable allocation of essential items, an overwhelming sense of loss through death or separation from family and home, deprivation of status and human rights, and continuing battles against sickness and disease (Dewey 1988).

While refugee women expect to find security and safety within the camps, sexual violence may follow them there, particularly if they lack support from male relatives. Women without husbands may be forced to trade sexual services for food or other necessities (Camus-Jacques 1989; Siemens 1988). Even women with husbands, however, may be at risk: violence against married women is increasing (Bonnerjea 1985; Chan 1984; Krumperman 1983; Lin 1986; Reynell 1988; Williams 1990).

The problems facing many unaccompanied women and women heads of household are being addressed in a few refugee camps by administrators sensitive to gender (Parker 1988; Stevens 1988). For example, in some camps, single women and women heads of household are housed in buildings separate from men. Some observers note, however, that most refugee camps continue to be male centered (Calloway 1987; Indra 1987; UNHCR 1987; Williams 1990:105).[8] Camp administrators, viewing women as dependents of men, select men to be the decision makers who control access to essentials. The effect of this structure of authority is two-fold: it enhances the position of potential and actual abusers, and it debases women and limits their control over their lives.

Women are also exposed to more potential health problems than are men in refugee camps (Bonnerjea 1985; Hutchinson 1985; Sundhagel 1981). Men are frequently given more food than pregnant and lactating women, resulting in female and child malnutrition (Berry 1988; Williams 1990). Inadequate food and nutritional supplements also jeopardize the development of unborn and nursing children (Jackson and Eade 1982). The inequitable distribution of goods continues because women have been removed from decision-making roles and positions of power that would ensure a less demeaning, more equitable distribution of essentials in the camps. In a study of camps in Africa, Williams (1990) found that refugee women were disempowered when power was shifted from the family to camp administrators. Thus, rather than being protected while in the camps, women are further abused.

To fully understand the impact of this abuse, the length of time spent in the camps must be considered. Crisp (1987:20-32) studied 673,000 refugees who, since 1975, have come to Thailand from Laos, Kampuchea, and

Vietnam, and found that nine percent of all refugees in Thailand have been in Thai camps for more than four years. This figure varies significantly with ethnicity: 69 percent of the Hill Tribe Laotians have been in refugee camps for more than four years; more than half of the Kampucheans have been in refugee camps for more than four years, and a large percentage have been there seven or more years. People who arrived as children have grown, married, and have had children of their own while living in the camps. Crisp (1987) suggests that the deadening monotony of long-term camp life, along with the tremendous sense of hopelessness that pervades the camps, often results in depression, even suicidal depression. Although Crisp's report concerns refugees in Thailand, there are indications that life in refugee camps is similar in its destructive and deadening effects throughout the world (Loescher 1989:1-2; Ruiz 1989:28-29).

Women arrive at the camps expecting their stay to be brief and secure, but they discover that the insecurity and uncertainty of their lives is prolonged. Urs Boegli, Director of the International Committee of the Red Cross, spoke of the continued abuse of Kampuchean refugees: "Unfortunately there are still abuses of human rights at the . . . sites. Despite a great deal of effort . . . the results have not met our goals for protection . . . more and more of the displaced people currently live a life that due to its absence of prospects has just stopped making sense" (cited in Crisp 1987:34).

Phase Three: Resettlement

Three rationales underlie much of the research on refugees. A great deal of work has been inspired by the need for host countries to assess how well refugees have adjusted to their new environment. A second catalyst for research has been the need for host countries to estimate the degree to which refugees have problems related to aging and physical and mental health. Finally, a third stimulus for research has been a general interest in refugee acculturation to the new socioeconomic environment; most of this work has focused on the role of the family in the adjustment process, changing gender roles, and the relationship between gender identification and ethnicity. For heuristic reasons, the following material covers each of these research areas separately; in actuality, however, there is a great deal of interplay among the areas, and this interaction is reflected in some of the discussion which follows.

Economic Adjustment

A common measure of refugee . ·‌·ustment is economic independence (Caplan, Whitmore, and Choy 1989), in which a refugee who leaves the welfare rolls and becomes economically self-sufficient is judged well-adjusted. The multitudes of refugees seeking sanctuary in the early 1970s inspired a number of studies on the employment of refugees.[9] These studies provided valuable baseline information, but they tended to be overly descriptive; rarely did they offer explanations for differential employment rates by ethnicity and gender (when they recorded such differences). Haines's work (1985) provides one exception to this pattern. He showed that participation in the labor force was a product of the length of time a refugee had been in the United States: "the combined labor force participation rate (both males and females) for 1975 arrivals was 64 percent, about the national average, whereas for 1979 arrivals, it was only 32 percent" (Haines 1985:27). Factors other than time, however, may affect entry into the paid-labor force.

Domestic responsibilities. Dorais, Pilon-Le, and Huy (1987) found that Vietnamese women had a lower rate of paid labor force participation than men, but that women who worked outside the home had more family responsibilities and worked longer hours than did men.[10] Many women did all the housework while holding down one or more jobs, thereby working 19 to 20 hours per day. Their findings seem to support those of Rumbaut (1989:149-151) who speculates that refugee women's low rate of participation in the labor force reflects their child care obligations and disadvantaged position in the labor market.

Although women's household responsibilities mediate their work status, Haines (1985:28) found that Cuban and Vietnamese women had "noticeably strong labor market involvement." Other researchers have suggested why this might be so. For example, Bach and his colleagues (1984) report that occupational background and household size and composition affect employment rates (although they do not provide precise figures to support this).[11] Moreover, Tenhula (1991:110) suggests that education and work experience, as well as household size and composition, are associated with a refugee's economic success in the host country. Thus, women's responsibility for the domestic sphere is not the sole determinant of their entry into the labor force.

Work preparedness. Competence in the English language and work skills are predictive of participation in the labor force. Haines (1985), for example, found that women were more lacking in these resources than men.[12] According to Rumbaut (1989), however, a low level of English language competence is more a function of age and pre-migration education than of gender. Yet educational level prior to resettlement is closely linked to economic success (Dunning 1989:64), and women consistently have lower educational levels than men.

The kind of skill refugees bring to the job market reflect their previous work experience, but this history is difficult to discern from secondary sources. Dunning (1989:60-61), for example, found that about 50 percent of

Vietnamese women living in California, Texas, and Louisiana had been white-collar workers prior to fleeing their country. Further, only seven percent of the women he interviewed indicated that they had been housewives, although Dunning classified another 37 percent, who reported that they had "no occupation," as housewives. A case can also be made for alternate interpretations: "no occupation" could be interpreted as "student" (as Dunning interpreted men's response of "no occupation"); or it could be interpreted as "working for a family-run business" or "working in the family field," that is, not working for outsiders. Dunning's interpretation may thus reflect an androcentric bias found in much of the literature on women refugees in the United States--a bias which obscures refugee women's previous work experience.

The literature on Southeast Asian women, for example, shows that they held an important economic position in the family (Laderman 1982:79-84; Van Esterik 1982:8-9) and played an important role in their home countries' informal economy as petty traders and entrepreneurs (Pas-Ong 1989:113). Many have brought the work skills accumulated during this experience to the United States, as DeVoe and Rynearson show in their work on Lao refugee woman in Missouri who participated in the informal economy (DeVoe and Rynearson 1983; Rynearson and DeVoe 1984).

Discrimination in the work force. Those few studies that focus on women refugees as wage earners indicate that they are discriminated against. Dunning (1989:66-69), for example, found that women were more likely to receive lower wages than men and to do piece work in the home. According to his findings, initial wages for women were $2.97 per hour while those for men were $3.66. Even having acquired work experience, refugee women did not gain parity with men; for example, wages for experienced workers averaged $4.09 for women and $5.40 for men. Rumbaut (1989:149-150) also found that women were over-represented in clerical work and garment industries paying low wages, although about 18 percent of women versus 20 percent of men were professional workers. Similarly, Caplan, Whitmore, and Choy (1989:210) found that women were as likely as men to hold high-status jobs (e.g., 13 percent of women compared to 11 percent of men).[13]

Discrimination in training programs. Because vocational training can be critical to securing appropriate employment, refugees seek skills they need in the labor market (Dunning 1989:72-73; Tenhula 1991:109). Men, however, are more frequently selected as participants in job-training programs than are women (Caplan, Whitmore, and Choy 1989:218), and in some instances women are not even considered potential clients. This may be so because administrative personnel believe that:

> men are more mobile, less socially restricted in the type of work they can undertake, and have more time at their disposal since they are

neither engaged in productive work nor encumbered by daily household responsibilities. . . . [Biased] policy-makers and aid workers . . . continue to consider the male-headed household as the norm even where female-headed households predominate; [it is assumed] that the man is invariably the primary producer for the family, whose economic welfare consequently depends on his efforts. The failure to take into account the value of women's work outside the formal economy has been matched by the widespread stereotyping of women's participation within the economy (Hall 1990:93).

Nevertheless, when women do receive job training they are often channeled into low-paying jobs. For example, Rumbaut (1989) found that job-training programs routed over half of the refugee women he studied to manufacturing jobs (see also Ng 1988). In contrast, Caplan, Whitmore, and Choy (1989:210-219) found a slightly different pattern among Vietnamese, Sino-Vietnamese, and Lao. While men were more likely than women to receive vocational and English training, women were more likely than men to work for wages and to hold high status jobs.[14] They found, however, that women's wages were about 20 percent less per hour than men's regardless of skill level. Women's access to employment and wages, therefore, is limited by the inherent characteristics of gender (Spero 1985:148-149).

Other factors. In contrast to the research discussed thus far, studies that move beyond a cursory examination of women's participation in the labor force render a more nuanced picture of women's economic adjustment. For example, Spero (1985) examined the effects of culture shock, depression, domestic violence, isolation, and the loss of family and community assistance on women's employment. Her data show how very vulnerable refugee women are in their attempt to adjust to new environmental conditions.

Many of the Vietnamese women in Kibria's (1989) study of how gender shapes women's employment and experience, were employed in the informal sector--a sector of the economy neglected in most surveys (see also Morokvasic 1984; Portes and Sassen-Koob 1987). Focusing on the impact of cultural traditions on women's roles, she found that male dominance, arising from Confucianism, coexisted with traditional expettations for women. In their home countries, for example, women owned property, expected an inheritance, participated in business and commerce, and had considerable informal power within the family (Bergman 1975; Hickey 1964). Women's work, therefore, was part of a family strategy, and, according to Kibria (1989), they are also expected to work in the United States to improve the family condition.

Family strategies were an explicit focus of a study of Asian women by Stier (1991). Using data from the 1980 Census, she looked at four variables that influenced women's employment decisions: (1) individual characteristics (opportunities and interest in work), (2) economic factors (family income and socioeconomic status), (3) family constraints, and (4) labor market conditions. Stier concluded that while the presence or absence of young children influenced a woman's entry into the job market, an extended family which included members who could assume women's child care responsibility released them for work. Moreover, she found that poverty forced women to enter the paid labor force, although there was considerable variation within each of the six Asian groups studied (see also Spenner and Rosenfeld 1990).

Women, Aging, and, Adjustment

While there is a paucity of material on aging among refugees, the general literature on ethnicity and aging could be applied to the refugee experience (e.g., Gelfand and Kutzik 1979; Gelfand 1982; Markides and Mindel 1987; Savishinsky 1990). A common theme emerges from studies of the relationship between change and aging, despite the differences among ethnic groups. Older individuals accentuate their ethnic heritage to maintain a sense of order, meaning, and continuity in the face of significant change. Such change may include loss of their indigenous languages, decline in traditional rituals, weakening of community solidarity groups, rising rates of intermarriage, increased geographic mobility, modified occupational struc-tures, and altered family values (Savishinsky 1990).

One of the rare studies available, that by Weinstein-Shr (1987), shows that refugees (from Southeast Asia, Latin America, Eastern Europe, Soviet Union, Africa and the Near East) shared problems similar to those described above. Moreover, she suggests that the experience of aging is culturally constructed, and the term "elderly" may be applied to a refugee in her 40s as well as to one in her 60s. If the onset of menopause is the mark of an elderly woman, it is likely that a woman in her 40s will be considered elderly and, therefore, retire. In the home country, such a woman would remain active, offering advice and counsel and caring for her grandchildren. When refugee women retire in the United States, however, they are isolated and feel useless and totally dependent on their families. Because they are unfamiliar with the new environment and the educational and employment systems and rarely speak the host-country language, their advice and counsel may appear useless or inappropriate to the younger generation. Consequently, they feel frustrated, alienated from younger generations, and suffer low self-esteem (Aylesworth, Ossorio, and Osaki 1980; Spero 1985; Weinstein-Shr 1987). If they are unable to adapt and modify their traditional expectations, they may insulate themselves within their families as protection from the outside world (Finck 1983:58), thereby creating a dilemma for the family, community, and host country.

Health in the Adjustment Process

The need to address health problems among refugees has prompted a number of studies (see Kulig 1990a and 1990b). Among the many issues encompassed by these studies, two are selected for discussion here: childbearing, and physical and mental health.

Childbearing. According to Rumbaut and Weeks (1986), Southeast Asian refugee women have a higher fertility rate than women in the United States (see also Zaharlick and Brainard 1988). This finding may be partly attributable to early age of marriage because Southeast Asian women marry when they reach puberty (Kubota and Matsuda 1982). Yet Kulig (1990b) reports, that the Cambodian women refugees she studied no longer marry this young, which may lead to fewer children per family.[15]

Practitioners need to be aware of traditional beliefs about conception and childbirth when dealing with clients of different ethnic backgrounds, as a number of studies demonstrate (Calhoun 1985; Faller 1985; Lee 1986; Manderson and Matthews 1981; Matthews and Manderson 1981; Sargent, Macucci and Elliston 1983; Wadd 1983). Kulig (1988; 1990a), for example, found that most (90%) Cambodian refugee women generally recognized the role of the menstrual cycle in the process of pregnancy but many thought they could only become pregnant every one to four years. Moreover, many women continue to rely on indigenous medicines and practices for birth control (although the effectiveness of these medicines remains unclear). Van Esterik (1980), however, reports that Southeast Asian refugee women know about Western methods of birth control and do not tend to rely on indigenous medicines. Consequently, practitioners need to be aware of differing traditional beliefs and practices in the medical care of refugee women, particularly regarding family planning and childbirth.

Physical and Mental Health. Research on the physical health of refugees usually does not address gender.[16] One exception to this pattern is the study of nutrition, which usually does focus on women. Reflecting women's role as caretakers, this work usually targets women because they are the ones who make nutritional decisions (Eldred 1985). For example, because contaminated milk may lead to acute diarrhea, and overly-diluted milk powder may lead to kidney failure and even death, research has concentrated on how refugee women use dried milk powder (e.g., UNHCR 1990).

The study of mental health among refugees--particularly research on stress and mental health--provides more information on women. In general, the literature suggests that differing stressors affect people in different ways (e.g., Baum and Grunberg 1991). For example, Barnett, Davidson, and Marshall (1991) argue that the work environment, its financial and social benefits, women's rights and responsibilities (at work and at home), and the quality of marriage are all implicated in a woman's perception of stress. Moreover, a significant factor associated with the experience of stress is the level of social support available to women. Shumaker and Hill (1991) suggest that lower levels of social support are associated with higher levels of health disorders, but this association is not the same for all women.

Kinzie and Fleck (1987) and Walter (1981), for example, studied how stress was perceived and experienced by Southeast Asian refugee women during the resettlement process. Women heads of household with several dependent children and no extended family were found to be particularly vulnerable to depression, insecurity, and anxiety (Aylesworth, Ossorio, and Osaki 1980; Fox 1985; Mitchell 1987). Because the sense of loss is so acute for refugee women, it underlies many, if not all, of these health problems; Van Esterik (1980) points to how this loss is further exacerbated by the absence of spiritual support provided by women's religious systems (e.g., Buddhism).

Westermeyer, first with Vang and Neider (1983) and then with Bouafuely and Vang (1984), reported that among Hmong refugees, men and women both experienced depression, but at different times. Whereas men were most likely to experience problems soon after resettlement, women's initial symptoms frequently appeared three years later, particularly if they worked outside the home. This association between outside work and stress may be related to women's loss of a sense of control over their time and work-product--which they had previously maintained in their home countries. Skartvedt (1989), in contrast, found that women were initially more isolated and depressed than men, but as they became more independent, their husbands became more depressed. Hirayama (1982) provides a possible explanation for this pattern, suggesting that when women are employed outside the home, their husbands help with housework. Although women remain primarily responsible for domestic work, the support they receive may ameliorate their stress.

The syndrome of depression is also different for men and women. Men's distress is often disabling and requires treatment, but men who are able to maintain their traditional roles fare better than those who cannot. Women, conversely, experience more phobic anxiety symptoms than men, a difference which may be associated with the post-traumatic symptoms that Kinzie and Fleck (1987) attributed to refugee women's rape experiences. Rumbaut (1989) also found significant differences in stress symptoms, depression, demoralization, and sense of well-being by gender and ethnicity among resettled refugees.[17] Men engage in more health-risk behaviors such as smoking and drinking than do women, yet women are consistently more demoralized than men. Paradoxically, both men and women indicate that they are satisfied with their work, financial situation, home life, neighborhood, social contacts, health, religion, and leisure.

As the foregoing indicates, health can only be understood in the context of the lived experience of men and women. Ethnicity and gender are inextricably linked to a refugee's ability to adjust to the host country, as is health status to adjustment. In addition, the different experiences of refugees prior to resettlement are implicated in the adaptation and illness process.

The Family's Role in the Adjustment Process

The family plays a central role in the adjustment process (Chan and Lamb 1987; Haines, Rutherford, and Thomas 1981; Indra 1987; Montgomery 1991; Skartvedt 1989; Stein 1986; Tienda and Booth 1991; Whitmore, Trautmann, and Caplan 1989).[18] As Haines (1985:20-21) notes, "the primary web of social relationships within which the adjustment of the individual refugee takes place is the family as a single household [and as an] extended set of kin." Refugees are not isolates but are embedded in a network of relationships. Their families are often larger, more structurally complex, and include more dependents than non-refugee families (Rumbaut 1989:151). Women, moreover, are pivotal to the stability of the family. In Africa, for example, the death of a mother often results in the disintegration of the family, while the death of the father does not affect its solidarity (Hall 1990).

Families, however, often change under conditions of resettlement. Dunning (1989:76), for example, reports that Vietnamese refugees consider their families to be fragmented because many family members remained in Vietnam or were killed when trying to escape. While men and women both suffer from the loss of their extended families (Spero 1985), this loss has very practical consequences for women, who can no longer count on their extended kin for assistance with their domestic responsibilities (Boserup 1970; Indra 1987; Montgomery 1991). The pressure created by these conditions may partially explain Rumbaut's (1989:155-156) finding that Southeast Asian refugee women were consistently more demoralized and more depressed than the men. The loss of an extended family severs women's ties to those who are critical for social support, guidance, nurturance, and reassurance (Bell 1991).

Gender Asymmetry

Rather than escaping the disaster they feared would befall them if they did not leave their home countries, women often find upon resettlement that, although they may be free of persecution and death, their social and economic positions do not improve, and may even worsen. Western society often creates greater gender inequalities than existed in the rural areas that women left behind. Tienda and Booth (1991) suggest that gender inequality remains, even when women's roles change; in fact, Boserup (1970) argues that inequality may even intensify.[19]

Despite this argument, women's roles in the host country are not necessarily a function of those held in their home countries. Prior to resettlement, some Southeast Asian women were doctors, lawyers, professors, and civil servants, or independent market peddlers or business owners (Van Esterik 1980). Upon resettlement, they suffered a loss of prestige as they found themselves isolated at home or working in low-paying, low-status jobs (Healy 1988; Ranard 1990). Other women (such as Mien and Hmong), may better their position in the host country and find themselves no longer vulnerable and powerless (Scott 1988; Waters 1990).

Gender and Ethnic Identity

Ethnicity is socially constructed and may have explicit objectives such as the creation of economically and politically influential groups (Sorenson 1991). In addition to evolving out of strategic goals, ethnic identity also emerges from the shared migration and refugee experience in the host country:

> symbols of ethnicity, such as language or linguistic style, dress styles, dietary preferences and religious behavior serve as reminders of their origin to the migrants themselves, while at the same time marking these people as outsiders in the sheltering locale (Gonzalez 1989:4).

The maintenance of ethnicity is closely associated with gender, and women play a particularly important role in preserving key markers of ethnic distinction. In addition to creating communities through biological and social reproduction, they establish a social environment. For example, they prepare and share traditional food (a symbol of common identity), thereby promoting solidarity within the community (DeVoe and Rynearson 1983).

Men are more likely than women to conform to host country norms and to change their style of dress. Even when women do alter their way of dress, they may continue to wear some items of their traditional clothing daily, and to always wear traditional fashions for special community events. Men, in contrast, do so only if they participate in such events.[20] Food and clothing are thus markers of ethnic identity, with women playing a critical role in the construction and maintenance of ethnocultural cohesion in a new environment.

Refugees are often quite conservative, focusing on "old ways" as key symbols of their ethnicity. Women's and men's traditional roles therefore take on an added symbolic meaning in the new setting (Epstein and Watts 1981). The maintenance of gendered responsibilities becomes critical to the very existence of the refugee culture (Hackett 1988), thereby producing stress for both the individual and the ethnic community. But what many fail to realize is that the refugees' home country is probably also changing, and these changes include transformations in men's and women's roles (Sorenson 1991). Thus, if the refugees had remained in their home countries, they also would have had to adapt to a social reorganization that challenged their cultural identity.

Conclusion: The Research Gaps

This review of the literature reveals a number of gaps in our knowledge about the experiences of women refugees during the three phases of their forced migration. Our understanding of the migration process from the home country to resettlement camps is incomplete. To comprehend and mediate the recovery process for individuals and their families, it is essential to obtain data about the flight from the home country. Such information is relevant to the resettlement process, and it can illuminate the conditions under which refugees do or do not effectively adapt to social change.

We also lack adequate information about life in resettlement camps. While it may seem frivolous to initiate investigations in a situation in which the survival of people is at stake, quantitative and qualitative research is key to creating policy and long-range understanding. For example, refugee resettlement programs usually target men rather than women,[21] assuming that families headed by men will adjust more easily to the new environment than will families headed by women. Data are required to foster understanding of the way in which refugee needs are ranked.

The implications of these decisions for refugees also demand attention. While the UNHCR literature argues that gender sensitivity has increased in refugee camps, this is not always the case. On the one hand, the participation of women in selected decisions in Philippine camps empowered them, while on the other, training programs to teach knitting techniques in an African camp did not. If knitting is not a marketable skill, such training is impractical and a waste of time and money that might otherwise be devoted to improving women's employment potential. Camp administrators need to be responsive to gender in order to plan appropriate job-training programs. Social scientists can help them achieve this objective by developing data necessary for informed decisions.

It also must be remembered that camps are not necessarily short-term places of refuge. Rather, they often become a home in which refugees live for several years, and in which some grow up and establish their own families. We lack information about how people and groups reorganize, the forces that motivate such reorganization, and the cultural systems that are created in camps. We also know little about the impact of long-term incarceration on refugees and the implications of a bureaucratic camp structure for their values, norms, and traditions. All of these issues demand attention.

As this review has shown, a large body of literature exists on the resettlement process. A number of issues, however, remain poorly understood. For example, although a sense of loss is an underlying theme in the literature on the adaptation of women refugees, women's loss of their culture has not been studied. Research has been reported on cultural bereavement among children (Eisenbruch, cited in Ferris 1991:9), and we need to build on this knowledge. Studies should be initiated to explore the meaning of cultural bereavement for women and to determine its implications for gender roles and women's adjustment. We also need more information on women's support networks (family, community, ethnic, and/or non-ethnic): the efficacy of network members in ameliorating the effects of earlier traumatic experiences, assisting in employment acquisition, and influencing women to embrace or reject change.

Finally, two critical areas remain neglected. First, while supplementing the literature on the refugee experience is important, the effort will be incomplete if the complexity of gender is not acknowledged. Women do not form a homogenous group and their experiences vary by age, ethnicity, work status, and country of settlement. The work of the few researchers who have analyzed census data on refugees has not recognized such variations among women. Detailed analyses are needed to lay the groundwork for qualitative studies which can illuminate the statistical relationships which emerge.

Second, much of the refugee research has originated in the need for information by governments, private organizations, and practitioners and, accordingly, it has a strong applied component. This focus often views women in their family roles, as mothers and wives who are responsible for the physical and mental health of their husbands and children. Women who work, for example, are perceived as responsible for their husbands' stress because their paid labor ostensibly challenges male dominance. The unit of inquiry in this type of research is the family and its dynamics. Such micro-level analyses ignore the role the greater society plays in generating stress via its ideology about women. Women are thus objectified as nurturers rather than as dynamic people who actively participate in society. More research is needed on the way the ideology and values of the host country shape women's experience as refugees in order to encourage greater understanding among practitioners and academics of the relationship between individual change and cultural change.

Notes

1. According to Minear (1990:13-19), other United Nations organizations, such as the UN World Food Program and the UN Development Program, as well as the World Bank and the International Fund for Agricultural Development, expanded their programs. Non-governmental organizations (NGOs) have also tried to respond to the growing number of crises caused by natural disasters or social and political strife.

2. Stevens (1988) found that two-thirds of the total refugee population in Somalia were female, while Williams (1990) reported that 90 percent of the total Ethiopian refugee population in Somalia were women with young children (under 15 years). Eighty percent of the Cambodian refugee families along the Thai-Cambodian border were female-headed (Williams 1990). In one Thai refugee camp 68 percent of the women refugees headed families with young children under age 15 (Sundhagel 1981). Women refugees from Central American countries often have the additional problem of not being recognized as refugees by the United States government. Those who are in the United States are not easily documented (or counted); however, as individuals and as members of solo families, undocumented Hispanic women, along with Cuban and Haitian women, constitute a significant block of Central American refugees in the United States and Central America (Golden and McConnell 1986; Roe 1987; Spero 1985).

3. Unfortunately, these data are not disaggregated to provide information about gender or family type (such as nuclear family or woman- or man-headed household).

4. The book, *African Refugees*, by Gaim Kibreab (1985) is just one example. In many ways, this is a good book on the dilemma of African refugees, despite its depiction of refugees as genderless and classless.

5. Social class, as well as gender, is ignored even though social class shapes the refugee experience. Further study is called for on the effects of class on the selection of people for resettlement and on the resettlement experience.

6. "To a certain extent the woman is used to appease the pirates, who go so far in their cruelty as to purposely transform witnesses into accomplices. Moreover, a certain amount of bargaining may take place. A young girl may be offered in exchange for the liberty of the group of boat people" (Amar 1985:31).

7. A country in the northeast part of Africa, adjacent to Somalia and Ethiopia.

8. An analysis of the ethnicity and dominant cultural values of participating individuals, countries, and international organizations which make policy decisions in these camps might illuminate this androcentrism.

9. For example, see Montero (1979) and Stein (1979) on the Vietnamese; Portes, Clark, and Bach (1977) on the Cubans; Feldman (1977) and Gilison (1979) on emigrées from the Soviet Union; and Bach and Bach (1980), Bach et al. (1984), DeVoe (in press), Haines (1985, 1987), Marsh (1980), and Whitmore, Trautmann, and Caplan (1989) on Southeast Asians.

10. Most men are content with this arrangement as long as their wives maintain their responsibilities as caretakers and housekeepers (Sen 1987, commenting on Lao men in Illinois).

11. On occupational background, see also Haines (1987:52-53).

12. See also Dunning (1989:62) on the Vietnamese; Haines (1987:51-52) and Rumbaut (1989:147) on Southeast Asians; and Spero (1985) on Southeast Asians, Haitians, and Hispanics.

13. Even with multiple adults working, refugee households remain below the poverty line (Rumbaut 1989:151-153). Caplan, Whitmore, and Bui (1985) suggest that increasing the number of workers in a household is a strategy that arises from a depressed economic condition.

14. Ethnographic studies are needed to provide explanations for findings which are based on larger census and quantitative materials.

15. Longitudinal studies involving age at marriage and total number of children among long-term refugees will determine the validity of such an assumption.

16. For example, see Parrish et al. (1987) on sudden death syndrome; Craft et al. (1983) on blood abnormalities among Southeast Asian refugees; and Pham (1986) on mental health problems among Vietnamese.

17. For example, on the self-rated health scale, 49 percent of the Khmer reported that their health was poor or fair, compared to 27 percent of the Hmong. On this same scale, 33 percent of the Vietnamese reported their health as poor or fair and 34 percent reported their health as excellent. Among women, 43 percent reported their health as poor or fair, while only 27 percent of the men did so; and only eight percent of the women and 26 percent of the men reported excellent health (this was not further divided by ethnicity) (Rumbaut 1989:154).

18. Angolan refugee women in Zambia represent an interesting contrast in that they assimilated more quickly than men (Spring 1982). A common method women adopted to assimilate and to achieve economic stability was to divorce their refugee husbands and marry Zambian men.

19. For example, even though gender inequality was present in Southern Africa, Tienda and Booth (1991:58) found that women were relatively autonomous farmers in their home villages. Upon moving to a major city, however, they found themselves disproportionately restricted to low paying

jobs in the informal economy; men were disproportionately employed in the formal and public sector. These women (who often had dependent parents and children back in their villages) thus became more dependent upon the more economically secure men.

20. In the eastern part of the United States refugee workers consider men more conservative in their clothing styles than women, and feel that women adopt United States clothing styles more rapidly (personal communication, Linda Camino). Research is needed to determine whether variations in rates of adaptation are related to variations in adjustment or whether such differences can be used to distinguish certain communities from other communities (e.g., by location, ethnicity, social class, education level).

21. An exception is a Canadian resettlement program for unaccompanied women or women who head households (Peteri 1988).

References

Adepoju, Aderanti
    1982   The Dimension of the Refugee Problem in Africa. *African Affairs* 81:21-35.

Amar, Meryem C.
    1985   Boat Women: Piracy's Other Dimension: Rape and Its Consequences. *Refugees* June:30-31.

Aylesworth, Laurence Saigo, Peter G. Ossorio, and Larry T. Osaki
    1980   Stress and Mental Health Among Vietnamese in the United States. In: *Asian American Social and Psychological Perspectives*, edited by R. Endo et al. Pp. 128-144. Palo Alto: Science and Behavior Books.

Bach, Robert L. and Jennifer B. Bach
    1980   Employment Patterns of Southeast Asian Refugees. *Monthly Labor Review* 103(10):31-38.

Bach, Robert L., Linda W. Gordon, David W. Haines, and David R. Howell
    1984   Geographic Variations in the Economic Adjustment of Southeast Asian Refugees in the U.S. In: *World Refugee Survey 1984*, edited by Rosemary E. Tripp. Pp. 7-8. Washington: U.S. Committee for Refugees (USCR) of the American Council for Nationalities Service (ACNS).

Barnett, Rosalind C., Harriet Davidson, and Nancy L. Marshall
1991   Physical Symptoms and the Interplay of Work and Family Roles. *Health Psychology* 10(2):94-101.

Baum, Andrew and Neil E. Grunberg
1991   Gender, Stress, and Health. *Health Psychology* 10(2):80-85.

Bell, Robert A.
1991   Gender, Friendship Network Density, and Loneliness. *Journal of Social Behavior and Personality* 6(1):45-56.

Bergman, Arlene Eisen
1975   *Women of Vietnam*. San Francisco: Peoples Press.

Berry, Angela
1988   Food for Thought. *Refugees* 56(Sept):34-35.

Bonnerjea, Lucy
1985   *Shaming the World: The Needs of Refugee Women*. London: World University Service.

Boserup, Ester
1970   *Women's Role in Economic Development*. London: George Allen and Unwin.

Burrows, Rob
1987   Pirate Arrests, Convictions Increase in 1986. *Refugees* 38(Feb):13-14.

Calhoun, Mary Atchity
1985   The Vietnamese Woman: Health/Illness Attitudes and Behaviors. *Health Care for Women International* 6(1-3):61-72.

Calloway, Helen
1987   Refugee Women: Specific Requirements and Untapped Resources. In: Third World Affairs, edited by Gaunar Altaf. Pp. 320-325. London: Third World Affairs Foundation.

Camus-Jacques, Genevieve
1989   Refugee Women: The Forgotten Majority. In: *Refugees and International Relations*, edited by Gil Loescher and Laila Monohan. Pp. 141-157. Oxford: Oxford University Press.

Caplan, Nathan, John K. Whitmore, and Quang L. Bui
1985 *Southeast Asian Refugee Self-Sufficiency Study: Final Report*. Ann Arbor: The Institute for Social Research.

Caplan, Nathan, John K. Whitmore, and Marcella H. Choy
1989 *The Boat People and Achievement in America*. Ann Arbor: The University of Michigan Press.

Chan, Kwok
1984 Indochinese Refugees and Social Support: The Theoretical Importance of the Family and Social Networks in Research and Social Intervention. In: *Refugee Resettlement: Southeast Asians in Transition*, edited by R. Nann, P. Johnson, and M. Beizer. Pp. 125-132. Vancouver, British Columbia: Refugee Resettlement Project.

Chan, K. and L. Lam
1987 Community, Kinship and Family in the Chinese Vietnamese Community: Some Enduring Values and Patterns of Interaction. In: *Uprooting, Loss and Adaptation: The Resettlement of Indochinese Refugees in Canada*, edited by K. Chang and D. Indra. Pp. 15-26. Ottawa: Canadian Public Health Association.

Coles, Gervase
1989 Approaching the Refugee Problem Today. In: *Refugees and International Relations*, edited by Gil Loescher and Laila Monahan. Pp. 373-410. Oxford: Oxford University Press.

Craft, J., D. Coleman, H. Coulter, R. Horwitz, and M. Barry
1983 Hematologic Abnormalities in Southeast Asian Refugees. *Journal of the American Medical Association* 249(23):3204-3206.

Crisp, Jeff
1987 Refugees in Thailand. *Refugees* 45:18-34.

De, Truong Thi Dieu
1989 *Vietnamese Women and Sexual Violence*. Report No. 1. Refugee Health Care Centre, Library and Documentation, P.O. Box 264, 2280 AG Rijswijk, The Netherlands.

DeVoe, Pamela A.
Southeast Asian Refugee Employees and Their Employers in the American Mid-West: Proponents, Picadors or Pawns?.   In: *Refugee Empowerment and Organizational Change: A Systems Perspective*, edited by Peter Van Arsdale. Westport: Greenwood Press. In press.

DeVoe, Pamela A. and Ann Manry Rynearson
1983   *Social Relations in a Refugee Neighborhood: Indochinese in St. Louis, MO.* Washington: Report for the Office of Refugee Resettlement.   Washington: Division of Health and Human Services.

Dewey, Arthur Eugene
1988   We Have to Be Tenacious in Our Protection Efforts. *Refugees* 56(Sept):19-20.

Dorais, Louis-Jacques, Lise Pilon-Le, and Nguyen Huy
1987   *Exile in a Cold Land: A Vietnamese Community in Canada.* New Haven: Council on Southeast Asia Studies, Yale Center for International and Area Studies and the William Joiner Center, University of Massachusetts.

Dunning, Bruce B.
1989   Vietnamese in America: The Adaptation of the 1975-1979 Arrivals. In: *Refugees as Immigrants: Cambodians, Laotians and Vietnamese in America* edited by David W. Haines. Pp. 55-85. Totowa: Rowman & Littlefield Publication, Inc.

Eldred, Patricia Lyons
1985   Changing Roles of Refugee Women: The Impact on Dietary Beliefs and Behavior.   Paper presented at the American Anthropological Association (AAA) Annual Meeting, Washington, D.C., December.

Epstein, T. Scarlett and Rosemary A. Watts
1981   *The Endless Day: Some Case Material on Asian Rural Women.* New York: Pergamon Press.

Faller, H.
1985   Perinatal Needs of Immigrant Hmong Women: Surveys of Women and Health Care Providers. *Public Health Reports* 100(3):340-343.

University of Ulster LIBRARY

Feldman, William
1977 Social Absorption of Soviet Immigrants: Integration or Isolation. *Journal of Jewish Communal Service* 54(1):62-68.

Ferris, Elizabeth G.
1985 Overview: Refugees and World Politics. In: *Refugees and World olitics*, edited by Elizabeth G. Ferris. Pp. 1-25. New York: Praeger Special Studies.

1991 Refugee Children: Hope for the Future. *Refugees* 112E, March. Published by the Commission on Inter-Church Aid, Refugee and World Service, World Council of Churches.

Finck, John
1983 The Indochinese in America: Progress Towards Self-Sufficiency. In: *World Refugee Survey 1983*, edited by Rosemary E. Tripp. Pp. 56-59. Washington: U.S. Committee for Refugees (USCR) of the American Council for Nationalities Service (ACNS).

Fox, R.
1985 The Indochinese: Strategies for Health Survival *International Journal of Social Psychiatry* 30(4):285-291.

Gelfand, Donald
1982 *Aging: The Ethnic Factor.* Boston: Little Brown.

Gelfand, Donald and Alfred Kutzik (editors)
1979 *Ethnicity and Aging: Theory, Research, and Policy.* New York: Springer Publishing Company.

Gilison, Jerome M.
1979 *Summary Report of the Survey of Soviet Jewish Emigres in Baltimore.* Baltimore: Baltimore Hebrew College.

Golden, Renny and Michael McConnell
1986 *Sanctuary: The New Underground Railroad.* Pp. 113-116. Maryknoll: Orbis Books.

Gonzalez, Nancie L.
   1989   Conflict, Migration, and the Expression of Ethnicity: Introduction.
          In: *Conflict, Migration and the Expression of Ethnicity*, edited by
          Nancie L. Gonzalez and Carolyn S. McCommon.   Pp. 1-10.
          Boulder: Westview Press.

Hackett, Beatrice Nied
   1988   Relative and Relational Power for Ethnic Chinese Cambodian
          Refugees: Economics with a Twist.   Paper presented at the
          American Anthropological Association (AAA) Annual Meeting,
          Phoenix, Arizona, November.

Haines, David W.
   1985   Initial Adjustment. In: *Refugees in the United States: A Reference
          Handbook*, edited by David W. Haines. Pp. 17-55. Westport:
          Greenwood Press.

   1987   Patterns in Southeast Asian Refugee Employment: A Reappraisal
          of the Existing Research. *Ethnic Groups* 7(1):39-63.

   1989   Introduction. In: *Refugees as Immigrants: Cambodians, Laotians,
          and Vietnamese in America*, edited by David W. Haines. Pp. 1-23.
          Totowa: Rowman & Littlefield.

Haines, D., D. Rutherford, and D. Thomas
   1981   Family and Community among Vietnamese Refugees. *International
          Migration Review* 15(1):310-319.

Hall, Eve
   1990   Vocational Training for Women Refugees in Africa. *International
          Labour Review* 129(1):91-107.

Healy, Mary T.
   1988   Lao Women as Crypto-Patrons: From Generalized Reciprocity to
          Patrons and Clients.   Paper presented at the American
          Anthropological Association Annual Meeting, Phoenix, Arizona,
          November.

Hickey, Gerald C.
   1964   *Village in Vietnam*. New Haven: Yale University Press.

Hirayama, K.
   1982   Evaluating Effects of Employment of Vietnamese Refugee Wives
          on Their Family Roles and Mental Health. *California Sociologist:
          A Journal of Sociology and Social Work* 5(1):96-110.

Hutchinson, Maria
   1985   Women Refugees and the U.N. Decade for Women. *Refugee
          Abstracts* 4:3-5.

Indra, Doreen
   1987   Gender: A Key Dimension of the Refugee Experience. *Refugees*
          6:3-4.

Jackson, Tony with Deborah Eade
   1982   *Against the Grain: The Dilemma of Project Food Aid* Oxford:
          Oxfam.

Kibreab, Gain
   1985   *African Refugees*. Trenton: African World Press.

Kibria, Nazli
   1989   Patterns of Vietnamese Refugee Women's Wagework in the U.S.
          Ethnic Groups 7(4):297-323.

Kinzie, J.D. and J. Fleck
   1987   Psychotherapy with Severely Traumatized Refugees *American
          Journal of Psychotherapy* 41(1):82-94.

Krumperman, Andre
   1983   Psychosocial Problems of Violence, Especially Its Effect on
          Refugees. In: *The Psychosocial Problems of Refugees*, edited by
          Ron Baker. Pp. 14-20. Luton, United Kingdom: L & T Press,
          Ltd.

Kubota and Matsuda
   1982   Family Planning Services for Southeast Asian Refugees. *Family
          and Community Health* 5(1):19-28.

Kulig, Judith C.
   1988   Conception and Birth Control Use: Cambodian Refugee Women's
          Beliefs and Practices. *Journal of Community Health Nursing*
          5(4):235-246.

· 1990a Childbearing Beliefs Among Cambodian Refugee Women. *Western Journal of Nursing Research* 12(1):108-118.

1990b A Review of the Health Status of Southeast Asian Refugee Women. *Health Care for Women International* 11:49-63.

Laderman, Carol
  1982 Putting Malay Women in Their Place. In: *Women of Southeast Asia*. Monograph Series on Southeast Asia, edited by Penny Van Esterik. Pp. 79-99. De Kalb: Northern Illinois University.

Lee, P.
  1986 Health Beliefs of Pregnant and Postpartum Hmong Women. *Western Journal of Nursing Research* 8(1):83-93.

Lin, Keh-Ming
  1986 Psychopathology and Social Disruption in Refugees. In: *Refugee Mental Health in Resettlement Countries*, edited by C. Williams and J. Westermeyer. Pp. 61-73. Washington: Hemisphere Publishing Co.

Loescher, Gil
  1989 Introduction: Refugee Issues in International Relations. In: *Refugees and International Relations*, edited by Gil Loescher and Laila Monahan. Pp. 1-33. London: Oxford University Press.

Manderson, L. and M. Matthews
  1981 Vietnamese Behavioral and Dietary Precautions During Pregnancy. *Ecology of Food and Nutrition* 11(1):1-8.

Markides, Kyriakos and Charles Mindel
  1987 *Aging and Ethnicity*. Newbury Park: Sage Publications.

Marsh, Robert E.
  1980 Socioeconomic Status of Indochinese Refugees in the United States: Progress and Problems. *Social Security Bulletin* 43(10):11-20.

Matthews, M. and L. Manderson
  1981 Vietnamese Behavioral and Dietary Precautions during Confinement. *Ecology of Food and Nutrition* 11(1):9-16.

Minear, Larry
1990 Civil Strife & Humanitarian Aid: A Bruising Decade. In: *World Refugee Survey 1989 in Review*. Washington: U.S. Committee for Refugees of the American Council for Nationalities Service.

Mitchell, R.
1987 From Refugee to Rebuilder: Cambodian Women in America. *Dissertation Abstracts International* 49:202.

Montero, Darrel
1979 *Vietnamese Americans: Patterns of Resettlement and Socioeconomic Adaptation in the United States*. Boulder: Westview Press.

Montgomery, R.
1991 Predicting Vietnamese Refugee Adjustment to Western Canada. *International Migration* 29(1):89-113.

Morokvasic, Mirjana
1984 Birds of Passage Are Also Women. *International Migration Review* 18(4):886-907.

Ng, Roxana
1988 The Documentary Construction of "Immigrant Women" in Canada. Working Paper on Women in International Development No. 160. East Lansing, MI: Women and International Development Program, Michigan State University.

Parker, Ann
1988 Support for Those Who Need It. *Refugees* 56(Sept):32-33.

Parrish, R., M. Tucker, R. Ing, C. Encarnacion, and M. Eberhardt
1987 Sudden Unexpected Death Syndrome in Southeast Asian Refugees: A Review of Communicable Disease Surveillance. *Morbidity and Mortality Weekly Reports* 36:43-53.

Pas-Ong, Suparb
1989 Selling for the World Market: The Peasant Petty Trader. *Sojourn: Social Issues in Southeast Asia* 4(1):113-126.

Peteri, Mary
1988 Resettlement of Refugee Women at Risk. *Refugees* 56(Sept):22.

Pham, T.
  1986 The Mental Health Problems of the Vietnamese Refugees in
        Calgary: Major Aspects and Implications for Service. *Canada's
        Mental Health* 34(4):5-9.

Portes, Alejandro, Juan M. Clark, and Robert L. Bach
  1977 The New Wave: A Statistical Profile of Recent Cuban Exiles to
        the United States. *Cuban Studies* 1:1-32.

Portes, Alejandro and Saskia Sassen-Koob
  1987 Marking It Underground: Comparative Material on the Informal
        Sector in Western Market Economies. *American Journal of
        Sociology* 93(1):30-61.

Ranard, Donald A.
  1990 A Buddhist Temple in Rural Virginia. *Refugees* 79(Oct):32-33.

Reynell, Josephine
  1988 *Socio-Economic Evaluation of the Khmer Refugee Camps on the
        Thai-Kampuchean Border.* Oxford: Refugee Studies Programme.
        University of Oxford, Queen Elizabeth House, 21 St. Giles, Oxford,
        OX1 3LA, United Kingdom.

Roe, Michael
  1987 Central American Refugees in the U.S.: Psychological Adaptation.
        Refugee Issues 3:21-30.

Ruiz, Hiram A.
  1989 *Peace or Terror: A Crossroads for Southern Africa's Uprooted.*
        Washington: U.S. Committee for Refugees. United States
        Committee for Refugees, 1025 Vermont Avenue NW, Suite 920,
        Washington, D.C. 20005.

Rumbaut, Ruben G.
  1989 Portraits, Patterns, and Predictors of the Refugee Adaptation
        Process: Results and Reflections from the IHARP Panel Study.
        In: *Refugees an Immigrants: Cambodians, Laotians, and
        Vietnamese in America,* edited by David W. Haines. Pp. 138-190.
        Totowa: Rowman and Littlefield.

Rumbaut, Ruben G. and John R. Weeks
   1986   Fertility and Adaptation: Indochinese Refugees in the United
          States. *International Migration Review* 20(2):428-465.

Rynearson, Ann Manry and Pamela A. DeVoe
   1984   Refugee Women in a Vertical Village: Lowland Laotians in St.
          Louis. *Social Thought* 10(3):33-48.

Sargent, C., J. Macucci, and E. Elliston
   1983   Tiger Bones, Fire and Wine: Maternity Care in a Campuchean
          Refugee Community. *Medical Anthropology* 7(4):67-79.

Savishinsky, Joel
   1990   Introduction: To Grow Old in a Foreign Land: Issues in Ethnicity
          and Aging. *Ethnic Groups* 8(3):143-146.

Scott, George M. Jr.
   1988   To Catch or Not to Catch a Thief: A Case of Bride Theft among
          the Lao Hmong Refugees in Southern California. *Ethnic Groups*
          7(2):137-151.

Sen, Srila
   1987   *The Lao in the United States Since Migration: An Anthropological
          Inquiry of Persistence and Accommodation.* Ph.D. dissertation.
          University of Illinois at Urbana-Champaign. Ann Arbor:
          University Microfilms International.

Shumaker, Sally A. and D. Robin Hill
   1991   Gender Differences in Social Support and Physical Health. *Health
          Psychology* 10(2):102-111.

Siemens, Maria
   1988   Protection of Refugee Women. *Refugees* 56(Sept):21-22.

Skartvedt, Elizabeth
   1989   The Impact of Gender Roles on the Psychosocial Adjustment of
          Refugee Women: Issues for Study. Paper presented at the Society
          for Applied Anthropology Annual Meeting, Santa Fe, New Mexico,
          (Dates).

Sorenson, John
   1991   Politics of Social Identity: 'Ethiopians' in Canada. *The Journal of Ethnic Studies* 19(1):67-86.

Spenner, Kenneth I. and Rachel A. Rosenfeld
   1990   Women, Work, and Identities. *Social Science Research* 19(3):266-299.

Spero, Abby
   1985   *In America and in Need: Immigrant, Refugee, and Entrant Women.* Washington: American Association of Community and Junior Colleges.

Spring, Anita
   1982   Women and Men as Refugees: Differential Assimilation of Angolan Refugees in Zambia. In: *Involuntary Migration and Resettlement: The Problems and Responses of Dislocated People,* edited by Art Hansen and Anthony Oliver-Smith. Pp. 37-48. Boulder: Westview Press.

St. Cartmail, Keith
   1983   *Exodus Indochina.* Auckland Exeter: Heinemann.

Stein, Barry N.
   1979   Occupational Adjustment of Refugees: The Vietnamese in the United States. *International Migration Review* 13(1):25-45.

   1986   The Experience of Being a Refugee: Insights from the Research Literature. In: *Refugee Mental Health in Resettlement Countries,* edited by C.L. Williams and J. Westermeyer. Washington: Hemisphere Publishing Co.

Stevens, Yvette
   1988   Refugee Women in Africa: The Key to Self-Reliance. *Refugees* 56(Sept):33-34.

Stier, Haya
   1991   Immigrant Women Go to Work: Analysis of Immigrant Wives' Labor Supply for Six Asian Groups. *Social Science Quarterly* 72(1):67-82.

Sundhagel, Malee
  1981   Situation and Role of Refugee Women: Experience and
         Perspectives from Thailand. *International Migration Review*
         19:102-107.

Tenhula, John
  1991   *Voices from Southeast Asia: The Refugee Experience in the United
         States*. New York: Holmes and Meier.

Tienda, Marta and Karen Booth
  1991   Gender, Migration and Social Change. *International Sociology*
         6(1):51-72.

UNHCR (United Nations High Commission on Refugees)
  1987   Women as Refugees. *Refugees* 41(May):5.

  1990   Breast Is Best. *Refugees* 74(April):24

USCR (United States Committee for Refugees)
  1990   1989 World Refugee Statistics. In: *World Refugee Survey 1989 in
         Review*, edited by Virginia Hamilton. Pp. 30-34. Washington:
         United States Committee for Refugees of the American Council
         for Nationalities Service.

Van Esterik, Penny
  1980   Cultural Factors Affecting the Adjustment of Southeast Asian
         Refugees. In: *Southeast Asian Exodus: From Tradition to
         Resettlement, Understanding Refugees from Laos, Kampuchea and
         Vietnam in Canada*, edited by Elliot L. Tepper. Pp. 151-171.
         Ottowa: The Canadian Asian Studies Association.

  1982   Introduction. In: *Women of Southeast Asia*, edited by Penny Van
         Esterik. Pp. 1-15. Occasional Paper No. 9. DeKalb: Northern
         Illinois University. Detroit, Michigan 48221.

Wadd, L.
  1983   Vietnamese Postpartum Practices: Implications for Nursing in the
         Hospital Setting. *Journal of Obstetrics and Gynecological Nursing*
         12(4):252-258.

Walter, I.
    1981   One Year after Their Arrival: The Adjustment of Indochinese
            Women in the United States (1979-1980). *International Migration*
            19:129-152.

Waters, Tony
    1990   Adaptation and Migration among the Mien People of Southeast
            Asia. *Ethnic Groups* 8(2):127-141.

Weinstein-Shr, Gail
    1987   Breaking the Linguistic and Social Isolation of Refuge Elders: An
            Intergenerational Model.   Paper presented at the American
            Anthropological Association (AAA) Annual Meeting, Chicago,
            Illinois, November.

Westermeyer, Joseph, Mayka Bouafuely, and Tou Fu Vang
    1984   Hmong Refugees in Minnesota: Sex Roles and Mental Health.
            Medical Anthropology 8(4):229-245.

Westermeyer, Joseph, Tou Fu Vang, and John Neider
    1983   Migration and Mental Health among Hmong Refugees.   *The*
            Journal of Nervous and Mental Disease 171(2):92-96.

Whitmore, John K., Marcella Trautmann, and Nathan Caplan
    1989   The Socio-Cultural Basis for the Economic and Educational
            Success of Southeast Asian Refugees (1978-1982 Arrivals).   In:
            Refugees as Immigrants: Cambodians, Laotians and Vietnamese in
            America, edited by David W. Haines.   Pp. 121-137.   Totowa:
            Rowman and Littlefield.

Williams, Holly Ann
    1990   Families in Refugee Camps. *Human Organization* 49(2):100-109.

Winter, Roger and Joseph Cerquone
    1984   Pirate Attacks Against Vietnamese Boat People Continue. In:
            World Refugee Survey 1984, edited by Rosemary E. Tripp. Pp. 8-9.
            Washington: U.S. Committee for Refugees (USCR) of the
            American Council for Nationalities Service (ACNS).

Wong, Diana
    1989   The Semantics of Migration. *Sojourn* 4(2):275-285.

Zaharlick, Amy and Jean Brainard
  1988   Fertility Transition and the Changing Status of Laotian Refugee
         Women.   Paper presented at the American Anthropological
         Association (AAA) Annual Meeting, Phoenix, Arizona, November.

Zolberg, Aristide R., Astri Suhrke, and Sergio Aguayo
  1989   *Escape from Violence: Conflict and the Refugee Crisis in the
         Developing World*. Oxford: Oxford University Press.

2

Gender, Development, and AIDS: A Political Economy and Culture Framework

Brooke Grundfest Schoepf

AIDS is a new fatal disease syndrome which poses a significant threat to the health and survival of millions in developed and less developed countries. The Human Immunodeficiency Virus (HIV) which causes immune system damage leading to AIDS, is transmitted through sexual intercourse, blood transfusion, and during pregnancy from mother to infant. Poverty and gender relations are central to the spread of HIV. By gender relations, I mean the processes, structures, and institutions by means of which societies order sex differences and invest them with cultural meanings for the people who act them out in daily life. In contemporary societies, gender relations are often relations of unequal power. Women's generally low status in family and society and their relative powerlessness in sexual relations make them particularly vulnerable to HIV infection. Linking a macrolevel analysis to microlevel studies of social interaction shows how political economy, gender, and culture shape responses to disease. These mutual determinations frame the symbolic representations of AIDS and influence prevention. They both render necessary, and offer possibilities for, wider social change.

I begin this chapter with an overview of the epidemiology and biology of HIV and then examine aspects of political economy and gender relations that propel the pandemic. The next sections offer a gendered perspective on AIDS prevention and a critical assessment of current debates and research strategies in the international arena. In the final sections I argue for community-based approaches to prevention that are grounded in actual conditions and that use what have become known as empowerment strategies. I call for further action-research to help reshape gender relations in support of both AIDS prevention and development. The discussion focuses primarily on Africa, where

I have worked since 1974. While some of the situations described are specific to Central and East Africa, others are more widely applicable.

An Overview of the Pandemic

HIV infection spread widely in the late 1970s, before the first cases were identified in the United States in 1981. By now, the slow-acting virus has become pandemic, with AIDS cases reported from 162 countries. Most of those now infected and 90 percent of the 15 to 30 million new infections expected to occur during the 1990s are and will be in less developed countries.

Nearly 447,000 cumulative cases of AIDS had been reported to the World Health Organization by the end of 1991, although the true figure is likely to be much higher.[1] By the year 2000, some 30 to 40 million people will have been infected, including 12 to 18 million children. Another ten to fifteen million children under age 15 will have been orphaned by the death of one or both parents. In high prevalence areas, ten to forty percent of young mothers are HIV-infected. Between 20 and 40 percent of their infants will develop AIDS; of these, 80 percent will die before age five.

AIDS is not just another disease, and the HIV virus is not just one among many new micro-organisms affecting humans. The biological processes involved are complex and difficult for lay people to understand. The virus uses the body's own immune system to reproduce itself and destroys its ability to resist other diseases, including tuberculosis, pneumonia, diarrheas, and various neurological disorders.

The virus is slow-acting; in the United States about half of those found to be infected have developed disease symptoms within ten years. Death generally occurs within two years following the onset of AIDS; the time depends upon availability of expensive drugs and skilled biomedical treatment. At present there is no cure for AIDS and no vaccine to prevent HIV infection. These are not likely to be discovered in the near future and when they do become available, access will be limited by inability to pay, especially in the Third World.

Different transmission patterns predominate in different parts of the world and in different population sub-groups within countries. Currently, about 70 percent of infections are believed to have been acquired during sexual intercourse with an infected partner (Chin 1990). Although AIDS was first detected in Western homosexual males, globally, one-third or more of the infected are women, most of whom were infected by men who had sex with multiple partners.

AIDS often provokes fear and hostility toward the afflicted. Families unable to dissemble the nature of the illness may find themselves isolated; AIDS orphans may be shunned and left to roam the streets, where they are particularly vulnerable to HIV infection. With numerous people falling sick and others demoralized by seeing so much death around them, the impact on all economic activities (particularly on season-sensitive, labor-intensive agriculture and food-processing) and on all social groups in the affected areas is likely to be severe (Barnett and Blaikie 1992; Gillespie 1989; Norse 1991; Obbo 1989a; Schoepf 1990). In the next sections, I argue for a development and gender relations approach to understanding the AIDS pandemic.

AIDS: A Disease of Development

An epidemic is an essentially social process, shaped by political economy and culture. Globally, AIDS is best regarded as a "disease of development"[2] and "underdevelopment" (Hunt 1989; Packard 1989; Schoepf 1988; Schoepf, Rukarangira et al. 1988). It has struck with particular severity in communities struggling under the burdens of economic crises caused by stagnation in the global economy, distorted internal production structures inherited from colonialism, unfavorable terms of trade, and widening disparities in wealth fueled by the channelling of public funds into private pockets.

In the late 1970s, Third World leaders urged restructuring the world economy to redress global inequality. Instead, the institutions of international finance restructured their lending policies. Structural adjustment and heavy debt service payments were imposed in the 1980s as a condition for further borrowing from the International Monetary Fund (IMF) and the World Bank (See Gladwin this volume). One result has been more intensive capital outflows that exceed new investments and drain away investable surpluses generated by the low-paid work force.

Where new investment occurs, it links Third World economies even more firmly to world markets on increasingly unfavorable terms, promoting "recolonization" (Tadesse 1991). Unpayable debts are repeatedly rescheduled, mortgaging the future. George (1988:21) terms this strategy, which shifts the brunt of crises from industrialized countries to the Third World, a "financial low intensity conflict." Cuts in already meager budgets for health, education, and social services have combined with inflation to further undermine living standards. The result is the impoverishment of tens of millions, especially women (Adedeji 1990; Cornia, Jolly, and Stewart 1987; Feldman 1989; Green 1985; Onimode 1989; Seidman and Anang 1992).

Investment in peasant agriculture and in rural social infrastructure has been extremely limited in many areas. "Production first" policies inspired by Western advisors increased credit and input availability for the large-farm sector in favorable ecological zones (Newbury and Schoepf 1989; Schoepf 1985). Population growth and increasing expropriation have led to land shortages in many areas (Davison 1988), and labor migration has increased.

Hard-pressed by state policies to sell more produce, families in many areas transfer the added labor burdens to women, who are seldom able to refuse patriarchal authority. Fewer girls go to school and sex differentials in education are widening; young women's future earnings, their status within the family, and their ability to care for children are thereby limited. Increasing numbers of young, overworked, and poorly remunerated women seek refuge from rural drudgery in the cities. Few find jobs. With the contraction of large-scale industry and government services, many city people are unemployed. Women and youth who are without special educational qualifications and powerful patrons are especially disadvantaged. Moreover, the incomes of most urban workers, already below subsistence levels in the early 1980s (Green 1985), are now hopelessly inadequate.

The burgeoning "informal sector," crowded with micro-enterprises, is relied upon to provide survival incomes and a base for capital formation. Vigorous though it appears in contrast to large-scale industry, the most prosperous operators are men with privileged access to capital and other scarce resources, including political protection (Rukarangira and Schoepf 1991; Schoepf and Walu 1991; Tadesse 1991). Wages in the informal sector are generally below legal minimums and social protection is lacking. Thus the informal sector cannot provide adequate living standards for most poor women and children. Their lives are made especially precarious by gender inequality, some special aspects of which are involved in the spread of AIDS.

Gender, Crisis and AIDS

Macroeconomic conditions operating in a context of pervasive gender inequality have different effects upon the lives of women in different regional, class, and family circumstances (Staudt 1988). Different circumstances also produce different negotiating strengths among women as well as different HIV risks (Bassett and Mhloyi 1991; Bond and Vincent 1990; Schoepf 1988, 1992b). Nevertheless, some common themes are found across classes and cultures (Caravano 1991; Krieger and Glen 1990).

Men whose incomes are low and uncertain or who are unemployed are often reluctant to start families or to assume responsibility for children. Engendering children, however, may be one of the few ways they have available to demonstrate their manhood (Campbell 1991; Gasch et al. 1991). As a result, many women, (Obbo 1989b) find themselves burdened with children whom they are hard-pressed to support.

In the absence of government support for social services, more burdens are placed on poor women, who turn to extended kin and community networks for help to "manage the crisis" and to shield their families from its most devastating effects (Antrobus 1989; Walu 1987). Family relations, however, have been severely strained, and deepening crises often render support networks more fragile. Propelled by civil wars, famine, and poverty, the wider social fabric in many areas is shredding, leaving many people without the safety net of social relations (UNECA 1989).

Women, who often lack access to cash, credit, land or jobs, engage in "off-the-books" activities in the informal sector.[3] Some exchange sex for the means of subsistence. Others enter sex work at the behest of their families, to obtain cash to purchase land or building materials, to pay a brother's school fees, or to settle a debt (White 1990).[4] Still others supplement meager incomes with occasional resort to sex with multiple partners (Obbo 1981; Schoepf 1981; Schuster 1979). Married or not, the deepening economic crisis propels many to seek "spare tires" or "shock absorbers to make ends meet." AIDS has transformed many women's survival strategies into death strategies (Schoepf 1988).

Many women are infected by husbands who have multiple partners.[5] Over time, the risks of unprotected intercourse with a single infected partner are considerable (Padian, Shiboski, and Jewell 1990). Wives' attempts to negotiate condom use can lead to domestic conflict, loss of support, and even violence (Kisekka 1990; Richardson 1988; Schoepf, Walu, Rukarangira et al. 1991). Many men interpret a wife's initiative as an accusation of infidelity or intent to restrict male prerogatives. Others say it means the wife intends to be unfaithful, a rationale which has also been used to oppose contraception. Unless she is prepared to end the marriage, a woman is obliged by her husband and his family to fulfill her "marital duty" by providing sex and children. In many countries this is part of the formal marriage contract; in others it is a "traditional" assumption.

The Difficulty of Prevention

The notion of "risk groups" has been used by epidemiologists to explain transmission patterns and target interventions to specific populations. Certain groups are particularly at risk for AIDS: sex workers and women in multiple partner relationships, and women whose human rights are abused. In the sections which follow, I discuss these groups of women, examine why assessing risk is problematic, and consider how attention to women's reproductive health might help to promote prevention of AIDS.

Sex Work and Multiple Partner Relationships

The myriad forms of sex work and other multiple partner relationships require prevention interventions tailored to specific social contexts (Alexander 1988; de Zalduondo 1991; Kane 1990a, 1990b; Schoepf 1988). Nevertheless, with high rates of infection present among young women who are not sex workers, categorizing women as "good women" versus "whores" is not only epidemiologically inadequate but counterproductive.

Women who view themselves as "good" because they provide for families as best they can, or as "normal" because they have sexual relations without being married, must reject the stigmatization which the labels attached to sex work imply. Rejecting the stigma, women may also deny their risk, including the necessity for condom protection and for treatment of sexually transmitted infections.

Failure to make realistic risk assessments contributes to the epidemic. Several studies have found that women tend to underestimate their risk of HIV infection (Miller, Turner, and Moses 1990; Thonneau et al. 1991). For change to take place, concern about infection must be coupled with perception that something can be done. Too much fear or a sense of helplessness often lead to denial rather than constructive action.

While prostitutes may be considered "reservoirs of infection" to be targeted for interventions, sex workers cannot be essentialized as a sub-culture in this manner (Kane 1990b; Kane and Mason 1992; Schoepf 1988; but see de Zalduondo 1991). When sex is exchanged for drugs, is illegal, or is not professionalized, condoms are rarely used and infection spreads rapidly (Plant 1991). Where prostitution is professionalized and condoms are used routinely, however, infection risk may be lower than in unprotected casual sexual encounters (Alexander 1988).

Once HIV is present, sex workers are at high risk when men refuse condoms (Moses et al. 1991; Nzila et al. 1991). Between 40 to 90 percent of low-income sex workers in East and Central African cities are HIV infected, and rates are rising rapidly in West Africa, the Caribbean, and South and Southeast Asia. Several studies (Moses et al. 1991; Nzila et al. 1991) report that between one-third and two-thirds of clients refuse condoms and are willing to pay higher rates for unprotected sex. Collective organization among sex workers and growing awareness among clients can raise acceptability; few are able to insist on protection. Moreover, many sex workers also have one or more non-paying partners with whom they are in stable relationships and, as in marriage, a woman's interest in maintaining the relationship inhibits condom use.[6]

Men's occupations may also create especially risky situations or environments that favor sex with multiple partners. For example, men who spend considerable time travelling or living away from home are especially likely to have multiple partners. Many poor men migrate long distances without their families in search of employment. In the South African mines, settlement restrictions, apartheid, and low wages oblige men to live in crowded, temporary quarters or dormitories. They often form liaisons or seek brief encounters with women who provide sexual and domestic services--what White (1990) terms "the comforts of home" (Jochelson, Mothibeli and Leger 1991; Packard and Epstein 1991).[7]

In addition to labor migrants, long distance traders, truckers and transport workers, seamen, fishermen, businessmen, government officials, technical consultants, teachers, students, and soldiers are at high risk. Seroprevalence rates of 30 percent and higher have been reported for some of these occupational categories in the most affected areas (Packard and Epstein 1991). Although few studies focus on high status men, those in positions of power are frequently consumers of commercial sex. They can also command the services of many who are not prostitutes.

International sex tourism is a major industry earning foreign exchange in some countries (Levy and Lerch 1991; Sabatier 1988; Truong 1990). Entertainment places are venues for casual sex and erotic adventures, including partner switching and practices not generally demanded of wives. The presence of military bases and ports also creates substantial demand. Governments and businesses that depend upon commercialized sex may be reluctant to institute a condom policy until reassured that business will continue. The resources devoted to AIDS prevention are meager, especially when compared to profits (Sabatier 1988).

More than being risky individual behaviors, these situations are rooted in the structures of underdevelopment and patriarchy. Some involve legal, socially approved activities; others are marginal and stigmatized; still others are outside the law. Nevertheless, they are widely practiced. Some of these common patterns of social interaction among people who find themselves in such circumstances are integral to activities such as smuggling and drug dealing, in which risk-taking is part of the life-style. At the same time, the structure of the wider political economy establishes the situations and restricts the options that people can choose as a means of survival. A focus on "sub-cultures," as on individual behaviors, tends to obscure the underlying causes of social interaction (Kane and Mason 1992; Quimby 1992). It also ignores the fact that the sex partners of those at high risk are not identifiable in terms of any shared social setting or identity (Kane and Mason 1992).

Abuse of Human Rights

AIDS raises special issues with respect to the human rights of women and youth (UNCHR 1991:22). Although not documented by statistics, several observers note that sexual harassment and violence against women have risen in the context of the economic crisis and of AIDS (Kisekka 1990; Richardson 1988). These are fundamentally power issues, and the presence of HIV renders rape more dangerous--potentially fatal--to women.

In theaters of war and military occupation, abuse of power by the military is common (Baldo and Cabral 1991; Giller, Bracken, and Kabaganda 1991). The high prevalence areas of Uganda and Tanzania have been linked to the presence of soldiers as well as to illegal cross-border trade. Throughout the region, military personnel have been found infected with HIV in excess of the general population. While men express concern chiefly over the implications for political stability, women note the special danger to girls and women. Kisekka (1990:45) writes that incessant warfare has "institutionalized brutalization of the populace, including sexual harassment with a concomitant rise in STDs [sexually transmitted diseases], particularly AIDS."

Where military and paramilitary men regularly harass the poor for money and sex, the city streets are not safe at night. Abuse of women prisoners is common in Zaire, and was so even before the current civil strife. In recent years, the threat of infecting women with HIV has been used as a form of political repression, a tactic designed to deter women from protesting their inability to feed their families in the face of galloping inflation. Just as women sought to politicize their role as mothers, so the state uses their vulnerability as women to intimidate and punish them for carrying their protests into the public sphere.

Sexual harassment by employers and educators became a public issue in the 1970s. As the crisis deepens, such harassment takes on a particularly sinister cast. Some seropositive men have boasted that they sought to make numerous sexual conquests. Their anger calls forth vengeance upon women in general because they contracted HIV through sex with a woman. Some are said to have left lists of female partners whom they tried to infect. True or not, the rumors heighten the repressive atmosphere. Some men now seek very young girls as sex partners, believing them to be free of AIDS risk (Bassett and Mhloyi 1991; Bledsoe 1990; Schoepf, Payanzo et al. 1988; SWAA 1989). The news media in one high prevalence area carried photographs of a mass marriage in which elder men were wedded to young brides.

Domestic violence is increasing as men's anger at poverty and hopelessness is vented upon their wives and children (Green 1985). In addition, men who perceive that AIDS interferes with their access to multiple sex partners may retaliate against women when deprived of other opportunities. Husbands who have heeded advice to practice marital fidelity have blamed women for their frustration. Some have committed acts of violence against wives. Kisekka (1990:46) quotes a newspaper columnist who excuses these men because they are not used to such "excessive domesticity." Other men accuse wives of "provoking" their sexual aggression by refusing to provide the sex owed to a husband, even when this is due to the women's realistic fear of contracting HIV.

Scapegoating of the afflicted by some members of a society is a worldwide practice; fear of AIDS has brought out many ugly forms. The combination of disease and sex exacerbates the situation because women are often blamed for sexually transmitted diseases (Fosu 1981; Kisekka 1990; Packard 1984; Roberts 1987; Vaughan 1991). Punitive measures, such as round-ups and witch-hunting of women who live independently of men, are an ever-present danger.

AIDS also has made child abuse of greater public concern. Although statistics are not often reported from developing countries, newspaper accounts provide anecdotal evidence. Rape of young girls appears to be increasing with the pandemic. (It is even rumored that some traditional healers have told men that sex with a virgin will cure them of AIDS.) Protection from sexual abuse and coercion into prostitution figure among the provisions of the new United Nations International Convention on the Rights of the Child (UNICEF 1991:77-96).

The discourse of rights, however, is effective only if enforced by legal sanctions and public opinion.[8] As with the rights of women, those of children are more likely to be acknowledged than observed. Until broad political support is mobilized, even the most basic rights to food, water, and health care may be violated (Scheper-Hughes 1987). The rights of women and children who are powerless to protect themselves from AIDS can only be guaranteed by developing a broad value consensus based on realistic risk assessment rather than on wishful thinking (Miller, Turner, and Moses 1990).

Assessing Risk

A number of cognitive and emotional factors make it difficult to assess risk. Denial is common when fear and anxiety levels are high, and AIDS is perceived by many people as a death sentence. Moreover, many people have pressing problems with which AIDS prevention is perceived to interfere. Awareness of vulnerability must be coupled with a feeling that prevention is possible. Some people do not know how to prevent infection; others have the knowledge but not the power to negotiate condom protection; still others are embarrassed to do so. Because infection is sexual and "silent," there is no immediately evident relationship between risk behavior and disease. Infected people look healthy for years, yet they are infectious to others. Knowing this in the abstract does not necessarily lead to integrating it in practice because emotions often interfere.

The only way to know with certainty whether or not one is infected is to be tested for the presence of antibodies to the HIV in the blood. Although this sounds like a simple technological solution, procedures currently available pose numerous problems. Due to the "window period" between infection and the production of antibodies, the test must be repeated. Further, confirmatory tests are mandatory when people are to be informed of a fatal diagnosis. At this time, most developing countries cannot afford to offer mass screening in a manner which is technically reliable and ethically justifiable.

Some public health professionals advocate that women undergo pre-pregnancy testing. Yet unequal gender relations create differential effects of such testing for women and men. Allen and Setlow (1991) recommend that husbands be tested simultaneously with their wives and that couples be counselled together. Few men agree to testing subsequent to learning of a wife's infection. The most common course is to repudiate the wife without considering that the husband might be the source of her infection. Intensive counselling has been successful in preventing divorce in some cases. It has rarely, however, kept such couples from having children (Allen and Setlow 1991).

In communities where child-bearing is central to the adult female role and childlessness tantamount to social death, it is seldom advisable to counsel women to refrain from having children; familial pressures and the woman's own expectations are too strong. A couple whose child has died may try again, hoping that the next one will be healthy. Under these conditions, unlinked screening (not tagged with the name of the donor) is useful to monitor the course of the epidemic, but it is of limited use in prevention (Bassett 1991).

Without access to expensive HIV/AIDS counseling support, most of those who are infected will have no knowledge of their condition. Consequently, people must make difficult personal risk assessments based on a review of their lives over the past few years, then decide if and how to protect themselves and others. They must also convince their partners and others in their social networks to accept and support these changes. The knowledge that their infection is not only likely to be transmitted to their wives but through them to the couple's children can act as a spur to protection for some men. It may also serve as a powerful message in communities where wider kin relations are concerned with continuity of the generations (Schoepf 1992c).

The emotional freight surrounding HIV makes it more feasible to introduce condom use in the context of birth spacing or after the desired number of children is reached. One-third of women in an experimental group in Kinshasa reported that they were able to do this; evidently their husbands' unspoken anxiety was sufficient to overcome their reticence and to get on with the difficult task of managing this unfriendly technology (Schoepf, Walu, Rukarangira et al. 1988, 1991). In this sense, personal risk-assessment is empowering because it can stimulate couples to address issues of sexuality and reproductive health that convention, male dominance, and shyness make difficult to discuss.

Several writers (e.g., Miller, Turner, and Moses 1990; Stein 1990) point to the need to develop contraceptive technology that women can control and that also prevents sexual transmission of HIV. One possible method is the "female condom," a bag which lines the vagina. Nevertheless, as noted above, many women will bear children despite the fact that their husbands are seropositive. New technology should offer protection from HIV while at the same time permitting conception (Caravano 1991). Long-term studies, however, are beginning to document infection among the previously seronegative wives of infected men. Thus, realistic appraisal by and responsibility among stable partners, and consistent condom use by those who have had multiple partners in the past, is imperative.

Reproductive Health and Prevention

Sexually transmitted diseases (STDs) may increase HIV risk as much as ten-fold (Piot and Hira 1990; Plummer et al. 1991). The mid-1970s and 1980s witnessed dramatic outbreaks of STD epidemics in many areas of the world at the same time that the HIV spread. Preventing and treating these sexually-transmitted diseases (STDs) are a powerful means of reducing the spread of HIV.[9] Antibiotic-resistant strains of gonorrhea and chlamydia, however, followed the wide non-prescription diffusion of drugs such as penicillin and tetracycline.

Women are more vulnerable than men to most STDs, and several of these diseases result in damage to their reproductive organs. Women's symptoms are often so subtle that they may be unaware that they are infected; men who experience symptoms often fail to notify their partners. In defiance of widespread stigmatization, some men may regard urethral discharge as an emblem of virility. Women may believe that vaginal discharge is "normal" because it is so widespread. Other beliefs and strong emotions frequently surround STDs, which may be attributed to witchcraft and generally raise the question of sex with multiple partners.

It is often dangerous for women to ask questions about their husbands' sexual activities. At the very least, acknowledgment is awkward and may threaten relationships based on maintaining a modicum of mutual trust. In some cultures, women with STDs are assumed to have had illicit sex and may be scapegoated; in others, the silence extends to many aspects of women's sexual and reproductive health. Lack of awareness, shame, stigma, and inaccessibility of affordable, respectful treatment keep many women from seeking treatment until they are incapacitated by pain. HIV has focused attention on this urgent health need which was deliberately avoided by some planners during the 1980s.[10]

Prostitutes and other women with multiple partners are regarded as "core transmitters," targeted for STD control and condom education to protect their clients, and hence, "the general population." Some countries have special clinics to screen and treat sex workers; more are being planned. Where prostitution is legal and unstigmatized, this may be an appropriate strategy. The widespread stigma attached to STDs, however, particularly their association with prostitution, makes it difficult for many women to seek treatment. Those who have multiple partners, but who do not identify themselves as prostitutes, are unlikely to go to special clinics. Married women, monogamous or not, are very rarely seen.

There is consequently a need for diagnosis and treatment of HIV in the community-based primary care facilities to which women go for other health concerns. Family planning (FP) and maternal-child health (MCH) clinics offer opportunities to provide integrated reproductive health services. In most African countries, unmarried teenagers and young adults have not been welcome at FP services and they rarely visit health centers. Contraception has been restricted to married women. Most teens, however, are sexually active and the consequences of unprotected sex have been heavy, especially for girls who become pregnant. They may die from illegal abortions or be expelled from school. Special efforts are needed to provide adolescent women with reproductive health care without shame, stigma, or strings attached. Conservative constructions of morality and the political power of their adherents often stand in the way.

Moralist Discourse and Prevention Policy

While biomedical discourse has attempted to situate AIDS prevention on the terrain of rational decision-making, conservatives in many countries have used AIDS to further their political objectives. In the United States, AIDS has provided a vehicle for crusades against homosexuals, drug users, and people of color, beginning with Haitians. Some construct AIDS as divine punishment for the sin of fornication. Their power has hampered prevention efforts. Leaders have to have courage to insist that protection from AIDS is a human right in the face of others' attempts to dictate "morality." Government officials at all levels have submitted to pressure to withhold prevention, despite the knowledge that similar measures have succeeded in saving many lives in Western Europe.

Youth and women have been special targets of political silencing in the name of a universal morality (Watney 1989). A historical pattern has been followed in which issues regarding sexually transmitted diseases are used for political manipulation (Brandt 1988). Between the "bad" sex worker and the "good" mother, there is now the "bad" mother who infects her children. The right of women to sexual autonomy with protection from disease has remained unaddressed (Caravano 1991), while moralizing discourse provides a pretext for claims to control disease by branding the afflicted and excluding them from society (Douglas 1972; Sabatier 1988; Treichler 1988).

Contemporary African societies embody a wide variety of values and practices. Their health services are heir to colonial traditions that incorporated powerful moralizing discourse against African sexuality (Vaughan 1991). Conservative providers frequently recast this discourse as biomedical advice about AIDS (Anonymous 1991). For example, some churches have imposed mandatory prenuptial screening and pronounce those found to be seropositive "unfit for marriage." Older African belief systems also treat many diseases as moral issues, and AIDS fits readily among those most feared and stigmatized. As in previous STD epidemics (and as in struggles over marriage in the 1930s [Hay and Wright 1982]), the subtext is control of women and youth by male elders.[11] Despite mounting concern with high and rising seroprevalence among teens, many adults believe that youth are malleable in ways that they themselves are not. Adult reluctance to recognize or accept the sexuality of adolescents leads to interventions with objectives such as "improving morality" and "promoting virginity."

Not all churches and not all religious leaders share these fundamentalist interpretations. Some have been quite realistic, even when they could not publicly promote condoms (see Schoepf, Rukarangira et al. 1988). In many countries, however, conservatives (whose hypocrisy and multiple partners are well known) have silenced realism in the media. In its stead, they diffuse ambiguous slogans about fidelity and partner numbers, that have been interpreted in ways other than those intended, and preach abstinence to sexually active youth.

Although AIDS information campaigns have greatly increased knowledge, few people at risk have changed their behavior. Addressing the complex constraints to change is not an easy task. There are no general solutions to problems of AIDS prevention. Experience with previous STD control campaigns and AIDS indicates that behavioral changes are hampered by authoritarian responses (UNCHR 1991). Moreover, moralizing about sex is likely to have unintended consequences. Many young people will continue to have sex and will have more than one lifetime partner. Those who are burdened by guilt or driven "underground" are unlikely to adopt safer sex practices. Enhancing people's capacities to understand problems and devise solutions is critical to the development of effective strategies.

Research/Knowledge Paradigms and Prevention Policy

The view of AIDS as a gender and development issue with ramifications beyond the health sector has gained considerable currency among the international community (NORAD 1991; UNDP 1991; UNICEF 1991; WHO 1991). This understanding, however, has yet to be translated into policy or to a change in the resource flow. For a decade, the field has been dominated by the technical approaches of laboratory medicine and epidemiology. A narrow biomedical vision of disease holds sway, despite acknowledgment that behavior change is the only way to prevent HIV infection and death.

There is little communication between the disciplines at the commanding heights of policy and resource allocation (author's interviews, September-December 1991). Further, a methodological gulf separates the biomedical from the social sciences in AIDS research (Ankrah 1989). The distance between epistemological paradigms is widened by the structure of power relations (Ackeroyd 1990). During the past decade, AIDS has been used by biomedicine to reassert its ideological authority (Glick-Schiller, Lewellen and Crystal 1990; Rosenberg 1988). With minor exceptions, support for social research and community-based interventions must pass through gates guarded by physicians who set criteria of scientific validity. Such screening has led to the publication of racist nonsense decked out as science (Leslie 1990) and to continuing neglect of community-based empowerment as a prevention strategy (e.g., Lamptey and Piot (1990), *The Handbook for AIDS Prevention in Africa*).[12]

Socially-oriented epidemiologists share the anthropologists' view that a focus on individual sexual behaviors deflects attention from sex as social relations, and from risky environments and situations especially conducive to HIV spread (Bassett and Mhloyi 1991; de Zalduondo 1991; Glick-Schiller, Lewellen, and Crystal 1990; Kisekka 1990; Schoepf 1991a, 1992b; Schoepf, Walu et al. 1991; Zwi and Cabral 1991). Nevertheless, the much-criticized notion of "primary risk groups"--categories of individuals defined by a special "risk behavior"--continues to hold sway or to be reintroduced as "groups of core transmitters" (see Piot and Harris 1990; Piot and Hira 1990). Many public health specialists continue to ignore the wider political economy and socio-cultural contexts and causes of the pandemic. Their failure to contextualize AIDS supports the creation of special programs that draw resources away from primary health care delivery.

The risk group paradigm facilitates racist stereotyping of the cultures and sexuality of peoples of color (Ahlberg 1991; Ankrah 1989; Dalton 1989; Farmer 1990; Fullilove 1991; Glick-Schiller, Lewellen, and Crystal 1990; Quimby 1992; Waite 1988). For example, heterosexual transmission of HIV in Africa and the Caribbean spurred a search for cultural factors to explain the "differences" from the original Euro-American pattern. A number of writers (e.g., Caldwell, Caldwell and Quiggin 1989; Hrdy 1987; Larson 1989) attribute the rapid spread of HIV in Africa to "traditional promiscuity." Such explanations are heir to a deeply-rooted legacy of Western racism which exoticises the sexuality of the "Other," objectifying men as superpotent and women as wild and uncontrollable (Bray 1991; Corbey 1988; Fullilove 1991; Gilman 1985, 1990; Monti 1987; Schoepf 1985, 1991a; Treichler 1989; Vaughan 1991; Watney 1989). (Such explanations also deflect attention from socioeconomic causes [Glick-Schiller, Lewellen, and Crystal 1990]).

Essentialist constructions of African "difference" have been challenged for their ethnocentrism and oversimplification of complex, diverse histories (Ahlberg 1991; Anonymous 1991; Conant 1987; Schoepf 1990, 1991a-d; Waite 1988). Portrayals of Africans as diseased and degenerate were created by European colonizers to justify the brutalities of the transatlantic slave trade, the plantation system, and lynching (Paula Giddens cited in Bray 1991). Such portrayals also underlie the commonly encountered assumption that little can be done to prevent sexual transmission of AIDS in Africa, thereby rationalizing the dearth of resources devoted to prevention. The current global spread of AIDS exposes the racist foundations of the notion that Africans, especially African women, are more "promiscuous" than people elsewhere.

Because AIDS is about sex, an essentialist view of sexuality as biologically driven contributes to pessimism with respect to prevention. Fortunately, this determinist view is wrong. Studies by African and Africanist feminists trace changing patterns of sexual relations during the colonial period and following Independence, and include two outstanding gender-sensitive reviews of sexuality in Africa (Pellow 1990; Standing and Kisekka 1989). This research, grounded in gender relations, does not succumb to the voyeurism criticized by Lyons and Lyons (1986) and Packard (1989). Rather, it takes seriously the need to address the risk of AIDS from sex.

Some development writers consider sex with multiple partners a product of the forces of an "unpeopled political economy," in which disembodied hegemonic structures act autonomously to determine the outcomes of social relations (e.g., Packard and Epstein 1991; Sanders and Sambo 1991).[13] Conversely, some writers on women and AIDS have followed the "women-left-out" approach criticized by

Antrobus (1989), Bujra (1984, 1990), Mbilinyi (1984, 1990), and Parpart (1989), neglecting the social relations of production and reproduction that create male supremacy and female risk and describing a timeless, seamless patriarchy which leaves little scope for change.

It is preferable to acknowledge that women's powerlessness to avoid risk and men's resistance to change are products of complex forces that will not yield to easy solutions--certainly not to berating men for their sexism (see Ankrah 1991). In patriarchal societies marked by competitive acquisitiveness, women are often objects of display whose possession enhances men's status. The psychodynamic processes of dominance and oppression are thus anchored in concepts of self, developed and reinforced by a lifetime of socialization to gender identities; the very thought of equality may be threatening (Mbilinyi 1985; Obbo 1989b).

Where women learn to accept the subordination of their own needs to those of others, refusing risky sex may be unthinkable. Where men are socialized to believe that virility is demonstrated by making sexual conquests and engendering numerous offspring, it is difficult for many to accept responsibility for protecting partners from conception or HIV risk. Such socialization to sexism is further compounded by the hopelessness of poverty and unemployment and by racism (Campbell 1991; Gasch et al. 1991).

Behavioral change can seldom be imposed by fiat, and exhortation seldom works for long. One can appreciate the new laws to punish rape and sexual harassment that have been instituted in countries hard-hit by AIDS. These must, however, be followed by changes in value consensus brought about through societal dialogue. The voices of poor young women engaged in daily struggles for existence have seldom been heard beyond the local level where they count for little. Moreover, appeals to "tradition" are likely to disempower them still further.

Community norms must change in favor of cultural survival; AIDS prevention must become a political act. Creative mass media productions and leadership from respected role models can prepare people for change. The next step is to work with people at risk to identify methods of prevention and to devise solutions. Yet, as noted above, relatively little research and even fewer demonstration projects have been funded to develop prevention based on individual and social empowerment.

Prevention Through Empowerment

The only immediate hope of limiting sexual transmission is to empower substantial numbers of people to alter behavior that is highly valued and considered normal and natural by many. There are numerous cultural constraints to AIDS prevention. Many of these constraints, however, can be overcome by discussing the problems with people at risk (Gasch et al. 1991; Schoepf 1992a-c; Schoepf, Walu et al. 1991). Some of the most "traditional" behaviors are relatively easy to change.   For example, elders in some communities of Uganda and Zambia have decided to abolish the custom of ritual purification of widows, substituting symbolic acts instead.[14] Zairian healers were able to "re-invent" complex traditional cosmological concepts to reduce AIDS risk. People who are apprised of the risks to self, family, and community can decide what they need to do to protect themselves.   The nature of the communication process holds the key to change.

The challenge is to break through the denial and "fatalism" (actually, a sense of powerlessness) which often accompany risk-taking before the mounting numbers of AIDS deaths make the need self-evident and protection relatively futile. Although many risky situations arise from women's powerlessness, rather than from their behavior, and although their socialization and all the institutions of society recreate that powerlessness (Obbo 1989b), it would be a mistake to consider these situations as permanent or to define for women the limits of their power.   While poor women of color "have to dig deep to find that power" (Antrobus 1989:195), women's groups in Latin America, Africa, and the Middle East have used the maternal role as a weapon, protesting that war, political repression, and economic crises make it impossible for them to fulfill their socially assigned responsibility to serve the family.

Political activism was spurred by critical reflection in women's groups. The same process can compel AIDS prevention. Some prototype outreach projects framed by feminist understandings have centered on women's responsibilities to their families.   Others, framed by biomedical discourse, focused chiefly on protecting clients. It is important to recognize this distinction and to be guided by the specific needs of actual groups of women, not some essentialist construct of "the prostitute." In San Francisco, peer counsellors worked with groups of prostitute women to encourage both clients and lovers to accept condom protection (Alexander 1988). In Vera Cruz, Mexico, where most commercial sex workers are also mothers, emphasis was placed on the need for women to stay healthy so they can care for their children. In Bulawayo, Zimbabwe, sex workers provide outreach to the "general population," many of whom are at risk (Wilson et al. 1990).

When empowerment workshops were offered in Kinshasa, wives grasped the opportunity to act. Although the women's options were limited in regular partner relations, about one-third of the wives were able to negotiate condom use as birth control; others were able to obtain husbands' consent to assist adolescent children in adopting safer sex practices, primarily, using condoms (Schoepf, Walu, Rukarangira et al. 1991). The women in this group pointed out that it is essential for AIDS to be appropriated as a community concern, rather than viewed simply as a problem for individual couples (Schoepf 1992c). They also began to organize around health care and economic survival issues.

Empowerment strategies that incorporate a deep understanding of local cultures and social group dynamics have the potential to bring about changes in sexual behavior and the social relations in which they are embedded (Kalumba et al. 1990) Problem-posing methods can be used by community groups to address broader issues of gender relations and to model more egalitarian behaviors, placing these within the context of social action in support of development and social change (Hope, Timmel and Hodzi 1984).

Conclusion

AIDS embodies unequal social relations, particularly gendered inequality in power and access to strategic resources. Throughout the world, patriarchal structures of economic, political, and social inequality limit the ability of most women to control independent incomes. These structures also promote women's socialization for subservience to men and limit the ability of most women to say "No" to risky sex. Given the diversity of norms and behavior, as well as the complex constraints noted above, prevention requires a deep understanding of culture and sensitivity to representations coming from many quarters.

While education campaigns promote recognition of AIDS as a serious health issue, the immediate survival needs of many women propel them to supply sexual services in risky situations and limit their ability to insist that their partners use condom protection. A dearth of reproductive health services led to epidemics of STDs and now to HIV. Women's vulnerability to AIDS and to economic crises are created by the same set of conditions.

The dangers of AIDS make necessary the linking of theory, method, and research that are often viewed as separate. Further research is needed to examine the differences in women's experience within the contexts of class and degrees of incorporation into the world market economy. Research is also needed to examine the processes of concert and conflict in interests among leaders of government and industry, and of North and South, that have supported rapid capital accumulation and class formation in recent years. These processes have vitiated the most promising development initiatives and bolstered the power of leaders unaccountable to their people. Finally, action-research with women is needed to develop and test social empowerment strategies; such strategies can take advantage of the political spaces being created by the delegitimation of the control of civil society by the state. This research agenda is made more urgent-- and perhaps can be facilitated--by the AIDS pandemic.

This review has relied chiefly upon data from Africa. Rapidly rising seroprevalence in South and Southeast Asia, however, highlights poverty and landlessness along with the subordination of women as integral to the spread of AIDS. Once we ask not only how AIDS spreads but why, we are brought to consider the history of colonialism and distorted development, buttressed by what Bassett and Mhloyi (1991:147), writing from Zimbabwe, term "an insidious combination of traditional and European patriarchal values."

The understandings on which the gender relations and development perspective are based, and the need for global redistribution of power and wealth, have not been readily accepted by policymakers. Rather, they tend to seek panaceas, limited interventions that appear to offer hope of interrupting the epidemic without threatening vested interests. Unless the underlying struggles of millions to survive in the midst of poverty, powerlessness, and hopelessness are addressed, and the meanings of AIDS understood in the context of gender relations, HIV infection will continue to spread. Because social structures circumscribe the choices people make, eradicating AIDS requires the elimination of the barriers that deny women control over their own sexual decisions.

Notes

1. AIDS is stigmatizing and difficult to diagnose, leading to under reporting. The majority of people in developing countries have little access to biomedical health services where diagnosis can be made and reported. Because in many countries people must pay to register deaths, an unknown number go unreported. Moreover, official reporting often is delayed. WHO periodically convenes a panel of experts in HIV epidemiology to review data and project probable figures.

2. Hughes and Hunter's (1970) term.

3. Discrimination in employment restricts women's labor force participation in most of sub-Saharan Africa to between four and ten percent of formal sector workers (Stichter 1990; Schoepf 1992b).

4. Under some conditions, sex work has provided women with considerable income and negotiating strength (White 1990) and brought trend-setting glamour to its more prosperous adopters. Many women spend several years in sex work, then marry or operate small businesses.

5. Attempts by researchers in several countries to create a special risk profile for pregnant women have failed. Most of the women tested in prenatal clinics are married and relatively few have multiple partners, yet eight to forty percent currently are infected in the cities of Central Africa. The highest risk is to women in their early twenties who report that they or their partner had a sexually transmitted disease (STD) during the past five years, and whose partners spend money drinking in bars, suggesting that the men had other partners (Allen and Setlow 1991).

6. A stable relationship is defined in WHO's partner-relations surveys as lasting one year or more (Adeokun 1990). Kane (1990a) suggests that regulated brothels in Belize are safer than bar pick-ups, in which a pretense of affection is made by both parties to the encounter and condoms are unlikely to be used. Nevertheless, the British fleet made brothels off-limits, which propelled even more seamen into casual sex with "quasi-prostitutes" without condoms. The example shows how policies based on flawed premises can lead to consequences other than those intended.

7. In the mining camps, sexual relations and domestic services may be sought from men as well.

8. Legal sanctions may be most significant. Some countries have made child rape punishable by death, but observers doubt that convictions will be obtained (Anonymous 1991).

9. Economic conditions often are the most powerful determinant of STD epidemics. In the United States reduced health care budgets in the 1980s caused services to be curtailed at the same time that joblessness, hopelessness, and crack (smokable cocaine) became prevalent in the inner cities inhabited by people of color. Exchange of sex for drugs became common. The drugs lower impulse control, making it difficult for men to use condoms even if they were to become culturally acceptable. The consequence is a rising epidemic of STDs and AIDS among young people of color (Handesfield 1990; Holmes, Karon and Kreiss 1990; Quinn et al. 1986).

10. In the 1980s, planners sought to provide coverage for a limited number of diseases through primary health care (PHC); STDs were not included. In 1981, I was a member of the planning team for Liberia's national PHC program. Liberian physicians identified the need for STD treatment in rural towns and villages. Our attempt to include this service in the plan was rebuffed by the USAID team leader. STD treatment was a politically inconvenient issue (as AIDS was to be later), because African governments were sensitive to the racist taint of "promiscuity." The international community considered treatment an unacceptable expense. There were foreign aid givers who (as several Liberian professionals suggested) sought to use infertility as a "passive" form of population control (Frank 1983).

11. Packard (1980) who (in a history of northeastern Zaire) wrote about women scapegoated for STDs is silent about gender issues in AIDS. He also minimizes the role of sexual transmission.

12. A forthcoming WHO conference and book on "success stories" will continue this limited perspective.

13. The phrase, "unpeopled political economy" is from Shula Marks (1987).

14. Elders in the rural community in Southeastern Zaire where I studied in 1975-1978 made this transformation in 1978.

References

Ackeroyd, Ann
   1990   "Useful" and/or "Interesting"? "Appropriate Methods for Whom and for What." Paper presented at the Overseas Development Administration workshop on AIDS in Developing Countries: Appropriate Social Research Methods, Brunel University, London, May 10-11, 1990.

Adedeji, Adebayo
   1990   *The African Initiative: Putting the People First.* Addis Ababa: United
          Nations Economic Commission for Africa.

Adeokun, Lawrence A.
   1990   Research on Human Sexuality in Pattern II Countries. In: *Human
          Sexuality: Research Perspectives in a World Facing AIDS*, edited by A.
          Chouinard and J. Albert. Pp. 112-134. Ottawa: Centre de Recherche
          pour le Développement International.

Ahlberg, Beth Maina
   1991   *Women, Sexuality and the Changing Social Order: The Impact of
          Government Policies on Reproductive Behaviour in Kenya.*
          Philadelphia: Gordon and Breach.

Alexander, Priscilla
   1988   *Prostitutes Prevent AIDS: A Manual for Health Educators.* San
          Francisco: Prostitutes Education Project.

Allen, James R. and Valerie P. Setlow
   1991   Heterosexual Transmission of HIV: A View of the Future. *Journal
          of the American Medical Association* 266(12):1695-1696.

Ankrah, Maxine E.
   1989   AIDS: Methodological Problems in Studying Its Prevention and
          Spread. *Social Science and Medicine* 29:265-276.

   1991   AIDS and the Social Side of Health. *Social Science and Medicine*
          32:967-980.

Anonymous
   1991   The Competing Discourses of HIV/AIDS in Sub-Saharan Africa:
          Discourses of Rights and Empowerment vs. Discourses of
          Control/Exclusion. Unpublished Manuscript.

Antrobus, Peggy
   1989   The Empowerment of Women. In: *The Women and International
          Development Annual*, volume 1, edited by Rita Gallin, Marilyn
          Aronoff, and Anne Ferguson. Pp. 189-207. Boulder: Westview Press.

Baldo, Mariella and Antonia Jorge Cabral
1991 Low Intensity Wars and Social Determinations of the HIV Transmissions: The Search for a New Paradigm to Guide Research and Control of the HIV/AIDS Pandemic. In: *Action on AIDS in Southern Africa*, edited by Z. Stein and A. Zwi. Pp. 201-228. New York: Committee for Health in South Africa (CHISA).

Barnett, Tony and Piers Blaikie
1992 *AIDS in Africa: Its Present and Future Impact*. London: Bellhaven Press.

Bassett, Mary T.
1991 Remarks at Workshop of the Pan African Action. Research Network. Arusha, Tanzania, August 15-29, 1991.

Bassett, Mary T. and Marvellous Mhloyi
1991 Women and AIDS in Zimbabwe: The Making of an Epidemic. *International Journal of Health Services* 21:143-156.

Bledsoe, Caroline
1990 The Politics of AIDS and Condoms for Stable Heterosexual Relations in Africa: Recent Evidence from the Local Print Media. In: *Births and Power: The Politics of Reproduction*, edited by P. Handwerker. Pp. 197-222. Boulder: Westview Press.

Bond, George and Joan Vincent
1990 Living on the Edge: Structural Adjustment in the Context of AIDS. In: *Structural Adjustment and Change*, edited by H.B. Hansen and M. Twaddle. Pp. 76-99. London: James Currey.

Brandt, Allan M.
1987 *No Magic Bullet: A History of Venereal Disease in the United States Since 1880*. New York: Oxford University Press.

1988 AIDS and Metaphor: Toward the Social Meaning of Epidemic Disease. *Social Research* 55(3):413-432.

Bray, Rosemary
1991 Taking Sides Against Ourselves. New York Times, Sunday Magazine, November 17, 1991.

Bujra, Janet
    1984   Class, Gender and Capitalist Transformation in Africa. *Africa
            Development* 17:42-53.

    1990   Taxing Development in Tanzania: Why Must Women Pay? *Review
            of African Political Economy* 47:44-63.

Caldwell, John C., Pat Caldwell, and Patricia Quiggin
    1989   The Social Context of AIDS in Sub-Saharan Africa. *Population and
            Development Review* 15(2):185-234.

Campbell, Cathy
    1991   Women, the Family and the ANC's Constitutional Guidelines. In:
            *Proceeding of the 1st Congress of the South African Health Workers'
            Congress (SAHWCO) Caring for a New Nation: Health Workers Meet
            the Challenge*. Pp. 63-78. Booysens, South Africa: SAHWCO.

Caravano, Kathleen
    1991   More than Mothers and Whores: Redefining the AIDS Prevention
            Needs of Women. *International Journal of Health Services* 21(1):131-
            142.

Chin, James
    1990   Current and Future Dimensions of the HIV/AIDS Pandemic in
            Women and Children. *Lancet* ii(336):221-224.

Conant, Francis P.
    1987   Surveying and Evaluating Social Science Research on AIDS in Africa.
            Paper presented at the Annual Meeting of the African Studies
            Association, Denver, Colorado, November.

Corbey, Richard
    1988   Alterity: The Colonial Nude. *Critique of Anthropology* 8(3):75-92.

Cornia, G.A., R. Jolly, and F. Steward (editors)
    1987   *Adjustment with a Human Face*. Oxford: Claredon Press.

Dalton, Harlon L.
    1989   AIDS in Blackface. *Daedalus*. Summer:205-227.

Davison, Jean (editor)
    1988   *Agriculture, Women, and Land: The African Experience*. Boulder:
            Westview Press.

de Zalduondo, Barbara O.
   1991   Prostitution Viewed Cross-culturally: Toward Recontextualizing Sex
          Work in AIDS Intervention Research. *The Journal of Sex Research*
          28(2):223-248.

de Zalduondo, Barbara O, Gerhard I. Msamanga, and Lincoln Chen
   1989   AIDS in Africa: Diversity in a Global Pandemic. *Daedalus.*
          Summer:165-204.

Douglas, Mary
   1972   Is Matriliny Doomed in Africa?   In: *Man in Africa*, edited by M.
          Douglad and P. Kaberry. Pp. 123-137.   Garden City: Anchor Books.

Farmer, Paul
   1990   Sending Sickness: Sorcery, Politics and Changing Concepts of AIDS
          in Rural Haiti. *Medical Anthropology Quarterly* 4(1):6-27.

Feldman, Rayah
   1989   *Women for a Change: The Impact of Structural Adjustment on Women
          in Zambia, Tanzania and Mozambique.* London: War on Want.

Fosu, Gabriel B.
   1981   Disease Classification in Rural Ghana: Framework and Implications
          for Health Behavior. *Social Science and Medicine* 15B(4):471-482.

Frank, Odile
   1983   Infertility in Sub-Saharan Africa: Estimates and Implications.
          Population and Development Studies 9(1):137-144.

Fullilove, Mindy T.
   1991   From Jungle Fever to Steatopygia.   Plenary address, Annual Meeting
          of the Society for the Scientific Study of Sex, New Orleans, Louisiana,
          October.

Gasch, Helen D., Michael Poulson, Robert Fullilove and Mindy Thompson
   Fullilove
   1991   Shaping AIDS Education and Prevention Programs for African
          Americans Amidst Community Decline. *Journal of Negro Education*
          60(1):85-96.

George, Susan
   1988   *A Fate Worse Than Debt: A Radical New Analysis of the Third World
          Debt Crisis.* London: Penguin Books.

Gillespie, Sheila
    1989   Potential Impact of AIDS on Farming Systems: A Case Study from
            Rwanda. *Land Use Policy* 6:301-312.

Giller, J.E., P.J. Bracken, and S. Kabaganda
    1991   Uganda, War, Women and Rape. *Lancet* ii(337):604.

Gilman, Sander
    1985   *Difference and Pathology: Stereotypes of Sexuality, Race and Madness.*
            Ithaca: Cornell University Press.

    1990   Plague in Germany, 1939/1989: Cultural Images of Race, Space and
            Disease. Paper presented for Wenner-Gren Foundation Symposium
            No. 111, "AIDS Research: Issues for Anthropological Theory, Method
            and Practice, Estes Park, Colorado, June 25 - July 1, 1990.

Glick-Schiller, Nina, Denver Lewellen, and Stephen Crystal
    1990   Culture or Politics? An Examination of the Culturological Analysis of
            AIDS Risk. Paper presented at the Annual Meeting of the American
            Anthropological Association, New Orleans, Louisiana, November.

Green, Reginald H.
    1985   From Deepening Economic Malaise Towards Renewed Development:
            An Overview.   Sub-Saharan Africa: Toward Oblivion or
            Reconstruction. *Journal of Development Planning* 15:9-44.

Handsfield, Hunter H,.
    1990   Old Enemies: Combatting Syphilis and Gonorrhea in the 1990s.
            Journal of the American Medical Association 264(11):1451-1452.

Hay, Margaret Jean, and Marcia Wright, eds.
    1982   African Women and the Law: Historical Perspectives. Boston: Boston
            University Papers on Africa, No 7.

Holmes, King K., J.M. Karon, and Joan Kreiss
    1990   The Increasing Frequency of Heterosexually Transmitted AIDS in the
            United States, 1983-1988.   *American Journal of Public Health*
            80:858-862.

Hope, Ann, Sally Timmel, and Peter Hodzi
    1984   *Training for Transformation: A Handbook for Community Workers.*
            Gweru, Zimbabwe: Mambo Press.

Hrdy, Daniel
1987 Cultural Practices Contributing to the Transmission of Human Immunodeficiency Virus in Africa. *Reviews of Infectious Diseases* 9(6):1109-1119.

Hughes, Charles C., and John M. Hunter
1970 Disease and 'Development' in Tropical Africa. *Social Science and Medicine* 3:443-493.

Hunt, Charles W.
1989 Migrant Labor and Sexually Transmitted Disease: AIDS Africa. *Journal of Health and Social Behavior* 30:353-373.

Jochelson, Karen, M. Mothibeli, and J.P. Leger
1991 Human Immunodeficiency Virus and Migrant Labour in South Africa. *International Journal of Health Services* 21:157-173.

Kalumba, Katele, Brooke G. Schoepf, Beth Maina Ahlberg, Justin Nguma, and Christine Obbo
1990 Pan-African Action Research Network for Community-Based HIV/AIDS Prevention. Concept Paper. November.

Kane, Stephanie
1990a AIDS, Addiction and Condom Use: Sources of Sexual Risk for Heterosexual Women. *The Journal of Sex Research* 27 (3):427-444.

1990b Reconceptualizing 'Risk Groups' in AIDS Intervention: An Analysis of Prostitution and the Military in Belize. Paper presented at the annual meeting of the American Anthropological Association, New Orleans, November.

Kane, Stephaine and Theresa Mason
1992 AIDS Research, Anti-drug Policies and Ethnography. In: *Social Analysis in the Time of AIDS* edited by G. Herdt and S. Lindenbaum. Pp. 192-222. Newbury Park: Sage Publications.

Kisekka, Mere N.
1990 AIDS in Uganda as a Gender Issue. *Women and Therapy* 10(3):35-53.

Krieger, Nancy, and Margo Glen
1990 AIDS: The Politics of Survival: Introduction. *International Journal of Health Sciences* 20:583-588.

Lamptey, Peter, and Peter Piot (editors)
   1990   *The Handbook for AIDS Prevention in Africa*. Durham: Family
           Health International.

Larson, Ann
   1989   The Social Context of HIV Transmission: A Review of Historical and
           Cultural Bases of East and Central African Sexual Relations. *Review
           of Infectious Diseases* 11(5):716-731.

Leslie, Charles
   1990   Scientific Racism: Reflections on Peer Review, Science and Ideology.
           Social Science and Medicine 31(8):891-906.

Levy, Diane, and Patricia B. Lerch
   1991   Tourism as a Factor in Development: Implications for Gender and
           Work in Barbados. *Gender and Society* 5(1):67-85.

Lyons, Andrew P., and Harriet D. Lyons
   1986   Savage Sexuality and Secular Morality: Malinovski, Ellis Russell.
           Canadian Journal of Anthropology 5(1):51-64.

Marks, Shula
   1987   *Not Either an Experimental Doll: The Separate Worlds of Three South
           African Women*. Bloomington: University of Indiana Press.

Mbilinyi, Majorie
   1984   "Women in Development" Ideology: The Promotion of Competition
           and Exploitation. *The African Review* 2(1):14-33.

   1985   Struggles Concerning Sexuality of Female Youth. *Journal of Eastern
           African Research and Development* 15:111-123.

   1990   A Review of Women in Development Issues in Tanzania. Report
           prepared for the World Bank.

Miller, Heather G., Charles H. Turner, and Lincoln E. Moses (editors)
   1990   *AIDS: The Second Decade*. Washington, DC: National Academy
           Press.

Monti, Nicholas
   1987   *Africa Then: Photographs 1840-1918*. New York: Knopf.

Moses, Steven, Francis A. Plummer, Elizabeth N. Ngugi, et al.
1991 Controlling HIV in Africa: Effectiveness and Cost of an Intervention in a High Frequency STD Transmitter Core Group. *AIDS* 5(4):407-411.

Mulemwa, Jane M.
1991 Achieving HIV/AIDS-related Behaviour Change. Paper prepared for the Pan-African Action-Research Network workshop, Arusha, Tanzania, August 15-29, 1991.

Newbury, Catharine, and Brooke G. Schoepf
1989 State, Peasantry and Agrarian Crisis in Zaire: Does Gender Make a Difference? In: *Women and the State in Africa*, edited by J.L. Parpart and K.A. Staudt. Pp. 91-110. Boulder: Lynne Reinner.

NORAD (Norwegian Agency for Development)
1991 *New Challenges for Development Cooperation*, edited by D. Leraand. Oslo: NORAD.

Norse, David
1991 Socioeconomic Impact of AIDS on Food Production in East Africa. Paper prepared for VII International Conference on AIDS, Florence, Italy, June 16-21, 1991.

Novello, Antonia
1990 Women and AIDS. Address to the United Nations General Assembly, (broadcast on US National Public Radio 10 March, 1991), 1 December.

Nzila, Nzilambi, M. Laga, A.B. Thiam, et al.
1991 HIV and Other Sexually Transmitted Diseases Among Female Prostitutes in Kinshasa. *AIDS* 5:715-722.

Obbo, Christine
1981 *African Women, Their Struggle for Economic Independence*. London: Zed Press.

1989a AIDS, Women and Children in Uganda. Paper presented at the Annual meeting of the African Studies Association, Atlanta, Georgia, November 5, 1989.

1989b Sexuality and Economic Domination in Uganda. In: *Women-Nation-State*, edited by N. Nyuval-Davis and F. Anthas. Pp. 79-91. London: Macmillan.

Onimode, Bade (editor)
  1989   *The IMF, World Bank and the African Debt.* London: Zed Press.

Packard, Randall, M.
  1980   Social Change and the History of Misfortune Among the Bashu of
          Eastern Zaire. In: *Explorations in African Systems of Thought,* edited
          by I. Karp and C. Bird. Pp. 237-267. Bloomington: Indiana
          University Press.

  1984   Maize, Cattle and Mosquitoes: The Political economy of Malaria
          Epidemics in Colonial Swaziland. *Journal of African History* 25(2):189-
          212.

  1989   Epidemiologists, Social Scientists and the Structure of Medical
          Research on AIDS in Africa. Working Paper No. 137. Boston:
          African Studies Center, Boston University.

Packard, Randall, and Paul Epstein
  1991   Epidemiologist, Social Scientists, and the Structure of Medical
          Research on AIDS in Africa. *Social Science and Medicine* 33(7):771-
          783, 793-794.

Padian, N.S., S.C. Shiboski, and N.P. Jewell
  1990   The Effect of Number of Exposures on the Risk of Heterosexual
          Transmission. *Journal of Infectious Diseases* 161:883-887.

Parpart, Jane L. (editor)
  1989   Women and Development in Africa: Comparative Perspectives.
          Lanham: University Press of America.

Pellow, Deborah
  1990   Sexuality in Africa. *Trends in History* 4(4):71-96.

Piot, Peter and Jeffrey Harris
  1990   The Epidemiology of HIV/AIDS in Africa. In: *The Handbook for
          AIDS Prevention in Africa,* edited by P. Lamptey and P. Piot. Pp. 1-19.
          Durham: Family Health International.

Piot, Peter, and Subhash Hira
  1990   Control and Prevention of Sexually Transmitted Diseases. In: *The
          Handbook for AIDS Prevention in Africa,* edited by P. Lamptey and P.
          Piot. Pp. 83-104. Durham: Family Health International.

Plant, M.A. (editor)
1991   *AIDS, Drugs and Prostitution*. London: Routledge.

Plummer, Francis A., Neil J. Simonsen, David W. Cameron et al.
1991   Cofactors in Male-Female Sexual Transmission of HIV-I. *Journal of Infectious Diseases* 163:233-239.

Quimby, Ernest
1992   Problems of African American Mobilization Against AIDS. In: *Social Analysis in the Time of AIDS: Theory, Method and Practice*, edited by G. Herdt and S. Lindenbaum. Pp.131-152. Newbury Park: Sage.

Quinn, Thomas C., et al.
1986   AIDS in Africa: An Epidemiologic Paradigm. *Science* 234(21):955-963.

Richardson, Diane
1988   *Women and AIDS*. New York: Nethuen Books.

Roberts, Penelope A.
1987   The State and the Regulation of Marriage: Sefwi Wiawso (Ghana), 1900-1940. In: *Women, the State and Ideology: Studies from Africa and Asia*, edited by H. Afshar. Pp. 48-69. London: Macmillan.

Rosenberg, Charles
1988   Disease and Social Order in America: Perceptions and Expectations. In: *AIDS: The Burden of History*, edited by E. Fee and D. Fox. Pp. 12-32. Berkeley: University of California Press.

Rukarangira, wa Nkera and Brooke G. Schoepf
1991   Unrecorded Trade in Shaba and across Zaire's Southern Borders. In: *The Real Economy of Zaire*, edited by J. MacGaffey. Pp. 72-96. Philadelphia: University of Pennsylvania Press.

Sabatier, Renée (editor)
1988   *Blaming Others: Prejudice, Race and Worldwide AIDS*. Washington: PANOS Institute.

Sanders, David and Abdul Rahman Sambo
1991   AIDS in Africa: The Implications of Economic Recession and Structural Adjustment. *Health Policy and Planning* 6(2):157-165.

Scheper-Hughes, Nancy
    1987   Child Survival: Anthropological Perspectives on Treatment and
            Maltreatment of Children. Norwell: Kluwer Academic Publishers.

Schoepf, Brooke G.
    1981   Cultural Sensitivity and the Dynamics of Sociocultural Change. In:
            Developing Nations: Challenges Involving Women, edited by B.
            Stoeker. Pp. 137-153. Lubbock: Texas Tech University.

    1985   Food Crisis and Class Formation: An Example from Shaba. *Review
            of African Political Economy* 33:33-43.

    1988   Women, AIDS and Economic Crisis in Zaire. *Canadian Journal of
            African Studies* 22(3):625-644.

    1990   AIDS in Eriaz. *Anthropology Today* 6(3):10-15.

    1991   Ethical, Methodological and Political Issues of AIDS Research in
            Central Africa. *Social Science and Medicine* 33(7):749-763.

    1992a   Gender Relations and Development: Political Economy and Culture.
            In: *Twenty-First Century Africa: Towards a New Vision of Self-
            sustainable Development*, edited by A. Seidman and F. Anag. Pp. 203-
            241. Trenton: Africa World Press.

    1992b   Women at Risk: Case Studies from Zaire. In: *Social Analysis in the
            Time of AIDS*, edited by G. Herdt and Lindenbaum. Pp. 259-286.
            Newbury Park: Sage.

    1992c   AIDS, Sex and Condoms--the Invention of Tradition: "Traditional"
            Healers and Community-based AIDS Prevention in Zaire. *Medical
            Anthropology* 13:1-18.

Schoepf, Brooke G. and Efngundu Walu
    1991   Women's Trade and Contribution to Household Budgets in Kinshasa.
            In: *The Real Economy in Zaire*, edited by J. MacGaffey. Pp. 124-151.
            Philadelphia: University of Pennsylvania Press.

Schoepf, Brooke G., Wa Nkera Kukarangira, Claude Schoepf, Ntsomo Payanzo,
and Engundu Walu
    1988   AIDS and Society in Central Africa: The Case of Zaire. In: *AIDS
            in Africa: Social and Policy Impact*, edited by N. Miller and R.
            Rockwell. Pp. 211-235. Lewiston: Mellen Press.

Schoepf, Brooke G., N. Payanzo, N. Rukarangira, E. Walu, and C. Schoepf
1988   AIDS, Women and Society in Central Africa. In: *AIDS, 1988: AAAS Symposium Papers*, edited by R. Kulstad. Pp. 175-181. Washington: American Association for the Advancement of Science.

Schoepf, Brooke G., Engundu Walu, Claude Schoepf, and Diane Russell
1991   Women and Structural Adjustment in Zaire. In: *Structural Adjustment and African Women Farmers*, edited by C. Gladwin. Pp. 151-168. Gainesville: University of Florida Press.

Schoepf, Brooke G., Engundu Walu, wa Nkera Rukarangira, Ntsomo Payanzo, and Claude Schoepf
1988   Community-based Risk-reduction Support. In: *AIDS Prevention Through Health Promotion: Changing Behavior*, edited by R. Bervens. Geneva: World Health Organization.

1991   Gender, Power and Risk of AIDS in Central Africa. In: *Women and Health in Africa*, edited by M. Turshen. Pp. 187-203. Trenton: Africa World Press.

Schuster, Ilsa
1979   The New Women of Lusaka. Palo Alto: Mayfield.

Seidman, Ann and Frederick Anang (editors)
1992   *21st Century Africa: Towards a New Vision of Self-Sustainable Development*. Trenton: Africa World Press.

Standing, Helen and Mary N. Kisekka
1989   *Sexual Behavior in Sub-Saharan Africa: A Review and Annotated Bibliography*. London: Overseas Development Administration.

Staudt, Kathleen
1989   State and Gender in Colonial Africa: Anthropological Perspectives. In: *Women, the State and Development*, edited by S. Charlton, J. Everett, and K. Staudt. Pp. 66-85. Albany: State University of New York.

Stein, Zena
1990   HIV Prevention: The Need for Methods Women Can Use. *American Journal of Public Health* 80:460-462.

Stichter, Sharon
    1990   Women, Employment and the Family: Current Debates. In: *Women,
            Employment and the Family in the International Division of Labour*,
            edited by Sharon Stichter, and Jane L. Parpart.   Pp. 11-71.
            Philadelphia: Temple University Press.

SWAA (Society for Women and AIDS in Africa)
    1989   Report of the 1st International Workshop on Women and AIDS in
            Africa, Harare, Zimbabwe, May 10-12.

Tadesse, Zenebrworke
    1991   Coping with Change: An Overview of Women and the African
            Economy. In: *The Future of Women in Development: Voices from the
            South*. Proceedings of the Association for Women in Development
            Colloquium. Pp. 44-64. Ottawa, Canada, October 19-20.

Thonneau, Patrick, Stephane Quesnod, Jean-Pierre Lhomme et al.
    1991   Evaluation by Women Consulting in a Family Planning Centre of
            Their Risk of HIV Infection. *AIDS* 5:549-553.

Treichler, Paula A.
    1988   AIDS, Homophobia, and Biomedical Discourse: An Epidemic of
            Signification. In: *AIDS: Cultural Analysis/Cultural Activism*, edited
            by D. Crimp. Pp. 31-70. Cambridge: MIT Press.

UNCHR (United Nations Centre for Human Rights)
    1991   New York: United Nations. Report of an International Consultation
            on AIDS and Human Rights, Geneva, July 26-28.

UNDP (United Nations Development Programme)
    1991   *The HIV Epidemic as a Development Issue*. New York: UNDP.

UNECA (United Nations Economic Commission for Africa)
    1989   *An African Alternative for Structural Adjustment Programmes: A
            Framework for Transformation and Recovery*. Addis Ababa: UNECA.

UNICEF (United Nations Children's Emergency Fund)
    1991   *The Situation of the World's Children*. New York: United Nations.

Vaughan, Megan
　1991　Syphilis, AIDS and the Representation of Sexuality: The Historical Legacy. In: *Action on AIDS in Southern Africa*, edited by Z. Stein and A. Zwi. Pp. 119-125. New York: Committee for Health in South Africa (CHISA).

Waite, G.
　1988　The Politics of Disease: The AIDS Virus and Africa. In: *AIDS in Africa: Social and Policy Impact*, edited by N. Miller and R. Rockwell. Pp. 145-169. Lewiston: Edwin Mellen Press.

Walu, Engundu
　1987　Women's Survival Strategies in Kinshasa. Consultant Report, Washington: World Bank.

Watney, Simon
　1989　Missionary Positions: AIDS, Africa and "Race" Differences. *A Journal of Feminist Cultural Studies* I:83-100.

White, Luise
　1990　*The Comforts of Home: Prostitution in Colonial Nairobi.* Chicago: University of Chicago Press.

Wilson, David, B. Sibanda, L. Mboy, and S. Msimanga
　1990　A Pilot Study of an HIV Prevention Programme Among Commercial Sex Workers in Bulawayo, Zimabawe. *Social Science and Medicine* 31:609-618.

WHO (World Health Organization)
　1991　Update: The Global Strategy for the Prevention and Control of AIDS. Geneva: WHO, GPA/GMC (2)/91-8, 11 October.

Zwi, Anthony B. and Antonio Jorge Cabral
　1991　Identifying "High Risk Situations" for Preventing AIDS. *British Medical Journal* 303(14 December):1527-1529.

3

Women and Structural Adjustment in a Global Economy

Christina H. Gladwin

During "the lost decade" of the 1980s, Africa and Latin America were plagued by trade imbalances and massive and snowballing debt, problems created by the rise in oil prices in 1973 and 1979 (Bacha 1988).[1] To reduce these trade imbalances and budget deficits, the International Monetary Fund (IMF) and the World Bank mandated structural adjustment programs (SAPs) and structural adjustment loans (SALs). As a result, growth rates of real per capita GDP (gross domestic product or output) in the Third World declined from 1979 to 1988, and they were negative for 50 of 82 developing countries during the mid-1980s (Cornia, Jolly, and Stewart 1987:17). Real wages and salaries decreased, inflation increased, per capita daily calorie consumption declined, and health, education, and nutrition standards deteriorated (Cornia, Jolly, and Stewart 1987:28).

The 1980s were also a time of economic expansion in the United States. Growth and consumption was financed by an unparalleled increase in the debt of individuals, corporations, and state and federal governments (*Philadelphia Inquirer* 1991). The national debt rose from $73.8 billion in 1980 to $3 trillion in 1991, and the trade balance became more negative as manufactured imports increased. In 1984, imports into the United States accounted for four-fifths of the increase in world imports (Cornia, Jolly, and Stewart 1987:14), and manufacturing plants closed and blue-collar workers lost unionized jobs in increasing numbers. The result has been labeled by some: "structural adjustment U.S. style" (Alt-WID 1992).

This chapter explores the phenomenon called "structural adjustment," and asks what were the factors necessitating SAPs in most Third World countries. What were the internal and external factors contributing to the crisis? Are there any connections between what occurred in the United States--"the North"--and the Third World or "the South"? And more to the point of this volume, why does it appear that women in the global economy, especially women of color, are bearing a disproportionately large share of the burden of these changes? The review is limited to Africa and Latin America. With the possible exception of the Philippines, Asia suffered only a modest decline in growth of per capita GDP from 1981 to 1985 (Cornia, Jolly, and Stewart 1987:19). The economies of Latin America and Africa, by contrast, deteriorated due to indebtedness and dependence on primary (agricultural) commodities for export.

I begin by discussing the factors that provoked the economic crises of the 1980s and led most economists to conclude that without some form of structural adjustment program, the situation might have been far worse in most recipient countries (Cornia, Jolly, and Stewart 1987:48; Lele 1991; O'Brien 1991). Then, I examine the impact of SAPs on subsistence women farmers in Africa and women wage laborers in Latin America. In the concluding section, I argue that SAP programs are *not* gender neutral and that complementary policies--credit, fertilizer subsidies, income-generation and micro-enterprise programs, job training programs, and nutritional supplementation programs for women and children, coupled with programs of debt forgiveness and reduced defense expenditures for their governments-- are needed to mitigate the adverse effects of SAPs on women now caught up in an increasingly-integrated and complex global economy.

Structural Adjustment Programs: A Necessary Evil?

Between 1981 and 1986, the global economy experienced the "most severe and prolonged recession since the 1930s" (Vickers 1991:2). Africa's economic performance was particularly bleak with an average annual growth rate in GDP of only 0.4 percent between 1980 and 1987. Per-capita incomes, already low in comparison to those in Asia or Latin America in the late 1970s, steadily declined by 2.6 percent per annum during the 1980s (Economic Commission for Africa 1989:i). Latin America experienced similar problems, and 21 of 23 countries had negative per capita GDP growth in 1982 (Cornia, Jolly, and Stewart 1987:17). Inflation ran rampant, increasing from 56 percent in 1980 to 473 percent in 1988 (Bacha 1988). Net capital transfers became negative (-\$19 billion) in 1982, the year Mexico declared a moratorium on its debt.

It is in this context--the context of a global recession--that structural adjustment programs and policies (SAPs), mandated by the IMF and the Bank and adopted by over 30 countries in Africa since 1982, should be examined (*The Economist* 1991).[2] Economists see structural adjustment as a way to invigorate stagnating agricultural and industrial sectors (Due 1991; Timmer, Falcon, and Pearson 1983). They argue that distorted "macro prices" (overvalued exchange rates, artificially low food prices, high wage rates, low interest rates, subsidized input prices) may improve income distribution and food intake in the short run, especially for the poor whose food consumption can least stand to be reduced. Distorted prices, however, also send signals that may negatively affect the efficient allocation of resources and may undermine the food supply system and economy in the long run.

Because most governments wish to affect income distribution in their societies, they are greatly tempted to use government policy in an effort to *set macro prices*, rather than allow them to be determined by market forces. If wage rates can be set high, labor is no longer cheap, and poverty is eliminated. If interest rates can be set low, capital is not scarce, and a country can quickly have a modern industrial sector. If food prices are kept low, food is abundant, and no one will be hungry. . . . It is no wonder that many countries have tried this approach. When it fails--as it must until the productivity base has been built that will support higher levels of living in the long run--the economy is riddled with serious price distortions. Resource allocations skew income distribution while much of the labor power of the work force is left untapped, and the government faces stagnant growth in both agricultural and industrial output. It is not easy to put such an economy back on track (Timmer, Falcon, and Pearson 1983:229).

These distorted macro prices were some of the *internal factors* which led to "the lost decade" of the 1980s. Clearly, there were others. The United Nations' Economic Commission for Africa (ECA), for example, mentions Africa's too-narrow production base, its ill-adapted technology, its over-dependence on subsistence agriculture, the urban bias of public policies, weak linkages between the modern formal sector and growing informal sector, and poor institutional management (1989:2-8). Similarly, Brazilian economist Bacha (1988) claims that the crisis was not due solely to external factors; internal factors specific to Latin America which predated the crisis were also responsible. In particular, Latin American countries had less openness to trade than East Asian countries, less exports and less manufactured exports, and more dependence on exports of primary (agricultural) commodities, whose terms of trade deteriorated in the 1980s.[3] Although Latin America in 1981 had as developed a manufacturing sector as did East Asian countries, generating 43.9 percent of GDP excluding services (vs. 47.2% in East Asia), its share in total merchandise exports in 1980 was only 22.2 percent while that of East Asia was 47 percent (Bacha 1988:4). Latin America's exports averaged only 13 percent of GDP in 1979, as compared to South Korea's 38 percent, of which 90 percent were manufactured products. Because debt is repaid with exports, this meant that Latin America was less able to absorb the external shocks of the late 1970s and early 1980s and repay its debt.

External factors included the oil price increases of 1973 and 1979 and the collapse of world prices of agricultural commodities, which accounted for 88 percent of exports in Africa and were responsible for sharp declines in the purchasing power of Africans and Latin Americans after 1981. This meant that a higher volume of exports became necessary to generate the same trade surplus. Both factors led to a doubling of total debt in Africa and Latin America. Although Africa's debt was a small percentage (10%) of global debt, it resulted in the total evaporation of commercial lending flows into Africa and the additional curtailment of loans--or switch to grants--by donor agencies. In Latin America, external debt rose from $231 billion in 1980 to $413 billion in 1988. Most countries borrowed to finance their mounting current account deficits, but even oil exporters, expecting growing energy prices in the future, borrowed heavily (Bacha 1988:7). During the petrol boom in Mexico, for example, in the period between 1980 and 1981, speculation and inflationary pressures increased; total capital flight reached 11 billion dollars before the currency was devalued in February 1982 (Arizpe, Salinas, and Velasquez 1987:113). Servicing the debt became burdensome, not only because debt service as a percent of exports rose from 34 percent in 1980 to 43 percent in 1988, but also because two-thirds of the debt was repayable in dollars at "floating" interest rates.

Here the interconnectedness of the new global economy came into play. Real interest rates rose in the early 1980s, due not only to the stringent monetarist policies adopted in the United States, United Kingdom, and other industrial countries in the late 1970s, early 1980s (Cornia, Jolly, and Stewart 1987:13), but also to the military expansion in the United States during the Reagan era. The United States Federal Reserve Board raised nominal interest rates (to 18-20% at their peak during 1980-82) to restrict the money supply, contract credit expansion, and curb inflation. Nevertheless, President Reagan decided to increase military spending from $143 billion in 1980 to $300 billion in 1990, and borrowed on world capital markets to finance the expansion. Although there were 50 percent cuts in social programs at the same time, these cuts were not enough and the United States budget deficit grew. This had to be financed, and the resulting competition for capital on world markets raised *real* interest rates. They have not declined, although nominal interest rates have declined since 1982 (Cornia, Jolly, and Stewart 1987:15). This aggravated the Third World debt crisis because so much of the debt was repayable at floating interest rates.

The result was a change in the level and direction of net capital flows during the 1980-85 period (Cornia, Jolly, and Stewart 1987:14-15). Due to the debt, commercial banks contracted lending to developing countries following the second oil shock. The United States became a magnet attracting capital flows from "the South" in order to finance its growing current account and budget deficits. Whereas in 1979 a net $40 billion flowed from northern-hemisphere countries to southern-hemisphere developing countries (Vickers 1991:4), in 1984 and 1985 the net capital transfer became negative; i.e., the developing world became a net exporter of resources to the industrial world.

Structural Adjustment Programs

To help developing countries cope with "financial strangulation, the curtailment of foreign finance, and increasing interest payments" (Bacha 1988:8), the IMF, World Bank, and bilateral donors (e.g., USAID) changed their lending policy, shifting from project-oriented funds to conditional funds. Infusions of capital were provided if countries agreed to undertake structural adjustment reforms such as devaluation of overvalued currencies, increases in artificially low food prices and interest rates, alignment of domestic prices with world prices, an emphasis on the production of exports (tradables) rather than subsistence crops (non-tradables), privatization of parastatals or large-scale government monopolies, reductions in public-sector employment and wages, elimination of food and fertilizer subsidies, and decreases in budget deficits (Economic Commission for Africa 1989:18-20).

SAP prescriptions are based on the neoclassical economic assumptions that markets work, that they are generally competitive, and that market signals are good guides to resource allocation (O'Brien 1991). On the positive side, SAPs introduce market-oriented policies into countries without markets (e.g., Malawi in 1987) and encourage entrepreneurial behavior and micro-enterprises. They demand that a public service be efficient, reliable, with transparent accounting for public moneys; they urge an end to one-party states. They mandate the divestiture of non-strategic public enterprises--parastatals--and require the removal of exchange rate and other biases against exports. From an economist's point of view, these measures are requisites for the functioning of a democratic market economy. On the negative side, however, SAPs mean deflationary stabilization policies aimed at reducing budget and trade deficits through fiscal and monetary measures. SAP conditions basically force governments to *cut back spending*, as well as reduce imports and promote exports to improve the balance of trade. (The measures mandated to achieve this end are often so draconian that even the United States has been unwilling to implement them.)

Impacts of Structural Adjustment on African Women Producers

Adjustment means change and change means costs as well as benefits, losers as well as winners (Elson 1989:60). For example, devaluation of an overvalued currency increases the cost of imported inputs, thereby working to the detriment of those who use imported goods (urban elites, industrial producers, agricultural implement users, truckers). In contrast, if devaluation is accompanied by increases in agricultural producer prices, it theoretically should benefit farmers who use few imported inputs, because their earnings should increase more than their costs. This should stimulate agricultural production, encourage import substitution of domestic goods in industrial production, and promote exports. In such a scenario, all farmers should benefit and although urban consumers would lose, the whole economy would be jump-started out of stagnation. In the long run, everyone should gain.

But in practice, does this happen? For the purposes of this paper, an important related question is: are SAPs *gender-neutral* (i.e., affecting men and women equally), or merely *gender-blind* (i.e., ignoring the impacts on women and assuming them to be the same as on men)?

I argue that in practice, structural adjustment programs do not benefit but hurt the majority of farmers, and their impacts are even harsher on women farmers. Such difference is critical in Africa where rural producers who might gain from an urban-to-rural redistribution of income are mainly women, who provide 46 percent of agricultural labor on average and produce most (60 percent or more) food crops (Dixon 1982). In practice, farmers in general and women farmers in particular rarely benefit from SAPs because the policies ignore power relations of all kinds (urban vs. rural power relations, patriarchal relations in the household and village).[4] Yet these power relations determine who gets access to shrinking resources of capital and foreign exchange, and who controls the surplus resulting from the added incentives to produce. Because urban elites have more power over the political process than peasant farmers, they have more influence over how budgets are cut and where. Due to inequality in gender relations, women producers do not have the resources to respond to improved price incentives (Mehra 1991). Subordinate to men in the household, women neither own land (Goheen 1991) nor have direct access to basic inputs of production such as credit and fertilizer (Gladwin 1991), extension advice (Staudt 1988), or labor, including their own (Due and Magayane 1990; Guyer with Idowu 1991). In many societies they do not have the right to grow cash or export crops (Lele 1991).

Women's relative lack of power constrains them even from allocating their own time differently between subsistence food crops (non-tradables) and cash crops (tradables). They can only increase their total hours of labor. Thus, western development schemes have been known to unintentionally double women's labor input while decreasing the size of their private fields and thus their autonomy (Gladwin and McMillan 1989). Given SAPs' greater emphasis on tradables, men who grow export crops will tend to appropriate *more* of these basic inputs, including women's labor, from the women who grow food crops, making their job of feeding the family more difficult and their opportunities to generate a marketable surplus even rarer (Meena 1991). The result will not be that men take over more of the food production, at least not in the short run; because as Boserup (1970:34) has pointed out, men usually refuse to do work which according to prevailing custom should be done by women. It is thus the African woman's role as provider of subsistence food within the family, coupled with her subordination to men, that causes her to lose out in the reshuffle known as structural adjustment.[5]

The Evidence

Unfortunately, there is some evidence supporting both camps: those who claim a positive impact of SAPs on African women farmers, as well as those who claim a negative impact. Guyer with Idowu (1991) shows how entrepreneurial Yoruba women were encouraged to start their own farms and cash in on higher producer prices produced by the Nigerian ban on all imported food as part of its SAP program. Ensminger's (1991) case study of Orma sedentarized pastoralists, who produce meat but do not consume it, also shows that the rise in Kenyan meat prices during the 1980s has meant greater incomes, education, nutrition, health, and political power for Orma women. But these appear to be the exceptions that prove the rule.

More studies show that higher producer prices can *hurt* women farmers, especially women heads of household, the smallest of the smallholders whose households are not usually self-sufficient in food production. Women-headed households (WHH) currently comprise 25 to 35 percent of both *rural* and *urban* households in most countries of tropical Africa, and may be either "de facto" or "de jure" (Due and Gladwin 1991; Due and White 1986). A de facto WHH is one in which the husband is away for long periods of time, making it necessary for the wife to do the decision-making and support the family, although there may be income coming from the husband irregularly from time to time. The wife makes decisions about family expenditures and farm operations when WHHs are rural. A de jure WHH is one in which the head is divorced, widowed or a single parent; in de jure WHHs the woman head must make all decisions and support the family; polygamous households are excluded.

There are major contrasts between WHHs and JHHs ("joint" households with both husband and wife present) in rural areas when both types of households are farming (Chipande et al. 1986; Due 1991; Due, Sikaponde, and Magayane 1991; Due and White 1986; Hudgens 1988; Mollel 1986; Phiri 1986; Sikaponde 1988). The major factor which differentiates these households is that women-headed households, with no able bodied male (or additional adult female) present are smaller in size than JHHs and therefore have less labor available for agricultural production in a farming system which is very labor intensive. With less labor available, WHHs have smaller crop acreages planted; this results in lower agricultural output, and a higher percentage of production is needed for family consumption, leaving less for sale. Therefore average and per capita net incomes are lower. Also, WHHs have less access to credit for hiring labor or labor saving devices and less access to extension services. WHHs plant more of their total crop acreage to food crops than do JHHs. But because they have smaller acreages, they are *net buyers* rather than net sellers of food products, and so they suffer when food prices rise.

How extensive are food-buying households in rural Africa? Peters claims that African peasants are not able to "withdraw" from the market into autarky--as posited by Hyden's (1983) "economy of affection"--in the cases of Tanzania and western Kenya (where 40 to 50 percent of households depend to a significant extent on purchased food), Malawi, and even some areas of Zimbabwe (a net exporter of maize) (Hyden and Peters 1991:312). In Malawi, for example, Peters and Herrera (1989) find that less than 15 percent of smallholders are fully self-sufficient in maize production. Lele terms the structure of Malawi's agriculture a "dualism-within-dualism" structure, whereby the small farm sector is distinct from the large "estate" sector and smallholders are split into two groups: a minority who have a farm size large enough "to produce a marketable surplus and capable of taking risks and a preponderant majority experiencing stagnation or near economic paralysis" (Lele 1989:16). Increasing the producer price of maize will thus be detrimental not only to the urban poor but also to the rural majority who buy maize. According to Harrigon (1987), the only hope of increasing their incomes is to encourage their use of fertilizer on "local" maize varieties, so that more of their land can be taken out of subsistence and planted to men's cash crops (hybrid maize, tobacco, cotton) or women's cash crops (groundnuts).

Advocates of SAPs now agree that structural adjustment programs "have ignored or given insufficient attention to the social costs of adjustment," especially for the poor (O'Brien 1991:35-37). O'Brien concludes that "the verdict is still out" on SAPs (1991:39), and more careful longitudinal impact studies such as Ensminger's (1991) study of the Orma need to be done. Yet the cross-sectional, ethnographic studies that have been done are also useful, and allow us to identify those components of SAP packages that negatively impact on women farmers and should either be dropped--or mitigated by the design of another intervention or targeted subsidy.

A fertilizer subsidy removal program--currently pushed by USAID in several African countries--is a component of a SAP package which should be dropped. It negatively impacts on African women farmers just now starting to use chemical fertilizers on subsistence food crops which are fertilizer-responsive, such as maize. Gladwin's (1991, 1992) results, based on a model of farmers' decisions between chemical and organic fertilizer in Malawi and Cameroon, show that women farmers want to use chemical fertilizer on maize, but are constrained from its use by lack of cash and credit in both countries, rather than their beliefs in organic substitutes (manure/compost or a fallow cycle with leguminous trees). In the view of women farmers, animal manures or leguminous trees are *not* substitutes for chemical fertilizer; they are complements, expensive ones, and very inconvenient, because maize fields are planted too far away from homes or roads. Fallow cycles (e.g., in Northwest Cameroon) are too short to be viable substitutes for chemical fertilizer in maize production.

Why can't credit be expanded to allow both married women and women heads of household to invest in fertilizer? Gladwin's (1991, 1992) credit decision models shows one of the main factors limiting women farmers' use of credit in Malawi is their aversion to the risks of not being able to repay loans in bad years. Poor women farmers do not want credit if they do not have a cash crop to sell in order to repay the loan; and they have learned not to sell subsistence crops needed by their families in the hunger period. From the perspective of the women, government's expanding credit is not a substitute for government's making fertilizer cheap enough, via a fertilizer subsidy, for poor women to get with cash provided by their own cash crops, husbands, sons, or savings.

What, then, do women do when fertilizer subsidies are removed and both fertilizer and food prices are allowed to increase, as they have in Malawi where the price of maize doubled and the price of fertilizer increased 66 percent since 1986/87? Aggregate data from Malawi show that, although the profitability of local (subsistence) maize has steadily increased, this increased profitability has not elicited an improved supply response of local maize, a non-tradable (Lukwago 1992). Yet the increased profitability of hybrid maize, the men's cash crop, has elicited a more than doubling of the supply. Where has this increased hectarage of hybrid maize come from? Groundnuts, the women's cash crop, has decreased drastically in hectarage. Men are thus responding to the increased profitability of their cash crop by drawing land resources away from the women's cash crop, leaving women less able to buy fertilizer for local maize and farm it more intensively. Yet more intensive farming of subsistence maize is the most effective way to increase cash crop production in Malawi (Harrigon 1987).

Meena's (1991) study of the Mwanza region, Tanzania, shows similar results. An increase in crop prices has not matched the increased price of farm implements and inputs which have risen due to devaluation and inflation. She also observed that women's food crops (vegetables, fruits, peas, and beans) do not get the necessary agro-chemical inputs, because women do not receive cash from the sale of cash crops.

In fact, increased producer prices for cash (export) crops may negatively affect women by forcing them to spend more of their time on men's cash crops and less on their own food crops. In Mwanza region, Meena (1991) claims women spend more of their time on cotton production and less on their own vegetables and fruits. In addition, men and women have previously been jointly responsible for harvesting crops. Now, however, men have been pulling out from ferrying harvested crops to market, due to the increased price of bicycles, ox carts, and wheel barrows to ferry cotton from the farms. When men do have a means of transport, they cooperate in this activity; otherwise it becomes women's business, adding to their labor burden. As a result, Meena (1991:175) concludes that:

> Price is thus an ineffective instrument to motivate agricultural producers in increasing production, if (1) there is a mismatch between increases in prices of necessary farm inputs and increases in producer prices, or if (2) there is no mechanism to ensure that the surplus which is accrued from the increased producer price benefits all the producers, including women. A price increase of cash crops whose income is not controlled by women cannot motivate women farmers who have nothing to gain from these increases.

Goheen's (1991) case study of land and gender in Nso, Northwest Cameroon, shows a similar institutional barrier which is exacerbated by the SAP crisis. Traditionally, land in Nso is owned by men; men and women labor on coffee, the export crop, while women, who grow virtually all the food consumed locally, have to "beg for land" for their crops. A decline in national food self-sufficiency over the past decade has intensified the government's interest in developing commercial agriculture in the region, so it has offered a "Young Farmers' Resettlement Program" with big tracts of previously unsettled land. But custom--and capital--dictates that only "big men" get the land, and women walk further and further away from the village to plant subsistence maize. This weakening of women's entitlements to land comes at a time when urban remittances have decreased, male relatives have not been paid for their coffee crop, and fertilizer subsidies are being removed. It "threatens the nutritional level not only of the rural household but also of a large proportion of the national population" (Goheen 1991:241).

Impacts of SAPs on Latin American Women

In most of Latin America, women do not have the same farming role as do African women; their role as food provisioner in the family does not include growing it.[6] Nevertheless, their roles as wage laborers and mothers made them vulnerable to the economic crisis of the 1980s. On the one hand, they were affected by the crisis because women's opportunities for employment and access to resources were more limited than men's (Deere et al. 1990:52-55). On the other hand, in countries where men's capacity to provide for their families was seriously eroded, women's participation in the waged labor force increased or intensified in an attempt to maintain the level of household income or at least contain its fall (Gonzalez de la Rocha 1988; Safa 1992a, 1992b). Poor women even cut their own food intake more than that of other family members during periods of declining food availability (Cornia, Jolly, and Stewart 1987:100; Raczynski and Serrano 1985). On a positive note, the crisis has allowed some women to battle gender ideologies portraying them either as dependent wives or "supplementary" workers even when fully employed (Safa 1992a:3). As their economic contribution to the family became more important relative to men's, more women resisted male dominance in the household and struggled for greater control over the budget, a greater share in household decisions, and control over their own fertility (Safa 1992a:26).

Impacts on Women's Employment

Women's job opportunities and access to resources were more limited than men's, and so women were vulnerable to the crisis (Deere et al. 1990:52-55). Not only were average earnings of women lower than those of men (e.g., J$68.3 vs. J$86.9 in Jamaica in 1985), but also women's unemployment rates were higher (e.g., 36.6% or over twice men's rate in Jamaica) (Deere et al. 1990:52). This was a setback for women who between 1950 and 1980 increased their labor force participation rates from 18 percent to 26 percent in Latin America as a whole, and still higher in some countries, e.g., from 11 percent to 37.5 percent in the Dominican Republic (Safa 1992a).[7] Yet most of this increased employment has occurred in unskilled, unstable, low-paying jobs in the informal economy or export-led industries (e.g., garment, electronics industries) encouraged by structural adjustment policies (Safa 1992a, 1992b, this volume; Tiano 1986, 1992).

Export manufacturers--transnational corporations (TNCs)--have shown a preference for women workers because they are perceived to be cheaper to employ, are more passive, compliant, and less likely to unionize, and have greater patience for the tedious, monotonous work of assembly operations (Deere et al. 1990:62; Fiala and Tiano 1991:5; Tiana 1986). They have proliferated in the Caribbean and Mexico due to their governments' urgent need of foreign exchange which led them to lift trade barriers, subsidize credit, and offer tax holidays, as well as unrestricted profit repatriation, export subsidies, and freedom from import duties on raw materials and machinery (Safa 1992b:2). On its part, the United States government supported export manufacturing in the area via United States Tariff Code 807 which limits United States tariffs on imports with United States components assembled abroad to only their "value added" portion; this encouraged United States firms to relocate the labor-intensive phases of manufacturing abroad to take advantage of cheaper wages.

When the crisis and structural adjustment policies hit in the 1980s, men's salaries fell--in percentage terms sometimes more than women's wages fell, as for example in the case of Jamaica (Davies and Anderson 1987, Table 14; Deere et al. 1990:53). This was due in part to devaluation, in part to sharp cuts in traditional export commodities such as sugar in the Dominican Republic, bauxite in Jamaica, and petroleum in Trinidad (Safa 1992b:4). Male unemployment also increased, and men were pushed into more marginal jobs in the informal economy. What effect did this have on women? They increased their labor force participation still further to maintain the level of household income or at least to contain its fall (Deere et al. 1990:53-67, Gonzalez de la Rocha 1988; Safa and Antrobus 1992).

One thus sees a seemingly-contradictory trend of increased labor force participation rates of women, and an increased intensity of work on their part, in response to SAPs and the crisis. In the Dominican Republic, for example, the number of "export platform" or export-assembly firms in the free-trade zones increased from 103 in 1983 to 224 in 1988 to 385 firms in 1992; and the number of employees more than quadrupled, reaching an estimated 85,000 in 1988 and 135,000 in 1992. Three-fourths of these jobs were held by women (Deere et al. 1990:63; Safa 1992a:11). In Jamaica between 1981 and 1985, the proportion of women employed in manufacturing rose from 7 percent to 8.7 percent of the female labor force (Davies and Anderson 1987, Table 12; Deere et al. 1990:62), while the overall growth of women's employment was 7.8 percent. In Guadalajara, a new center for export-led electronics and data-entry firms in Mexico, a longitudinal study of 100 households by Gonzalez de la Rocha (1988:214-215) shows that urban women of age 15 or more increased their labor force participation by 25.4 percent over the period from 1982 to 1985, while men aged 15 or more increased their labor force participation only slightly (10.5%). In other countries, similar changes were observable but not measurable because labor force participation rates were not disaggregated by gender, e.g., Costa Rica, Chile, and Uruguay (Cornia, Jolly, and Stewart 1987:94).[8]

Much of this increased employment appears to have occurred in the informal sector, which in Latin America as a whole grew in size from 29 percent to 32 percent from 1980 to 1985 (Tokman 1986). Households engaged in informal income-earning activities of all kinds: part-time marketing, subcontracting for the formal sector and export-led industries, small-scale manufacturing, retail trade, small-scale transport, personal services, self production (cultivation of small family gardens, subsistence production, cooperative child-care and health clubs--*clubes de madres*, voluntary labor exchanges for house construction), as well as illegal or quasi-legal activities (beer-brewing, smuggling, prostitution, begging, drug cultivation) (Cornia, Jolly, and Stewart 1987:90-97; Vickers 1991:25). Usually, such activities are characterized by low wages and earnings, the smallness of markets, and locational advantage. The expansion of the informal sector depends in part on interactions with the formal sector, which may siphon off the productivity gains of the informal sector through various mechanisms (e.g., subcontracting, price determination, oligopolistic market control, etc.)

Arizpe, Salinas, and Velasquez (1987:120) also claim that Mexican rural women have increased their farming, although traditionally they have not had a farming role. The 1980 census confirms that 12.3 percent of the total female work force was employed in agriculture; in some states, e.g., Campeche, the female labor force increased from 11 percent of total number of workers in 1970 to 25 percent in 1980. Women began to enter paid agricultural work as male family members increased their seasonal out-migration during the crisis and they could no longer afford to pay for wage labor. Younger women who had in the 1970s migrated to cities for service employment now could find nothing better than seasonal agricultural labor. Women thus comprised one-third of the 4.5 million rural day-laborers in the 1980s.

Impact on Women's Consciousness

In an analysis of patriarchal relations at three levels (the household, the workplace, and the state), Safa (1992a) argues that the erosion of men's roles as economic providers during the crisis of the 1980s and the increase in women's contributions in the workplace, especially in export-led industries, has led to one positive impact: more women workers are negotiating with their men to acquire more authority in the household. Although men still control women's labor, with industrialization there is increasing competition for control of women's labor, and men at the household level increasingly lose out to men in the workplace and the state. In Caribbean countries such as Jamaica and the Dominican Republic where men's role as economic provider is being eroded through unemployment, "women are acquiring more authority in the household not just because they are employed, but because of the importance of their economic contribution" (Safa 1992a:26). While the men are doing odd jobs in the informal sector like selling cooked food, driving cabs or doing construction work part-time, women working for a wage in export-led industries are becoming less dependent on them and are more prone to leave an unsatisfactory relationship.

Women's job satisfaction in export-led industries has also been examined by Tiano (1986, 1992) and Fiala and Tiano (1991), who compare women in export processing plants to women in the service sector in Mexicali, Northern Mexico. In 1983-84, they interviewed 194 women: 66 in electronics *maquilas*, 58 in garment manufacturing plants, and 70 waitresses, maids, cashiers, cooks, and other service providers. When asked whether they agreed or disagreed with job-attitudinal statements, respondents were not highly critical of their material conditions on the job; they were only modestly critical about what they were paid and whether they could feel proud on the job (Fiala and Tiano 1991:8). Family roles occupied a central place in their lives, and they were concerned that their work might jeopardize their ability to perform family roles effectively. Tiano (1992) notes that these results, shared by Stoddard (1987:51), Lucker and Alvarez (1984), and Ong (1987), contradict ethnographic results that paint a dreary picture of working conditions in export assembly plants (Fernandez-Kelly 1983). The latter describe conditions for women workers as "squalor, deprivation, and exhaustion," and claim they are worse in the apparel maquilas than in large TNC electronics firms.

Tiano's (1992:14) results, however, show that workers in apparel occupations are more likely than those in electronics and service occupations to profess universal employment satisfaction, with 65 percent stating they dislike nothing about their jobs as compared with 34 percent of the electronics assemblers and 27 percent of the service workers. Apparel assemblers are also less likely than others to have considered quitting their jobs. Yet working conditions are worse in the apparel industry. Why are they the most satisfied?

To resolve these debates, Tiano (1992) posits that workers dynamically develop "job coping mechanisms" similar to the survival strategies discussed below, e.g., making a game out of quota competition. These strategies allow workers not only to increase productivity but also to generate a satisfying sense of personal achievement from their work tasks. Although these satisfactions do little to transform the objective realities of the workplace, they do enable workers to meet the challenges of their work, exercise some creative control over their labor, and maintain their health. She concludes that such adaptability and complacency could be a reflection of apparel workers' labor market vulnerability and their limited employment alternatives. If they considered themselves fortunate to have secured jobs in apparel manufacturing because they were older, or had more children, or less education, they might be more likely to find creative ways to adapt to the rigors of their jobs in a way which enabled them to evaluate their jobs in a positive light (Tiano 1992:17). Further, if their mothers have worked previously, women may acquire from these role models an effective arsenal of coping strategies. Using multiple regression analysis, she then finds support for this hypothesis. She concludes that job satisfaction has less to do with job tasks and the conditions of the workplace and more to do with who the women are and what learned abilities they have to cope with the demands of their work roles (Tiano 1992:26).

Impacts on Women as Food Provisioners

Women in Latin America and the Caribbean usually work a "double day" as wage earners and as food providers. Their ability to provide food for the family has been complicated by the economic crisis and mandated SAP reforms which have doubled the cost of the family food basket in the 1980s (Deere et al. 1990:55). The impact of rising food prices has been a particular hardship for women-headed households, which in Latin America

University
of Ulster
LIBRARY

are estimated to range from 14.4 percent in Brazil and Guatemala (Kennedy 1992) to 39 percent in Jamaica (Deere et al. 1990:52). Most women faced with reduced incomes and escalating food prices have adopted personal survival strategies--grass-roots adaptations developed indigenously by the women themselves and not by government agencies--to help them feed their families (Deere et al. 1990:70-72; Gonzalez de la Rocha 1988). According to Cornia, Jolly, and Stewart (1987:98-99), these survival strategies involve changes in:

(1) *purchasing habits*. Families in Chile have abandoned monthly purchases at wholesale prices of non-perishables such as sugar, tea, flour, cooking oil. Instead, they shop frequently and purchase in small quantitites at high prices in neighborhood stores.

(2) *food preparation habits*. Women from 15 to 20 households in Lima have been preparing *comedores populares* (collective meals). They buy food in bulk and prepare and cook it together. Working in shifts, the women use their release time to increase their wage labor and family income.

(3) *overall consumption patterns*. Some families eliminate the purchase of non-essential items (clothing, consumer durables, leisure). Under continuing pressure, they suspend payment on essentials such as water, fuel, and rent. Families try to delay cut backs in staples and children's education.

(4) *dietary patterns*. Poor households substitute high caloric foods for protein-rich foods, thereby replacing expensive sources of calories. Over a period of time, however, per capita calorie intake usually declines (Raczynski and Serrano 1985).[9]

(5) *intrahousehold food distribution*. Women in poor households reduce their own food intake, making it available to other family members (Raczynski and Serrano 1985).

Although innovative, Cornia, Jolly, and Stewart (1987:102) caution that women's survival strategies should not be interpreted as inexpensive solutions to the problems of the poor nor as an excuse for policy inaction. Some of them are even non-adaptive in the long run, e.g., the reduction of women's own food intake.

Impact on Women's Reproductive Roles

Conventional approaches to adjustment have usually slashed funding for child-welfare services which affect women in their reproductive roles as mothers and caretakers. Expenditures on education, nutrition, health (including family planning) have been cut in real terms by most SAPs in Latin America (Commonwealth Secretariat 1989). (In Africa, these cuts have locked increasing numbers of women-headed households into a permanent cycle of poverty in both urban and rural sectors [Due 1991; Meena 1991].)

According to Cornia, Jolly, and Stewart (1987:131-139), this is unfortunate and unnecessary. It is unfortunate because the nutritional level of children has worsened: malnutrition and infant mortality rates have either increased or their previous decline has been decreased. It is unnecessary because alternative adjustment packages--"with a human face"--are possible. Stabilization efforts that are deemed successful in terms of conventional measures (e.g., a decrease in the budget deficit) but have inhuman consequences (e.g., a 46% decrease in wages) can be replaced by "expansionary adjustment." The latter would employ a different timing or more gradual correction of imbalances, or would target interventions at the poor, and employ compensatory programs to protect their basic living standards.

The Chilean case shows that it is possible to have adjustment "with a human face." Because Chile had a historic commitment to the health and education of children, it geared social policy to moderating the effects of the recession from 1981 to 1986 via a series of public work schemes, nutritional supplementation programs, primary school feeding programs, and food subsidies to children under 8 years of age and pregnant women in poverty. As a result, malnutrition among pre-school children and pregnant women continued to decline during the 1980s, as did the incidence of communicable diseases (Cornia, Jolly, and Stewart 1987:110-111).

Conclusion

The 1980s revealed a new vulnerability in the global economy resulting from greater international interdependence, which had previously had positive impacts in the form of greater economic growth (Joekes 1990). The new vulnerability was discussed via some complicated macroeconomic terms (e.g., deteriorating terms of trade, overvalued exchange rates, increasing debt-to-export ratios, distorted macro prices). But basically the story was simple. When the second oil price hike occurred in 1979, oil-importing countries had to cut back spending. When they dragged their feet, as Latin American countries did (Bacha 1988:14), the IMF and World Bank mandated structural adjustment programs (SAPs). When the United States dragged its feet, and borrowed on world money markets to finance its growing deficits, real interest rates increased. Because much of Third World debt was financed at floating interest rates, this further exacerbated their debt crisis and mandated even more draconian "stabilization" programs for the southern hemisphere.

Eventually, this vulnerability was passed on to farmers, both men and women farmers, usually in the form of removal of input (fertilizer) subsidies.

In some African countries, SAPs also mandated higher farm product prices that aimed to encourage greater agricultural production. These higher prices, however, did not help but hurt women-headed households, as little of their production was sold. To the extent that SAPs have been successful in switching resources from non-tradable (food) crops to tradable (export) crops, women farmers suffered. In the squeeze for scarce resources, they lost land, capital, and labor from their own cash crop to men's cash crops, and so lost the cash needed to buy fertilizer to grow the non-tradable crop more intensively.

What should be done? Some components of SAP packages should just be dropped completely, e.g., fertilizer subsidy removal programs (Gladwin 1991, 1992). Other reforms, e.g., increased food prices, which impact negatively on women-headed households but benefit smallholders in general, should not be dropped but should be mitigated by a consumer subsidy or nutritional-supplement program targeted especially at them.

The vulnerability was also transfered to workers via cuts in employment, wages, and child-welfare services. In Latin America and the Caribbean, as men's wages and employment decreased and men were pushed into more marginal jobs in the informal economy, women increased their own labor force participation to try to maintain the level of household income (Safa 1992a). As their economic contribution to the family became more important, they struggled for greater control over the family budget, a greater share in household decisions, greater autonomy, and control over their own fertility (Safa 1992a).

Proponents of SAPs have defended them by claiming that without some form of adjustment, the situation might have been far worse in most Third World countries during the 1980s and 1990s. I agree. It is not enough to describe the impact of "the crisis" on women without understanding the origin of the crisis or the need for some kind of adjustment. The real issue, as Cornia, Jolly, and Stewart (1987) rightly claim, is that alternative adjustment packages--"with a human face"--are possible. Draconian stabilization efforts can be replaced by expansionary adjustment packages employing a more gradual correction of imbalances and targeting interventions at women, children, and the poor.

Ironically, such an expansionary adjustment path has been taken by the United States. It was allowed by the G7 partners (Great Britain, France, Germany, Japan, Italy, and Canada) to gradually devalue its currency in the 1980s. Indeed, in some respects the United States has yet to adjust: to date, the government has still not decided how and when to reduce its budget and trade deficits. In the words of Paul Volcker, past chairman of the Federal Reserve Board,

We say to all kinds of countries in Latin America and Europe, "Fix up your budget deficit and do it by Tuesday." We ask them to do all kinds of things we are not prepared to do ourselves. It sounds hollow for us to lecture on their budgets when we're frozen on this issue (Volcker, McNeil-Lehrer News Hour, June 22, 1992).[10]

If the poorest countries of the world were allowed to adjust as gradually as the U.S., the world's largest debtor nation, what would adjustment "with a human face" look like? As Moser (1989:1802) argues, adjustment policies for developing countries must be based on *their* interests, their prioritized concerns; and these are not often homogeneous but vary with class and ethnicity and gender. They are therefore the focus of intense power struggles which women often lose due to patriarchal relations and gender inequalities. To benefit women, interventions should be targeted directly at the women themselves and might include income-generation programs, job-training programs, credit and fertilizer subsidies, and nutritional-supplementation programs. Nevertheless, women remain responsible for family food provision, health, and education as well as community maintenance, and interventions should relect these responsibilities (Moser 1989:1803-1804). Policy interventions that strengthen the household survival strategies developed by the women themselves may be the best way to mitigate the adverse effects of structural adjustment on them.

Notes

1.   I am grateful to the authors of my edited book, *Structural Adjustment and African Women Farmers*, University of Florida Press, 1991, especially Jean Due, Jean Ensminger, Miriam Goheen, and Uma Lele. I am especially grateful to Helen Safa who introduced me to the Latin American literature and macro-economist Ed Tower who explained the reasoning behind Malawi's SAP. Naturally, I take full responsibility for any views expressed in this chapter.
2.   From 1980 to 1985, there were 47 countries, on average, with IMF stabilization programs. From 1980 to 1986, 21 countries have had SALs or SACs (structural adjustment credits) with the World Bank; $4.5 billion was allocated to these programs over the period, compared to a cumulative net flow of $30.3 billion from the Fund (Cornia, Jolly, and Stewart 1987:49).
3.   "Terms of trade" refer to a measure of the relative level of export prices compared with import prices.
4.   Following Hartmann (1976:138), and much of the women's studies literature, patriarchy is defined as "a set of social relations which have a material base and in which there are hierarchical relations between men, and solidarity among them, which enable them to control women" (Hartmann

1976:138). Patriarchy also is taken to mean "male control over female labor" (Hartmann 1981).

5. Elson's (1991) argument is slightly different. She claims that the sexual division of labor in Africa, expressed in rules about work which is suitable for women but unsuitable for men, is a barrier to an important SAP objective--the reallocation of labor from the production of food crops (non-tradables) to the production of cash crops (tradables). The assumption of most SAPs, that human resources can be treated as if they were costlessly transferable between different crops, ignores these rules. This treatment of labor as ungendered may mean that SAPs fail to achieve their objectives. In contrast, my argument is that SAP objectives are succeeding, and at an incredible cost to women food producers.

6. Yet in some rural areas women also farm. In Jamaica, women farmers produce 60 percent to 75 percent of locally produced food; but this represents only 14 percent of total food consumed. (Deere et al. 1990:56).

7. In the English-speaking Caribbean, women's labor-force participation rates traditionally have been higher than in the Spanish-speaking Caribbean, e.g., 62 percent in Jamaica in 1985 for women over 14 years of age (Deere et al. 1990:62).

8. Cornia, Jolly, and Stewart (1987:94) also mention that women's labor force participation rates increased in the Philippines from 43.7 percent to 48.3 percent between 1982 and 1984.

9. In Nigeria, where all food imports were eliminated under structural adjustment, the number of meals decreased to one per day, and people would refer to the time of their one meal by formula:010 meant they would eat at lunch, 001 dinner, 100 breakfast (Elabor-Idemudia 1991).

10. For a video or transcript of Volcker's comments of June 22, write McNeil-Lehrer News Hour, 1320 Braddock Place, Alexandria, VA 22314.

References

Alt-WID (Alternative Women in Development)
    1992   Reaganomics and Women: Structural Adjustment U.S. Style - 1980-1992. Washington: Alt-WID.

Arizpe, Lourdes, Fanny Salinas, and Margarita Velasquez
    1987   Effects of the Economic Crisis on the Living Conditions of Peasant Women in Mexico. In: *The Invisible Adjustment: Poor Women and the Economic Crisis*, edited by Lola Rocha, Eduardo Bustelo, Ernesto Lopez, and Luis Zuniga. Santiago: UNICEF.

Bacha, Edmar L.
  1988 Latin America's Economic Stagnation: Domestic and External Factors. Paper prepared for the Conference on Comparative Development Experiences in Asia and Latin America. East West Center/University of Hawai, Honolulu, April 20-22.

Boserup, Ester
  1970 *Woman's Role in Economic Development*. New York: St. Martin's Press.

Chipande, G. H. R., M. M. Mowezalamba, L. S. Mwaisanoc, and M. W. Mhango
  1986 Income Generating Activities for Rural Women in Malawi: A Final Report." Centre for Social Research, Zomba: University of Malawi.

Commonwealth Secretariat
  1989 *Engendering Adjustment for the 1990s*. London: Commonwealth Secretariat.

Cornia, Giovanni A., Richard Jolly, and Frances Stewart
  1987 *Adjustment with a Human Face*. Oxford: Clarendon Press.

Davies, Omar, and Patricia Anderson
  1987 The Impact of the Recession and Adjustment Policies on Poor Urban Women in Jamaica. Paper prepared for UNICEF. Kingston: University of the West Indies.

Deere, Carmen Diana, Peggy Antrobus, Lynn Bolles, Edwin Melendez, Peter Phillips, Marcia Rivera, and Helen Safa
  1990 *In the Shadows of the Sun: Caribbean Development Alternatives and U.S. Policy*. Boulder: Westview Press.

Dixon, Ruth
  1982 Women in Agriculture: Counting the Labor Force in Developing Countries. *Population and Development Review* 8:558-559.

Due, Jean M.
  1991 Policies to Overcome the Negative Effects of Structural Adjustment Programs on African Female-Headed Households. *Structural Adjustment and African Women Farmers*, edited by C. Gladwin. Pp. 103-127. Gainesville: University of Florida Press.

Due, Jean M., and Christina Gladwin
1991   Impacts of Structural Adjustment Programs on African Women
        Farmers and Female-Headed Households. *American Journal of
        Agricultural Economics* 73(5):1431-1439.

Due, Jean M., and Marcia White
1986   Contrasts Between Joint and Female-Headed Farm Households in
        Zambia. *Eastern Africa Economic Review* 2:94-98.

Due, Jean M., and Flavianus Magayane
1990   Changes in Agricultural Policy Needed for Female-Headed Farm
        Families in Tropical Africa. *Agricultural Economics* 4:239-253.

Due, Jean M., Enock Sikaponde, and Flavianus Magayane
1991   Does the T & V Extension System Assist Female-Headed
        Families? Some Recent Evidence from Zambia. *Eastern African
        Economic Review* 7:36-52.

Economic Commission for Africa (ECA)
1989   African Alternative Framework to Structural Adjustment Programs
        for   Socio-Economic   Recovery   and   Transformation,
        E/ECA/CM.15/6/Rev.3. New York: United Nations.

The Economist
1991   Sisters in the Wood: A Survey of the IMF and the World Bank.
        The Economist 321(7728):1-48.

Elabor-Idemuda, Patience
1991   The Impact of Structural Adjustment Programs on Women and
        Their Households in Bendel and Ogun States, Nigeria. *Structural
        Adjustment and African Women Farmers*, edited by C. Gladwin.
        Pp. 128-150. Gainesville: University of Florida Press.

Elson, Diane
1989   The Impact of Structural Adjustment on Women: Concepts and
        Issues. *The IMF, the World Bank, and the African Debt*, Vol. 2,
        edited by Bade Onimode. Pp. 56-74. London: Zed Books.

Elson, Diane (editor)
1991   *Male Bias in the Development Process*. London: Zed Books.

Ensminger, Jean
  1991   Structural Transformation and Its Consequences for Orma Women
          Pastoralists. *Structural Adjustment and African Women Farmers*,
          edited by C. Gladwin. Pp. 281-300. Gainesville: University of
          Florida Press.

Fernandez-Kelly, Maria Patricia
  1983   *For We Are Sold: I and My People*. Albany: SUNY Press.

Fiala, Robert, and Susan Tiano
  1991   The World Views of Export Processing Workers in Northern
          Mexico: A Study of Women, Consciousness, and the New
          International Division of Labor. *Studies in Comparative
          International Development* 26(3):3-27.

Gladwin, Christina
  1992   Gendered Impacts of Fertilizer Subsidy Removal Programs in
          Malawi and Cameroon. *Agricultural Economics*, forthcoming.

Gladwin, Christina H.
  1991   Fertilizer Subsidy Removal Programs and Their Potential Impacts
          on Women Farmers in Malawi and Cameroon. *Structural
          Adjustment and African Women Farmers*, edited by C. Gladwin.
          Pp. 191-216. Gainesville: University of Florida Press.

Gladwin, Christina, and Della McMillan
  1989   Is a Turnaround in Africa Possible without Helping African
          Women to Farm? *Economic Development and Cultural Change*
          37(2):345-69.

Goheen, Miriam
  1991   The Ideology and Political Economy of Gender: Women and
          Land in Nso, Cameroon. *Structural Adjustment and African Women
          Farmers*, edited by C. Gladwin. Pp. 239-256. Gainesville:
          University of Florida Press.

Gonzalez de la Rocha, Mercedes
  1988   "Economic Crisis, Domestic Reorganization and Women's Work
          in Guadalajara, Mexico." *Bulletin of Latin American Research*
          7(2):207-223.

Guyer, Jane, with Olukemi Idowu
1991 Women's Agricultural Work in a Multimodal Rural Economy: Ibarapa District, Oyo State, Nigeria. *Structural Adjustment and African Women Farmers*, edited by C. Gladwin. Pp. 257-280. Gainesville: University of Florida Press.

Harrigon, Jane
1987 Price Policy in Malawi. Report of Ministry of Agriculture, Lilongwe, Malawi.

Hartmann, Heidi
1976 Capitalism, Patriarchy, and Job Segregation by Sex. *Signs* 1(3):137-169.

Hartmann, Heidi
1981 The Family as the Locus of Gender, Class and Political Struggle: the Example of Housework. *Signs* 6(3):366-394.

Hudgens, Robert
1988 A Diagnostic Survey of Female-Headed Households in the Central Province of Zambia." *Gender Issues in Farming Systems Research and Extension*, edited by S. Poats, M. Schmink, and A. Spring. Pp. 373-388. Boulder: Westview Press.

Hyden, Goran
1983 *No Shortcuts to Progress*. Berkeley: University of California Press.

Hyden, Goran, and Pauline Peters
1991 Debate on the Economy of Affection: Is It a Useful Tool for Gender Analysis? *Structural Adjustment and African Women Farmers*, edited by C. Gladwin. Pp. 301-336. Gainesville: University of Florida Press.

Joekes, Susan
1990 Women and Structural Adjustment: Operational Implications for the JCGP Member Agencies. Brighton, UK: Institute of Development Studies.

Kennedy, Eileen
1992 Effects of Household Structure on Women's and Children's Nutritional Status. Paper presented at the 14th Annual Conference on Economic Issues, Middlebury College, Middlebury, VT, April 3-4, 1992.

Lele, Uma
   1989   Structural Adjustment, Agricultural Development, and the Poor:
          Some Lessons from the Malawian Experience. Washington:
          World Bank, 1989.

   1991   Women, Structural Adjustment and Transformation: Some
          Lessons and Questions from the African Experience. *Structural
          Adjustment and African Women Farmers*, edited by C. Gladwin.
          Pp. 46-80. Gainesville: University of Florida Press.

Lucker, G. William and Adolfo Alvarez
   1984   Exploitation or Exaggeration: A Worker's-Eye View of
          Maquiladora Work." *Southwest Journal of Business and
          Economics* 1(4):11-18.

Lukwago, George
   1992   Structural Adjustment in Malawi: The Fertilizer Subsidy Removal
          Program. M.S. Thesis, University of Florida, Gainesville, Florida.

Meena, Ruth
   1991   The Impact of Structural Adjustment Programs on Rural Women
          in Tanzania. *Structural Adjustment and African Women Farmers*,
          edited by C. Gladwin. Pp. 169-190. Gainesville: University of
          Florida Press.

Mehra, Rekha
   1991   Can Structural Adjustment Work for Women Farmers? *American
          Journal of Agricultural Economics* 73(5):1440-1447.

Mollel, Naftali, M.
   1986   An Evaluation of the Training and Visit (T&V) System of
          Agricultural Extension in Muheza District, Tanga Region,
          Tanzania. M.S. Thesis, University of Illinois.

Moser, Caroline O.N.
   1989   Gender Planning in the Third World: Meeting Practical and
          Strategic Gender Needs. *World Development* 17(11):1799-1825.

O'Brien, Stephen
   1991   Structural Adjustment and Structural Transformation in sub-
          Saharan Africa. *Structural Adjustment and African Women
          Farmers*, edited by C. Gladwin. Pp. 25-45. Gainesville: University
          of Florida Press.

Ong, Aihwa
  1987 *Spirits of Resistance and Capitalist Discipline: Factory Women in Malaysia*. Albany: SUNY Press.

Peters, Pauline, and M.G. Herrera
  1989 Cash Cropping, Food Security, and Nutrition: The Effects of Agricultural Commercialization Among Smallholders in Malawi." Harvard Institute of International Development.

Philadelphia Inquirer
  1991 America: What Went Wrong? *Philadelphia Inquirer*, Tuesday, Oct. 22.

Phiri, C.
  1986 Women and Their Economic Activities: A Comparative Analysis of Male-Headed and Female-Headed Households in Thekerani Rural Growth Centre. Department of Rural Development, Bunda College, Zomba, Malawi.

Raczynski, D., and C. Serrano
  1985 Vivir la Pobreza: Testimonio de Mujeres. Santiago: Corporacion Investigacciones Economicas Latino America (PISPAL-CIEPLAN).

Safa, Helen
  1992a Gender Inequality and Women's Wage Labor: A Theoretical and Empirical Analysis. Paper presented at United Nations/World Institute of Development Economics Research Conference on Trajectories of Patriarchy and Development, Helsinki, July, 1992.

  1992b The Social and Economic Consequences of Export Led Industrialization in the Caribbean Basin. Paper presented at the UCLA Conference on the Garment Industry in the Pacific Rim, Los Angeles, May, 1992.

Safa, Helen, and Peggy Antrobus
  1992 Women and the Economic Crisis in the Caribbean. In: *Economic Crisis, Persistent Poverty and Gender Inequality*, edited by Lourdes Beneria and Shelley Feldman. Chapter 3. Boulder: Westview Press.

Sikaponde, Enock
   1988   An Evaluation of the Training and Visit (T&V) System of
          Agricultural Extension in Eastern Province, Zambia. M.S. Thesis,
          University of Illinois.

Staudt, Kathleen
   1988   Women Farmers and Inequities in Agricultural Services. *Rural
          Africana* 29(1975):81-93.

Stoddard, Ellwyn
   1987   *Maquila: Assembly Plants in Northern Mexico*. El Paso: Western
          Press.

Tiano, Susan
   1986   Women and Industrial Development in Latin America. *Latin
          American Research Review* 21(3):157-170.

   1992   Satisfaction, Commitment, and Pride: Job-Related Orientations
          of Women Maquila Workers. Paper presented at the 14th Annual
          Conference on Economic Issues, Middlebury College, Middlebury,
          VT, April 3-4, 1992.

Timmer, C. Peter, Walter Falcon, and Scott Pearson
   1983   *Food Policy Analysis*. Washington: World Bank.

Tokman, V.E.
   1986   Ajuste y Empleo: Los Desafios del Presente.   Oficina
          Internacional del Trabajo. Santiago: PREALC.

Vickers, Jeanne
   1991   *Women and the World Economic Crisis*. London: Zed Books.

World Bank
   1990   *Structural Adjustment and Poverty: A Conceptual, Empirical, and
          Policy Framework*. Washington: World Bank.

Part II

Trend Report

4

Women and Human Rights

Margaret E. Galey

Human rights achieved an international legal status in the United Nations Charter (Henkin 1978:21-101; Sohn and Buergenthal 1973:505-513). In conferring this status, the Charter created a prospective link between women's rights and human rights by declaring, in four articles, that a major purpose of the United Nations is "the promotion and protection of human rights and fundamental freedoms for all without distinction as to race, sex, nationality or religion" (McDougal, Lasswell, and Chen 1975:497).

The link between women's rights and human rights was subsequently strengthened by the 1948 Universal Declaration on Human Rights and the 1966 International Covenants defining men's and women's rights. Nonetheless, the adoption of the Convention on the Elimination of All Forms of Discrimination Against Women (hereafter the Women's Convention), in concert with the efforts of private international organizations, legal scholars, and feminists, have shaped the perception that women's rights are human rights.[1]

This report traces this trend by considering the past and current status of the Women's Convention, the first comprehensive international treaty on women's rights. First, the background and substance of the Women's Convention are described. Then, its impact is assessed in three settings, using different notions of impact: impact as participation (United States); impact as international implementation (the Committee on the Elimination of Discrimination Against Women); and impact as domestic implementation (Egypt). In the concluding section, suggestions for future research are offered.

Background

The Women's Convention was prepared by the United Nations Commission on the Status of Women (CSW). Established in June 1946 by the United Nations Economic and Social Council (ECOSOC), CSW has recommended numerous resolutions on women's rights for incorporation into private and public law. The Commission has also prepared several conventions, including the Political Status of Women, the Nationality of Married Women, and the Consent to Marriage and Registration of Marriage, and it developed the Declaration on the Elimination of Discrimination Against Women (Galey 1979; Guggenheim 1977). The International Labour Organization (ILO) and the United Nations Education, Scientific and Cultural Organization (UNESCO) have also adopted conventions on specific areas of women's rights (Colliver 1989:25-49; Hevenor 1983, Lubin and Winslow 1991; Reanda 1982; Tinker 1981).

Despite these measures, CSW recognized that gender discrimination persisted and it thus decided that an international legally-binding treaty was necessary to end it. In 1974, Commission members began to prepare the Women's Convention and, in 1976, they recommended it for approval to ECOSOC and the United Nations General Assembly (UNGA). UNGA's Third Committee on Social and Humanitarian Affairs discussed the instrument from 1977 to 1979, and the UNGA plenary unanimously approved the Women's Convention on December 18, 1979. The Convention entered into force on September 3, 1981 upon ratification by 20 states, which thereby became, in international legal terms, states parties to the instrument. A decade later, in October 1991, 110 governments, almost two-thirds of the United Nations membership, were states parties. At this writing, 117 governments have ratified or acceded to the Convention.[2]

Substance of the Women's Convention

The Women's Convention is structurally similar to other international human rights instruments and consists of a preamble and thirty articles.[3] The Preamble states the purpose of and rationale for the Women's Convention and affirms men's and women's equal rights and the dignity and worth of the person. In the words of the Preamble (paragraph 7), "extensive discrimination against women continues to exist," despite the many provisions condemning the practice in United Nations instruments and measures. According to the Preamble, such discrimination is an obstacle to "the full and complete development of the potentialities of women in the service of their countries," and the "full and complete development of a country, the welfare of the world and cause of peace" (paragraph 12).

Provisions

Article 1 of the Women's Convention defines, for the first time in any international legal instrument, sex discrimination. In the words of Article 1, the practice is constituted by:

> any distinction, exclusion or restriction made on the basis of sex that has the effect or purpose of impairing or nullifying the recognition, enjoyment or exercise by women, irrespective of their marital status, on a basis of equality of men and women, of human rights and fundamental freedoms in the political, economic, social, cultural, civil or any other field.

By ratifying the Women's Convention, states agree (in Article 2) to condemn such prejudice and to pursue, by "all appropriate measures" and without delay, a policy to eliminate discrimination against women. States also agree (Article 2) to incorporate the principle of men's and women's equality into their national constitutions, to adopt legislation that prohibits discrimination against women, to refrain from engaging in any discriminatory act or practice, and to modify or abolish laws, regulations, customs, and practices that discriminate against women. These measures are designed to promote "the full development and advancement of women" (Article 3), to modify culturally-patterned behaviors such that maternity is understood as a social function (Article 5), and to suppress all forms of traffic in women and exploitation of women by prostitution (Article 6).

The emphasis in the Women's Convention on "all appropriate measures" is comprehensive yet flexible, permitting states to take those measures that are within their ability (British Commonwealth 1975:4, 16; Cook 1990a:670-673). For example, Article 34 specifies that no provision of the Women's Convention "shall affect any provisions that are more conducive to achieving equality," such as those included in state legislation or in any other international convention, treaty, or agreement.

Article 4, nonetheless, calls for temporary measures, such as affirmative action policies, to speed *de facto* equality between men and women; these measures, however, are not intended to discriminate against men and are to be discontinued once women have achieved equal opportunity and equal treatment. Additionally, Article 24 enjoins states parties to adopt all necessary measures at the national level to achieve "the full realization of the rights recognized in the Convention."

Political Rights of Women. The provisions of the 1952 Convention on the Political Rights of Women, insuring women the right to vote in all elections, to stand for election, and to hold public office, are reaffirmed in Article 7, which also confirms women's right to be involved in the formulation and implementation of government policy and to participate in associations concerned with public and political life. Women's right to represent their countries at the international level is affirmed in Article 8, while Article 9, incorporating provisions of the 1957 Convention on the Nationality of Married Women, declares that marriage will not alter a woman's nationality.

Social and Economic Rights. The Women's Convention also acknowledges women's right to education, including training in sports and physical education (Article 10), and their right to employment (Article 11).[4] Access to health care services is addressed in Article 12, which directs that family planning and appropriate services in connection with pregnancy, birth, and the post-natal period be provided to women. Article 13, added by the UNGA's Third Committee on Social and Humanitarian Affairs, is intended to ensure women equal rights in other areas of economic and social life that may have been omitted elsewhere in the Women's Convention (Cook 1990a; Tinker 1981). Among the rights identified are family benefits, bank loans and financial credit, and participation in all aspects of cultural life.

Article 14 is the first provision in an international instrument to address the problems faced by rural women, the majority of whom perform most agricultural work in developing countries. It specifies that states are to ensure women's right to participate in development planning and to have access to health care facilities, social security programs, education, and agricultural credit and loans (UN 1988:22).

Civil Rights. According to the Women's Convention, any contract and private instrument that restricts women's legal capacity is null and void (Article 15). Women's rights in several areas in which they face particular discrimination are also confirmed by validating their right to equality with men before the law, to equal opportunity to conclude contracts, to administer property, and to freedom of movement and choice in residence and domicile (UN 1988:22; Cook 1990a:699-702).[5]

Article 16 draws on the 1962 Convention on the Consent to Marriage and charges states to end discrimination in "all matters of marriage and family relations." According to Article 16, men and women have equal rights to marry and to divorce, as well as equal rights and responsibilities as parents, guardians, and trustees. To these ends, the Article declares that women have the right to choose a spouse and enter marriage with free and full consent, to decide on the number and spacing of children, to choose a family name, a profession, and an occupation, and to own, acquire, manage, and administer property. Article 16 also outlaws child marriages and requires states to set and enforce a minimum age for marriage and to register marriages (Cook 1990a:702-706; UN 1988:23).

Final Clauses. Every international treaty defines a procedure by which ratifying governments assume legal responsibility for fulfilling obligations they undertake. Such provisions describe how ratification is to be achieved, under what circumstances, when the treaty will enter into force, the permissibility of reservations, and where states' instruments of ratification are to be deposited (usually with the Office of the United Nations Secretary General).

According to the Women's Convention, thirty days after the twentieth state deposits the instruments of ratification or accession with the United Nations Secretary General, the provisions of the document enter into force (Articles 25 and 27). The Women's Convention may be revised upon the request of any state party (Article 26). Reservations may be taken if they are compatible with the purpose of the Women's Convention (Article 28), although a standard for determining compatibility is not provided. Finally, disputes over the interpretation of the Women's Convention must be settled by negotiation, arbitration, or referral to the World Court (Article 29).

Enforcement

The United Nations cannot compel states to observe a treaty. Rather, the world organization tries to persuade members to fulfill their obligations through several means: international fact-finding, considering petitions from states or individuals, reviewing reports submitted by states parties, and/or establishing an international committee to supervise reports from states parties (Schwelb 1977; Sohn 1985; Vasak 1981; Wolf 1985).

The Women's Convention provides no administrative avenue for individuals to petition or file complaints or for specially-appointed experts to fact-find. Rather, the Committee on the Elimination of Discrimination Against Women (CEDAW) was established in 1981 to monitor the progress of states parties in achieving the goals of the Women's Convention (Colliver 1989; Cook 1990a; Galey 1984). Byrnes (1989) refers to this Committee (CEDAW) as "the other human rights body" to distinguish it from the more well-known Human Rights Committee established under the International Covenant on Civil and Political Rights.

CEDAW is made up of 23 members whose governments have ratified the Women's Convention.[6] The Committee is not a judicial body. Rather, it is a committee made up of experts who offer suggestions to help reporting states implement the Women's Convention (Byrnes 1989; British Commonwealth 1975:45).

The Committee meets once every year for two weeks to review reports submitted by states parties and to make recommendations to improve their performance.[7] During the two-week session, Committee members question states regarding their compliance with reporting guidelines and request that they provide any missing information in subsequent reports. At the end of each session, CEDAW reports its activities to the United Nations Secretary General for transmittal to the UNGA.

Legal Status of the Women's Convention

The Women's Convention entered into force less than two years after approval by the United Nations General Assembly, a pattern consistent with related conventions. For example, the earlier Convention on the Political Rights of Women, Convention on the Nationality of Married Women, and Convention on Minimum Age for Marriage, Consent to Marriage, and Registration of Marriage entered into force within two years of adoption by the UNGA (UN 1987a:237, 313, 330; see also UN 1988:269-272, 358-360, 361-366). The International Covenant on Civil and Political Rights, in contrast, required about ten years to enter into force (UN 1987a:25), while the Convention on the Elimination of Racial Discrimination required four years (UN 1987a:95), the Genocide Convention three years (UN 1987a:175), and the Torture Convention three and a half years to enter into force (UN 1987a:228). Conversely, the United Nations Charter required only four months to enter into force and the 1926 Slavery Convention only six months (Goodrich, Hambro, and Simons 1969:8-9; UN 1987a:200).

The prompt entry into force and ratification of the Women's Convention suggests an international commitment to the principles it embodies. Nevertheless, a large number of states have not ratified the instrument. Among those which have not are the United States, South Africa, Burundi, Cambodia, the Cameroon, Gambia, India, Jordan, Lesotho, and Switzerland. More states parties also have entered reservations to the Women's Convention than to any other international treaty. According to CEDAW's 1991 Report, 41 states parties entered reservations to the Convention (six have since withdrawn them) (Cook 1990a; UN 1990:84-86), and several entered reservations to more than one article. In contrast, only six of the 123 countries which ratified the Convention on the Elimination of All Forms of *Race* Discrimination, entered reservations on their obligations to eliminate such prejudice (UN 1987a:99-118).

The numerous reservations to the Women's Convention suggest that states do not agree on the meaning of discrimination against women or on how to eliminate it (Cook 1990a). Several governments that have entered reservations, for example, maintain that the culturally-defined social roles of women in their respective societies are not discriminatory. Sixteen ratifying states will not accept the proviso for the elimination of discriminatory family laws contained in Article 16. Their reservations could be interpreted as a rejection of the Women's Convention (Cook 1990a:702-707) because judicial and administrative means are available to resolve discrepancies between the Women's Convention's objectives and those of reporting states. Governments, however, have not yet compelled their use (Cook 1990a:707-712).

Assessing the Impact of the Women's Convention

One way to measure the impact of a convention is to analyze the extent to which it has been implemented. In this case, legal scholars define the term "implementation" as the international actions and the national legislative, executive, and judicial measures that are adopted to secure the provisions of a convention. The assumption that underlies this definition is that such measures promote change in domestic law and practice. The impact of a convention, however, is broader than legal implementation.

For example, Alger (1963, 1965) reports that participation in meetings of international organizations can be a learning experience with the potential to change awareness and understanding of a particular institution, procedure, or issue. Others (Hadwen and Kaufman 1960; Jacobson 1984; Kaufman 1989: Soroos 1986) indicate that involvement in international negotiating processes can foster acceptance of international decisions, including treaties and their provisions. These findings suggest that the meaning of impact should be broadened to include participation in international organizations. More specifically, participation in the processes of treaty making (negotiation, signature, ratification, and implementation) should be explored to determine how involvement in them affects thinking and action.

A range of individuals participate in the making of treaties, including government delegates, United Nations Secretariat staff, and representatives of accredited non-governmental organizations (NGOs). At any time during the treaty-making process, these participants may alter their views about the United Nations and the issues with which it deals and/or may modify their position on women's rights. As a result of their changed beliefs, they may also press for ratification of a treaty by joining an association, undertaking a letter-writing campaign, or publicizing the instrument. All of these changes are measures of the impact of an international convention.

The impact of a treaty, however, may extend beyond official participants. Citizens of nations whose governments have ratified a convention may be affected by legislation adopted to secure the instrument's provisions. Some may benefit from these measures, while others may not. Who benefits from ratification of a convention and why deserves study. Pending such an investigation, it is useful to recognize that the impact of domestic laws on individuals is likely to be a function of several factors, including the type of laws enacted, the extent to which they are enforced, the nature of the society's cultural practices, and the class and gender of the individual.

In the sections that follow, the impact of the Women's Convention is assessed in three settings by using different notions of impact: impact as participation (United States), impact as international implementation (CEDAW), and impact as domestic implementation (Egypt). In the absence of specific data on the topic, a range of materials, including official reports, personal observations, and historical and sociological sources, is drawn upon.

Impact as Participation

The debate, negotiation, and adoption of the Women's Convention brought together a number of participants, including members of the United Nations Commission on the Status of Women (CSW), government delegates in the Economic and Social Council (ECOSOC) and the General Assembly, United Nations Secretariat support staff, and official observers affiliated with accredited NGOs. Participation became a learning experience for many of these individuals. Members of CSW, for example, gained an understanding of the formal and informal workings of the United Nations as well as the provisions of the Women's Convention. Those in ECOSOC and UNGA became aware of the existence and scope of discrimination against women.

Civil and foreign service officers and politically-appointed officials (such as ministers and secretaries of state) also participated in negotiations, albeit indirectly. Based in ministries located in national capitals, they communicated regularly with their delegates to the United Nations, instructing them about government positions on provisions being negotiated and hearing the outcomes of daily negotiating sessions. As a result of these reciprocal communications, ministry officials' appreciation of the problems confronting women deepened. To illustrate this process, a chronicle of the Women's Convention in the United States is offered.

The Women's Convention and The United States. In 1974, CSW met in New York to begin drafting the Women's Convention. Prior to the meeting, United States member, Pat Hutar consulted with high-level Department of State officials and obtained approval to negotiate the treaty for the United States. This consultation allowed Ms. Hutar to make these officials aware of the importance of the Women's Convention to the United States.

Her successor, Koryn Horbal, had a similar opportunity to influence opinion. In 1979, the Swedish representative on the UNGA's Third Committee on Social and Humanitarian Affairs proposed the establishment of the Committee on the Elimination of Discrimination Against Women (CEDAW). Ms. Horbal sat in during the Committee's discussion. She subsequently consulted legal advisors at the United States Mission about the Swedish proposal and they, in turn, conferred with officials at the Department of State. The outcome of these multiple consultations was a heightened awareness of the Women's Convention and the CEDAW proposal among United States Mission and State Department staff.

Once a convention has been negotiated, it is adopted by the General Assembly and opened for signature and ratification by governments. This process also provides an opportunity for changes in opinions to occur. After the Women's Convention was adopted by the UNGA, for example, a number of delegations agreed to hold a ceremony at the 1980 United Nations Conference in Copenhagen, at which heads of delegations would sign the Convention. Between the time of adoption in 1979 and the Conference, governments had to decide whether or not to sign the Women's Convention at the ceremony. In deliberations about this decision, government officials gained new understanding of the meaning and scope of the Women's Convention.

In the United States, for example, signature of a treaty is considered an intent to ratify. After the Women's Convention was adopted by the UNGA, President Carter authorized the Department of State to review it and to advise him whether or not to sign. The then Secretary of State, Cyrus Vance, requested the Office of the Legal Advisor to coordinate the effort, and the Women's Convention was circulated among government departments with jurisdiction over its provisions for opinions. (The Departments of Education, Health and Human Services, Justice, and Labor and the Office of Equal Employment Opportunity responded.) On the basis of their comments and the State Department's internal review, President Carter instructed Sarah Weddington, head of the United States delegation to the 1980 Conference, to sign the treaty for the country and, shortly thereafter, he transmitted the Women's Convention to the United States Senate for advice and consent. The chamber has not yet acted on it, however.

The Senate's delay has three roots (Hevenor and Whitman 1990; Tinker 1981). First, the Senate has been reluctant to ratify human rights treaties. It took members forty years to ratify the Genocide Convention and fifteen years to ratify the International Covenant on Civil and Political Rights. Further, three human rights conventions have remained pending before the chamber since 1977.[9] In large part, the Senate's reluctance stems from its members' hesitation to commit the United States to an international treaty whose provisions fall within the jurisdiction of the fifty states of the federal union. Second, the Senate's hesitation reflects the belief that ratification and subsequent domestic implementation could erode national sovereignty or detract from the supreme authority of the United States government.

Third, some legislators view the Women's Convention as an international Equal Rights Amendment (ERA). Indeed, United States ratification of the Women's Convention may ultimately serve some of the purposes of an ERA. There are, however, two key differences between the ERA and the Women's Convention. One, the ERA was intended as a constitutional amendment, requiring ratification by three-fourths of the states for it to achieve legal force. In contrast, the Women's Convention is an international treaty, requiring ratification by 20 governments of the world community to gain the force of law. Two, the required number of state legislatures failed to approve ERA, but the Women's Convention was adopted by the UNGA and entered into force.

White House support for ratification of the Convention has not been forthcoming, although unofficial support has grown dramatically in the last decade. In 1984, the American Bar Association recommended Senate ratification of the Women's Convention with reservations (ABA 1984). A year later, consensus approval of the Forward Looking Strategies (the principal document of the 1985 United Nations women's conference) spurred B'nai B'rith and other organizations to form the National Committee on UN/CEDAW. A coalition of thirty national groups, it publicizes the Forward Looking Strategies and presses for ratification of the Women's Convention (National Committee on UN/CEDAW 1990).[10]

The activities of the National Committee prior to the 1990 Congressional and Senate elections helped encourage Senator Pell (Democrat from Rhode Island and Chair of the Senate Foreign Relations Committee) to convene hearings on the Women's Convention. Senator Pell subsequently informed Secretary of State Baker that he considered Convention ratification long overdue (National Committee on UN/CEDAW 1990).

Several Republican Senators also contacted President Bush to urge prompt action on the Women's Convention. In the House, Representative Yatron (Democrat from Pennsylvania) introduced House Resolution 116 urging the President to complete the review of the Women's Convention and to recommend Senate advice and consent. Co-sponsored by the Congressional Caucus for Women's Issues, the House overwhelmingly approved the resolution on October 22, 1991.

President Bush, in the interim, forwarded the International Covenant on Civil and Political Rights to the Senate for advice and consent, thus following the informal rule of transmitting conventions in the order in which the United States signed them. The Covenant, adopted by the UNGA in 1966, was signed by the United States in 1977, three years before the Women's Convention.[11]

Because the Covenant affirms the individual rights of both men and women, it may advance women's human rights. Having ratified the instrument, the United States is obliged to report to the Human Rights Committee, the supervisory body established by the Covenant. The nation's first report, showing the country's progress in realizing the rights recognized in the Covenant, is due within the year, and others are required at subsequent intervals thereafter (UN 1987b:32). Human rights groups and women's groups that have monitored human rights abroad may now expand their attention to the United States (AI 1991; ILRH 1991).

Ratification by the United States of the conventions dealing with race and gender discrimination would signal the country's commitment to end such prejudice, thereby strengthening its credibility as a great power with a strong human rights tradition. Pending such action, United States representatives to international meetings maintain that the nation's laws provide for such rights or establish standards higher than those included in international conventions.

Although the United States Constitution and the Bill of Rights excluded women, women worked vigorously during the 19th and 20th centuries to obtain civil, political, and economic equality with men (Chafe 1991; Deckard 1975; Hoff 1991:7-36). Progressive legislation in the early 1900s enabled women to enjoy improved working conditions and, following World War I, they achieved the right to vote when three-quarters of the states approved the 19th amendment to the United States Constitution in 1919.

In the years since, substantial legislation has been enacted to protect women's rights, including laws that address employment, education, health and health insurance, child care and support, birth control and abortion, and pensions and social security (US Congress 1989). In addition, the Congressional Caucus on Women's Issues, established in 1977 as a bipartisan organization to advance women's position, made the omnibus legislative package, the Economic Equity Act of 1981, the heart of its legislative effort during the 1980s (Rix 1990:325-346).

Executive measures have been initiated as well. For example, in 1963 President Kennedy established the first National Commission on the Status of Women to develop a unified agenda for women's rights (Harrison 1989:109-165). Increasing numbers of women have been appointed to positions in the Federal and State court systems. President Reagan also nominated, and the Senate confirmed, the first woman, Jean J. Kirkpatrick, to be United States Ambassador to the United Nations and the first woman, Sandra Day O'Connor, to be a Supreme Court Justice (Schmittroth 1991:449).[12]

Several women have served as governors of states and a rising number have been elected to state legislatures. Nevertheless, less than five percent of the 435-member United States House of Representatives and the 100-member Senate are women. Moreover, no woman has been elected President or Vice-President of the United States, although in 1984 the Democratic Party nominated Geraldine Ferraro as the first woman candidate for Vice-President.

In contrast to the small proportion of women in public life, the percentage of women in wage employment has increased, rising from 42.4 percent in 1980 to 45.4 percent in 1990. Many of these women workers have children under age 18, and their proportion is growing (56.4% in 1980 to 66.3% in 1990). While more women occupy managerial positions than previously (32% in 1983 to 40% in 1990), in 1980 only two women were chief executive officers (CEOs) of the Fortune 500 companies (Katherine Graham, chief executive of the Washington Post, and Marion O. Sandler, co-chief executive of Golden West Financial Corporation). Ten years later, only one woman had joined their ranks (Linda Wachner of the Warnaco Group) (Marsh 1991:B3).

The inequality which underlies figures such as these was highlighted during the confirmation hearing of Judge Clarence Thomas to be an associate justice of the Supreme Court. The hearing drew national and international attention to one kind of gender discrimination, sexual harassment, and it kindled an outpouring of public and press discussion (Abramson and Shirbman 1991; AS 1991; PS 1992; Sandroff 1992).[13]

The Thomas hearing also invigorated the women's movement in the United States and inspired large numbers of women to speak out on issues such as harassment, abortion, family leave, and the dearth of women in public office. Women's militancy converged with anti-incumbency sentiment and reapportioned electoral districts to create an environment favorable to women candidates. As a result, women may make historic gains in the 1992 House and Senate elections (Kurtz 1992:66-69).

To sum up, the United States has not ratified the Women's Convention. Nonetheless, gender discrimination is not necessarily a part of every woman's experience and the country has satisfied several of the standards set forth in the Women's Convention. It is apparent, then, that factors other than signature of a convention contribute to women's advancement. In the case of the United States, these include reformative legislation, a vital women's movement, a strong human rights tradition, and the belief in participatory democracy.

Impact as Implementation

McDougal, Lasswell, and Chen (1975:531) maintain that, prior to the adoption of the Women's Convention, provisions for implementing international measures to secure women's equality with men were more primitive than those adopted to minimize race discrimination.[14] For example, reporting by states parties under the Declaration of the Elimination of All Forms of Discrimination Against Women and other conventions relevant to women were the only international means available to secure women's interests. Once the Women's Convention entered into force, however, CEDAW was established and given responsibility for the implementation of women's rights.

In the sections that follow, the impact of the Women's Convention is assessed by using two measures of implementation: international and domestic. The performance of CEDAW in fulfilling its purpose is taken as an example of international implementation, while the actions of one ratifying state, Egypt, is selected as an illustration of domestic implementation.

Impact as International Implementation. According to CEDAW's guidelines, states must submit a report within one year after ratification, at least every four years thereafter, and subsequently at the request of the Committee. Initial reports must be submitted in two parts. The first part is to include a summary of the social, economic, political, and legal structure of the nation and a discussion of the effects of ratification on the structure of the state. The second part is to contain information about the constitutional, legislative, administrative, and judicial measures adopted to fulfill the goals of the Women's Convention.

Data disaggregated by gender, descriptions of any violations of human rights, and summaries of barriers that inhibit women from participating in society on a basis equal to men must also be included (Byrnes 1989:12-17; UNGA 1983:1-3). In subsequent reports, states are expected to identify significant changes in their countries, to describe any remaining obstacles to the realization of the Women's Convention's goals, and to demonstrate how the government has responded to recommendations made by the Committee (Byrnes 1989:15-16; UNGA 1987, 1988, 1989, 1990, 1991).

CEDAW began reviewing initial reports from states parties in 1984. By 1991, it had considered 69 initial reports and 31 second reports (Byrnes 1989; UNGA 1991:88-94). Several problems arose, however, in the review process. First, a number of states did not submit their first and second reports by the deadline. By 1991, initial reports of 35 countries and second reports of 41 countries were overdue (Byrnes 1989; UNGA 1991:88-94). Second, even when a state had submitted a report in a timely manner, CEDAW's overwhelming workload sometimes prevented it from considering the report promptly, periodically forcing it to postpone discussion for as long as two or three years (Byrnes 1989:27-28; UNGA 1991:88-94).

Third, CEDAW members originally relied exclusively on reports from states parties to evaluate progress. They recently realized, however, that materials produced by specialized United Nations agencies and non-governmental organizations could be useful in augmenting information included in country reports. As a result, they have begun to request reports from these agencies and bodies (Byrnes 1989; UNGA 1987:80), thereby enhancing their ability to evaluate reports.

Despite these problems, the Committee has approved eighteen recommendations for states parties. These have ranged from providing general guidelines for reporting (UNGA 1986:46), to requests for statistical data on women and on violence against women (UNGA 1989), to suggestions that women's unremunerated domestic work be measured and quantified (UNGA 1991:1-3). In this sense, then, the Committee is moving the goal of the Women's Convention forward by helping states parties to improve their data collection and the quality of their reports on measures taken to eliminate discrimination against women.[15]

Impact as Domestic Implementation. Egypt signed the Women's Convention at the 1980 United Nations conference. In ratifying it on September 18, 1981, the Egyptian Peoples Assembly entered reservations to four articles: Article 2 (the advancement of women), Article 9 (nationality), Article 16 (marriage), and Article 29 (dispute settlement) (UN 1988:20-24; UNGA 1987:3). President Sadat subsequently decreed signature and ratification. A National Commission on Women, established in 1977 within the Ministry of Social Affairs, was given responsibility for preparing Egypt's reports for CEDAW (UNGA 1987).[16]

Egypt submitted its first report to CEDAW in 1983 (UN CEDAW 1983:45) and its second in 1987. A third report was due in 1991 (UNGA 1991:95). The initial three-page report (UN CEDAW 1983) contrasts with the second, more substantial 33-page report, which benefitted from CEDAW's Guidelines (UN CEDAW 1987:1-33). The 1987 report contains information on women's advancement in education, employment, health care, and the government. Some understanding of Egypt's recent history is necessary, however, to appreciate the significance of these achievements.

Advances reported in 1987 actually are the result of social, economic, and political trends begun long before Egypt ratified the Women's Convention. For example, since the late 19th century, Egypt has been fostering nationalism and anti-imperialism, educational opportunity, economic development, and feminism (El Saadawi 1984:170-171; Jawayardena 1987:43, 49; Morsy 1991:142). The Egyptian women's movement began in 1919 when veiled gentlewomen and working women joined the nationalist cause against the British. They were led by Hoda Shaarwi, who founded the Egyptian Feminist Union (EFU) to seek legal and social reforms in marriage, education, employment, and politics (Goldschmidt 1988:57, 60; Jawayardena 1987:51-56). The Union achieved some success, establishing equal educational opportunities for boys and girls and a legal age of marriage of 16 for girls and 18 for boys. It failed, however, to alter the 1929 Personal Status Law governing marriage and divorce, inheritance and child custody--a law considered the most backward in Arab countries (Badran 1988:16; Hatem 1986:24; Sadat 1987:352-353).

Following independence and the creation of the democratic republic of Egypt (1952) under President Gamal Abdel Nasser, women gained the right to vote and to hold public office in 1956 (Goldschmidt 1988:110; Sullivan 1986:33). They were elected to Parliament for the first time in 1957 and, in 1959, they helped to adopt Labor Law 91, which prohibited employment discrimination based on sex and protected women against employment in harmful occupations (Sullivan 1986:80). Under Nassar's direction, a Supreme Council on Family Planning was created in 1965 which, with the Ministry of Public Health, managed family planning centers, most of which were located in rural areas. Nassar also enacted a 1962 declaration advocating that women shed the remaining shackles that impeded them from taking a constructive and vital part in shaping Egyptian society (Hopwood 1982:169).

Nasser did not consider, however, reforming the 1929 Personal Status Laws until after the 1967 Arab-Israeli War (Hatem 1986:21; Goldschmidt 1988:119; Hopwood 1982:168-169). The 1929 laws treated marriage as a contract, not a sacrament, and exhibited various double standards. Muslim women were permitted free consent in marriage, but were prohibited from marrying non-Muslim men. Muslim men, in contrast, were permitted to marry Christian or Jewish women. In addition, a Muslim man could marry as many as four wives if he could provide for them, but a Muslim woman could only marry one man at a time (El Kharbouty and Hussein 1977:35-50; Nasir 1990:43; Sadat 1987:352-363).

Marriage also could be terminated at will by a husband, by mutual consent, or by judicial decree through annulment. A woman, however, was often unable to gain her spouse's consent to divorce, and some were unwilling to appear in public before the courts to plead for annulment. Moreover, the father traditionally was given responsibility for children, unless proven unable to support them.

Anwar Sadat succeeded Nasser in 1970 and attempted to balance his support for the advancement of women with his respect for the conservative opposition. The balance, reflected in Egypt's 1971 Constitution, affirmed that:

> The state shall be responsible for making the balance between a woman's duties toward her family and her activity in society, as well as maintaining her equality with men in the fields of education, political, social, economic and cultural life, without detriment to the laws of the Islamic Sharia (Sullivan 1986:820).

According to Egypt's 1987 Report to CEDAW, the country had moved women closer to equality with men. Increases in the enrollment of girls in primary and secondary schools, and particularly in universities and institutions of higher education, were noted. Further, women were reported to be employed in almost all fields, including government, where 80 percent of all women workers were employed in health and educational services (UN CEDAW Report 1987:4).

Egypt's 1987 Report also indicated that the employment of women in the agricultural sector had increased dramatically, from 8.8 percent in 1980 to 40.8 percent in 1983. (The increase may be due to better statistical recording of women's work.) Dramatic decreases, however, were recorded for professionals (from 40.6% in 1980 to 19.7% in 1983) and clerical workers (from 28.2% in 1980 to 14.7% in 1983) (UN CEDAW 1987:4).

With the 1981 enactment of Law No. 137, the Egyptian Report added, women workers have the protection they need to reconcile family and work without detriment to employers' interests. While they have had maternity leave since 1959, Law No. 137 gave them 18 months leave after the birth of a baby and leave without pay three times during their working life (UN CEDAW 1987:5-6).

Although women's wages in public institutions were equal to those of men, Egypt's 1987 Report indicated that equal opportunity for promotion, appointment to responsible jobs, and training for higher posts did not exist (UN CEDAW 1987). Egyptian law also allowed a husband the right to prevent his wife from working if he wished (El Saadawi 1980:189-191). In addition, according to the 1987 Report, illiteracy prevented many women from finding gainful employment, exercising their political rights, educating their children, and practicing family planning (UN CEDAW 1987).

To underscore the importance of family planning in reducing Egypt's population growth, government leaders took several steps to promote acceptance of the practice. Family planning centers were already in place; they provided contraception, although they were prohibited from performing abortions, except in medically necessary situations (El Saadawi 1980:69, 72). To encourage women to practice family planning, the Minister of Health established a new midwifery program, employing traditional midwives (*dayas*), who were better able than men to speak to women about birth control.

Sadat's wife, Jehan, played an important role in many of her husband's decisions. For example, she convinced her husband to endorse family planning, which he did in 1978. At her behest, Sadat also authorized food allotments to families with no more than five members and, in 1980, he proposed a small monthly pension to those over age sixty, thereby enabling them to live out their lives independently of their children (Sadat 1987:321).

Mrs. Sadat became a role model for Egyptian women when she won a seat on the People's Council. President Sadat, as part of the new peace constitution of 1978, had created a new consultative Assembly--a 210-member upper chamber similar to the United States Senate, to which seven women were elected in 1980 (Sullivan 1986:175). Mrs. Sadat subsequently persuaded her husband to allot legislative seats for women in the Parliament. In his decree on June 20, 1979, Sadat earmarked 30 seats in the People's Assembly and 20 percent of all seats in the 26 local People's Councils for women. On July 3, 1979, the newly elected People's Assembly approved the quotas in Law No. 21 (Sadat 1987:364-365).

Despite these gains, women were still considered too emotional to serve as judges, and they were not permitted to hold executive positions as governors, mayors of towns, or heads of villages (El Saadawi 1980:186-187; Sullivan 1986:35). Nonetheless, Egypt's 1987 Report to CEDAW indicated that women were being appointed to judicial posts and to police work for the first time, a measure of their advancement since ratification (UN CEDAW 1987).

During Sadat's Presidency, Mrs. Sadat also encouraged him to change the 1929 Personal Status Laws. To speed approval, President Sadat decreed that the reforms be implemented. On July 3, 1979, the People's Assembly approved them by enacting Law No. 44 (Sullivan 1986:82).

According to Law No. 44, the court may appoint arbiters to attempt to reconcile differences between a divorcing couple. A husband must inform his wife that he has divorced her and that he intends to take a new wife. The first wife gains the right to seek a divorce within a year, to retain custody of sons until age ten and daughters until age twelve, to obtain an extension of this period if beneficial to the children, and to keep the family home. The divorced woman also has the right to collect alimony from her former husband as well as a lump sum, whose amount increases in proportion to the length of their marriage (Hatem 1986:38; Sullivan 1986:36-37).

Law No. 44, however, did not address inheritance law, a man's right to take four wives, and to divorce a wife at will. A woman's testimony in court also remains worth only half that of a man's, and a man has the right to remarry following divorce while a woman must wait three months (Sadat 1987:358).

Despite the unanimous approval of Law No. 44, it remained controversial (Sullivan 1986:67). In December 1982, the constitutionality of the law was challenged on procedural grounds and referred to a Constitutional court, after which Egyptian courts refused to enforce it. In May 1985, Law No. 44 was ruled unconstitutional by the Constitutional Court, which argued that the emergency decree initiating it was issued in the absence of an emergency (Sullivan 1986:37).

Shortly thereafter, the Mubarak government proposed new legislation similar to that decreed by Sadat in 1979. A broad coalition of political leaders from government and the opposition as well as religious leaders arrived at a compromise before Mubarak's proposal reached the People's Assembly. This compromise was enacted as the 1985 Family Law immediately prior to the United Nations women's conference in Nairobi. Hijab (1988:35) argues that the law was passed to make the Government look "modern" at the Conference. Nonetheless, the 1985 Family Law, in contrast to the 1979 law, establishes penalties to enforce its provisions (Hijab 1988:35; Sullivan 1986:35-37).

These debates on family law and women's personal rights helped raise Egyptian women's consciousness. Women lawyers now argue women's rights in civil courts. Women have also formed networks through which they have worked, for example, to end the practice of female circumcision--which still prevails in rural villages (Morsy 1991:29-30). Moreover, they have organized demonstrations, petitions, media campaigns, and new associations.

One of these was the Arab Women's Solidarity Association (AWSA), a feminist organization of professional women which was established in 1982.

The Government of Egypt recognized AWSA in 1984 but, in September 1991, it dissolved the group, froze its bank accounts, and allocated its funds to Women of Islam. One month later, AWSA contested the dissolution before the State Council Court (Middle East Watch News 1991:1-4).[17]

AWSA's problems sparked international interest among human rights and women's groups, which publicized its plight, and they encouraged a worldwide letter-writing campaign. Nevertheless, in May 1992, the Court upheld the disbandment on the grounds that AWSA had violated rules of law, public order, and morality (Middle East Watch News 1992:1).

Events, international in scope, have also contributed to the growing awareness of women's issues in Egypt (Hijab 1988:1). These events include hundreds of seminars, meetings, and conferences concerning the integration of women in development. Among these were the first conference of African and Arab women, convened in 1974 in Cairo to discuss women's issues and to exchange information on projects supporting women. Two hundred women from thirty countries attended (Sadat 1987:323-324).

In sum, Egypt's reports to CEDAW and other materials indicate that women's movement toward equality with men has progressed. As this review illustrates, it is difficult to determine how much of this advancement is due to government efforts to implement the provisions of the Women's Convention and how much ensues from other factors (such as the work of women's organizations and international women's conferences, ratification of other human and labor rights conventions, or a more general drive toward political and economic reform).

Conclusion

The subject of this paper has been the Convention on the Elimination of All Forms of Discrimination Against Women, the first comprehensive international treaty on women's rights. Approved in 1979, the Women's Convention is one of a growing number of treaties that promote the United Nations Charter's goal--the advancement of human rights and fundamental freedoms for all, without distinction to race, gender, nationality, or religion.

The growing recognition that women's rights are human rights was demonstrated by assessing the impact of the Women's Convention by means of two different measures of impact. The first was defined as participation in negotiation, signature, and ratification of the Women's Convention. As illustrated here, participation by United States government officials, delegates, and representatives apparently altered their views of the United Nations as an institution and increased their awareness of the content of the Women's Convention. The second measure of impact was defined as implementation. CEDAW was chosen as an example of international implementation, while Egypt served as an illustration of domestic implementation. Measurement of impact both as participation and as implementation was difficult due to the dearth of data on the issue. Nonetheless, a number of propositions emerged from the discussion that call for empirical study.

Participation

• heightens awareness of the United Nations as an institution and of the role of the nation-state in it;

• increases perception of the links between subsidiary bodies (the Commission on the Status of Women), treaty bodies (the Committee on the Elimination of Discrimination Against Women), and larger political organs (the United Nations Economic and Social Council and General Assembly);

• results in practical knowledge of how to influence other participants in treaty negotiations and expands the willingness to do so;

• augments understanding of women's rights as human rights;

• creates an incentive to find ways to alter discriminatory domestic laws;

• increases understanding of the barriers that impede governments' resolution of treaty disagreements by compromise;

• facilitates communication between participants in United Nations processes;

• encourages non-governmental organizations to press for ratification and implementation of a treaty;

• produces heightened awareness such that those involved in the process of treaty ratification extend their efforts to include activities such as public lectures about a convention.

These emergent propositions require testing. In doing so, two issues must be considered. The first concerns variables. As the Egyptian case has shown, indigenous factors may be as responsible for change as exogenous ones. Moreover, any number of factors can intervene during the participation process, thereby determining whether or not change occurs. Incumbency, for instance, can affect opinions, with those who hold positions longer espousing different views from those who do not (Alger 1963). These selected examples highlight the need to factor in variables carefully in any study.

The second issue concerns methodology. Experience is a product of class, ethnicity, and nation as well as gender. These differentiating social categories must be acknowledged and incorporated into any study. While such incorporation may be difficult, in-depth interviews can produce the necessary nuanced data. Studies based on these considerations are likely to develop a data base capable of offering a more precise assessment of the role of the Women's Convention in achieving the elimination of all forms of discrimination against women.

Notes

1. See, for example, Bayefsky (1990), Bruce (1971), Bunch (1990), Burrows (1989), Cook (1989, 1990a, 1990b), Eisler (1987), Elder (1986), Ireland (1978), McDougal, Lasswell, and Chen (1975), Reanda (1982), Taubenfeld and Taubenfeld (1975), and Tinker (1981).

2. Accession is an alternative means of undertaking the obligations of a treaty. Rather than signing and ratifying, a government may accede, that is, join a treaty.

3. To obtain a copy of the Women's Convention, contact your local United Nations Information Office. In the United States, write to the office at 1998 F Street, N.W., Washington, DC USA. See also, UN 1988:17-24.

4. Articles 10 and 11 are based on the conventions adopted by UNESCO and the ILO (Hevenor 1983; UN 1988).

5. The Women's Convention, in addressing civil rights in Article 16, neither invokes nor replicates the International Covenant on Civil and Political Rights, which provides broader civil rights protection to women and men.

6. Members of CEDAW are elected by virtue of their individual attributes and by a vote of all ratifying states. Candidates must have "high moral standing and competence in the fields covered by the Convention" and reflect a broad geographic range of countries at different stages of development and with varying legal systems. The majority of Committee members have been women, of whom half have been lawyers. The remainder have held professional posts in the health sciences, political science, trade and labor organizations, education, and social work (Byrnes 1989:8-9). A number have been career diplomats, government officials, and feminist activists (Byrnes 1989).

7. Ratifying states also meet every two years. They initially convened in 1981 after the Women's Convention entered into force, and met in 1982 to elect members to CEDAW and again in 1983 to discuss rules of procedure

and guidelines for initial reports of states parties. Currently, they meet in even-numbered years to discuss matters of mutual concern. The fifth meeting of states parties took place in 1992, when delegates discussed the problem of reservations to the Women's Convention.

8. Fourteen states entered reservations to Article 16 (the family), nine to Article 15 (legal capacity), eight to Article 9 (Nationality); seven to Article 7 (public life); six to Article 11 (employment); five to Article 2 (policy), three to Article 13 (economic and social life), two to Article 5 (stereotyped roles), and one to Article 1 (definition of sex discrimination) (Cook 1990a:714-716).

9. The three treaties are: the Inter-American Convention, the Convention of the Elimination of all Forms of Racial Discrimination, and the International Covenant on Economic, Social, and Cultural Rights.

10. For information about the Committee, contact: Billie Heller, Chair, National Committee for UN/CEDAW, 520 North Camden Drive, Beverly Hills, CA 90210, USA.

11. The Senate Foreign Relations Committee convened a hearing on the Covenant on April 2, 1992, and President Bush completed ratification on June 5, 1992.

12. The presence of a woman on the Supreme Court has proved important. Following the Court's 1973 decision (Roe vs. Wade), opposition to legalized abortion reached militant proportions. Lower court judgements have begun to reach the Supreme Court and, in the summer of 1992, the Court upheld its 1973 decision with some restrictions.

13. A new civil rights bill approved shortly after the Thomas hearing failed to address sexual harassment per se, although it did deal with discrimination against women in the workplace. The bill, however, set a ceiling on damages claimed for such discrimination. Representative Barbara Kennelly (Democrat from Connecticut) and Senator Edward Kennedy (Democrat from Massachusetts) subsequently introduced legislation to remove the ceiling on damages for such discrimination.

14. For discussion of international implementation generally see Schwelb 1977:141-186; Sohn 1985; Sohn and Buergenthal 1973:505-992; Vasak 1981:215-230.

15. Data are not available to analyze how Committee members' ideas about women's rights and human rights have been affected by their work. Data are also not available on the relationship between a member's position in her government or society and her actions to achieve the goals of the Women's Convention there. Studies on these topics could illuminate the impact of the Women's Convention.

16. Experts from Egypt have participated in annual meetings of CEDAW since 1982 as well as in biennial meetings of states parties to the Women's Convention. Dr. Marvat El-Tallawy, a career diplomat, was Egypt's first nominee for election to CEDAW in 1982. After being elected, Dr. El-Tallawy resigned her CEDAW seat and joined the United Nations staff; Ms.

Farida Abou El-Tegouh was appointed as her successor. In 1986, Dr. El-Tallawy, then Minister Plenipotentiary with Egypt's Foreign Affairs Ministry, was nominated to CEDAW. She was elected and then re-elected for a two-year term in 1990.

17. The International Women's Rights Action Watch (IWRAW) also has reported on this case. The IWRAW publishes monthly newsletters and an annual report summarizing the activities of the Committee on the Elimination of Discrimination Against Women. For information, contact: IWRAW/WPPD, Humphrey Institute of Public Affairs, University of Minnesota, 301 19th Street South, Minneapolis, MN 55455, USA.

References

ABA (American Bar Association)
   1984   Recommendation. Section of International Law and Practice. Report to House of Delegates, 1-4. (Available from Section on International Law, American Bar Association, 1800 M Street, Washington, DC, USA.)

Abramson, Jill and David Shirbman
   1991   High Court Drama: Sex Harassment Furor Jeopardizes Thomas, Hurts Republicans Too. *Wall Street Journal* October 9, A1, A7.

Alger, Chadwick
   1963   The United Nations as a Learning Experience. *Public Opinion Quarterly* 27(Fall):411-426.

   1965   Personal Contact in Intergovernmental Organizations. In: *International Behavior: A Social-Psychological Analysis*, edited by Herbert Kelman. Pp. 521-547. New York: Holt, Rinehart and Winston.

AS (American Survey)
   1991   The Charge Against Clarence Thomas. *Economist* 12(October):25-26.

AI (Amnesty International)
   1991   *Women on the Front Lines*. New York: Amnesty International.

Badran, Margot
   1988   Dual Liberation: Feminism and Nationalism in Egypt, 1980-1925. *Feminist Issues* Spring:15-34.

Bayefsky, Anne F.
  1990 The Principle of Equality of Non-Discrimination in International
        Law. *Human Rights Law Journal* 11:1-34.

British Commonwealth
  1975 *The Convention on the Elimination of All Forms of Discrimination
        Against Women: A Commentary on the Convention.* London:
        Commonwealth Secretariat.

Bruce, Margaret
  1971 Work of the United Nations Relating to the Status of Women.
        Revue de Droits de l'Homme 4:365-412.

Bunch, Charlotte
  1990 Women's Rights as Human Rights. *Human Rights Quarterly*
        12:486-498.

Burrows, Noreen
  1989 The 1979 Convention on the Elimination of All Forms of
        Discrimination Againsst Women. *Netherlands International Law
        Review* 31:332-354.

Byrnes, Andrew
  1989 The "Other" Human Rights Body: The Work of the Committee on
        the Elimination of Discrimination Against Women. *Yale Journal
        of International Law* 14(Winter):1-67.

  1991 CEDAW's Tenth Session. *Netherlands Quarterly of Human Rights*
        3, Appendix I.

Chafe, William
  1991 *The Paradox of Change: American Women in the 20th Century.*
        New York: Oxford University Press.

Colliver, Sandra
  1989 United Nations Machineries on Women's Rights. How Might
        They Better Help Women Whose Rights Are Being Violated? In:
        New Directions in Human Rights, edited by Ellen Lutz, Hurst
        Hannum, and Kathryn J. Burke. Chapter 3. Philadelphia:
        University of Pennsylvania Press.

Cook, Rebecca J.
   1989   The International Right to Nondiscrimination on the Basis of Sex:
          A Bibliography. *Yale Journal of International Law* 14(Winter):161-
          181.

   1990a Reservations to the Convention on the Elimination of All Forms
          of Discrimination Against Women. *Virginia Journal of International
          Law* 30(Spring):643-716.

   1990b International Human Rights Concerning Women: Case Notes and
          Comments. *Vanderbilt Journal of Transnational Law* 23:779-818.

Deckard, Barbara
   1975   *The Women's Movement*. New York: Harper and Row.

Eisler, Riane
   1987   Human Rights: Toward an Integrated Theory for Action. *Human
          Rights Quarterly* 9(Spring):287-308.

Elder, Betty G.
   1986   The Rights of Women: Their Status in International Law. *Crime
          and Social Justice* 25:1-39.

El Kharbouty, Maitre Attiat and Aziza Hussein
   1977   Law and the Status of Women in the Arab Republic of Egypt. In:
          Law and the Status of Women, edited by Luke T. Lee. Pp. 35-50.
          New York: United Nations.

El Saadawi, Nawal
   1980   *Hidden Face of Eve*. (Translated and edited by Dr. Sherif Hetata.)
          Boston: Beacon Press.

   1984   Egypt: When a Woman Rebels. In: *The Sisterhood is Global*,
          edited by Robin Morgan. Pp. 194-206. Garden City: Doubleday.

Galey, Margaret E.
   1979   Promoting Non-Discrimination Against Women: The UN
          Commission on the Status of Women. *International Studies
          Quarterly* 23:273-302.

   1984   International Enforcement of Women's Rights. *Human Rights
          Quarterly* 6:463-490.

Goldschmidt, Arthur, Jr.
 1988 *Modern Egypt: The Formation of a Nation-State.* Boulder: Westview Press.

Goodrich, Leland, Edouard Hambro, and Anne Simmons
 1969 *The Charter of the United Nations: Commentary and Documents.* New York: Columbia University Press.

Guggenheim, Malvina H.
 1977 The Implementation of Human Rights by the UN Commission on the Status of Women: A Brief Comment. *Texas International Law Journal* Winter:161-181.

Hadwen, John G. and Johan Kaufmann
 1960 *How United Nations Decisions are Made.* Leyden: A.W. Sithoff.

Harrison, Cynthia
 1989 *On Account of Sex: The Politics of Women's Issues, 1945-1968.* Berkeley: University of California Press.

Hatem, Mervat
 1986 The Enduring Alliance of Nationalism and Patriarchy in Muslim Personal Status Laws: The Case of Modern Egypt. *Feminist Issues* Spring:19-43.

Henkin, Louis
 1978 *The Rights of Man Today.* Boulder: Westview Press.

Hevenor, Natalie
 1983 *International Law and the Status of Women.* Boulder: Westview Press.

Hevenor, Natalie and David Whitman
 1990 Opposition to Human Rights Treaties in the US Senate: The Legacy of the Bricker Amendment. *Human Rights Quarterly* 10:309-338.

Hijab, Nadia
 1988 *Womanpower: The Arab Debate on Women at Work.* New York: Cambridge University Press.

Hoff, Joan
   1991   *Law, Gender and Injustice: A Legal History of US Women.* New
          York: New York University Press.

Hopwood, Derek
   1982   *Egypt, Politics and Society, 1945-1981.* London: George Allen and
          Unwin.

Hosken, Fran P.
   1981   Toward a Definition of Women's Rights. *Human Rights Quarterly*
          3:1-10.

Ireland, Patricia
   1978   International Advancement and Protection of Human Rights for
          Women. *Lawyer of the Americas* 10:87-98.

ILRH (International League for Human Rights)
   1991   *Human Rights Abuses Against Women: A Worldwide Survey.* New
          York: International League for Human Rights.

Jacobson, H.K.
   1984   *Networks of Interdependence: International Organization and the
          Global Political System.* 2nd edition. New York: Alfred Knopf.

Jawayardena, Kumari
   1987   *Feminism and Nationalism in the Third World.* Atlantic Highlands:
          Zed Press, Ltd.

Kurtz, Howard
   1992   Capitol Gains. *Working Women* February:66-69.

Lubin, Carol and Anne Winslow
   1991   *Social Justice for Women.* Chapel Hill: Duke University Press.

Marsh, B.
   1991   Women in the Work Force. *Wall Street Journal.* October 18, 1992.
          Page B3.

McDougal, Myres S., Harold D. Lasswell, and Lung-chu Chen
   1975   Human Rights for Women and the World Public Order: The
          Outlawing of Sex-based Discrimination. *American Journal of
          International Law* 69:497-523.

Middle East Watch News
  1991   Egyptian Government Moves to Dissolve Prominent Arab
         Woman's Organization. *News from Middle East Watch* 1:1-9.

  1992   Court Upholds Closure of Women's Organization. *News from
         Middle East Watch* 4:1-8.

Morsy, Soheir A.
  1991   Women and Contemporary Social Transformation in North Africa.
         In: *The Women and International Development Annual*, Volume 2,
         edited by Rita S. Gallin and Anne Ferguson. Pp. 129-175.
         Boulder: Westview Press.

Nasir, Jamal J.
  1990   *The Status of Women Under Islamic Law*. London: Graham and
         Trotman, Ltd.

National Committee on UN/CEDAW
  1990   Fact Sheet 1,1.

Picker, Jean
  1977   Law and the Status of Women in the United States. In: *Law and
         the Status of Women*, edited by Luke T. Lee. Pp. 311-344. New
         York: United Nations.

PS (Political Science)
  1992   Politics, Values and the Thomas Nomination. *Political Science and
         Politics* XXV(3):471-473.

Reanda, Laura
  1982   Human Rights and Women's Rights: The UN Approach. *Human
         Rights Quarterly* 3:11-31.

Rix, Sara (editor)
  1990   *The American Woman 1990-1991: A Status Report*. New York:
         W.W. Norton.

Sadat, Jehan
  1987   *A Woman of Egypt*. New York: Simon and Schuster

Sandroff, Ronni
  1992   Sexual Harassment: The Inside Story. *Working Woman* 47-51, 78,
         June 1992.

Schwelb, Egon
  1977   The International Measures of Implementation of the International
         Covenant on Civil and Political Rights and of the Optional
         Protocol. *Texas Journal of International Law* 12(Summer):141-186.

Schmittroth, Linda (editor)
  1991   *Statistical Record of Women Worldwide*. Detroit: Gale Research
         Inc.

Sohn, Louis B.
  1985   Human Rights: Their Implementation and Supervision by the
         United Nations. In: *Human Rights in International Law: Legal
         and Policy Issues*, edited by Theodore Meron. Chapter 10. New
         York: Oxford University Press.

Sohn, Louis B. and Thoman Buergenthal
  1973   *International Protection of Human Rights*. New York: Bobbs-
         Merrill.

Soroos, Marvin
  1986   *Beyond Sovereignty: The Challenge of Global Policy*. Columbia:
         University of South Carolina Press.

Sullivan, Earl
  1986   *Women in Egyptian Public Life*. Syracuse: Syracuse University
         Press.

Taubenfeld, Rita and Howard Taubenfeld
  1975   Achieving the Human Rights of Women. *Human Rights* 4:125-169.

Tinker, Catherine
  1981   Human Rights for Women: The UN Convention on the
         Elimination of All Forms of Discrimination Against Women.
         Human Rights Quarterly 3:32-41.

UN CEDAW (United Nations Committee on the Elimination of all Forms
  of Discrimination Against Women)
  1983   Initial Report of Egypt.

  1987   Second Report of Egypt.

UNGA (United Nations General Assembly)
1981- Report of Committee on The Elimination of All Forms of
1991 Discrimination Against Women (CEDAW).

UN (United Nations)
1987a *Human Rights: A Compilation of International Instruments.* New York: United Nations Secretariat, Division of Human Rights.

1987b *Human Rights: Status of International Instruments.* New York: United Nations Secretariat, Division of Human Rights.

1988 *Compendium of International Conventions Concerning the Status of Women.* New York: United Nations Secretariat, Center for Social Development and Humanitarian Affairs.

1990 *Multilateral Treaties Deposited with the Secretary-General and Addendum.* New York: United Nations Secretariat, Office of the Legal Advisor.

US (United States) Congress
1989 Congressional Research Service. *Selected Women's Issues Legislation Enacted Between 1932-1988.* (Write your United States Senator or United States Representatiave, U.S. House of Representatives, Washington, DC, 20515, USA to request this.)

Vasak, Karel
1981 Distinguishing Criteria of Institutions. In: *The International Dimensions of Human Rights.* Revised and edited by Philip Alston. Westport: Greenwood Press.

Wolf, Francis
1985 Human Rights and the International Labour Organization. In: *Human Rights in International Law: Legal and Policy Issues,* edited by Theodore Meron. Chapter 7. New York: Oxford University Press.

Part III

Forum: Women in the Caribbean

5

Women's Status in Contemporary Cuba: Contradictions, Diversity, and Challenges for the Future

Marie Withers Osmond

The picture of Cuban women derived from publications written in English is varied and contradictory. While some authors claim that women have made tremendous progress in Cuban society, others argue that the barriers to positive change in their status are increasing. These different perspectives often emerge from ideologically-based comparisons of the condition of women in Cuba to that of women in the close-neighboring United States. Frequently, politically inspired propaganda pervades the literature: American writers portray Cuba in an economic and political downslide, while Cuban reports emphasize outstanding and continuing revolutionary progress. There appears to be some truth in each account. One can live in Cuba in different areas, talk to different people, and find evidence for multiple views on the condition of women.

This chapter emphasizes differences among women, an emerging trend in the field of women and international development. Whether the focus of a study is a single society (such as Cuba) or the global women's movement which emerged during the United Nations Decade for Women, the issue of difference is glaringly apparent. Thus, I follow the guidelines set forth by Gallin, Aronoff, and Ferguson (1989) to encourage appreciation of the multiple approaches adopted to address problems and the implications of these approaches for strategies of change.

As a number of writers have demonstrated (e.g., Tinker and Jaquette 1987), the needs and goals of professional and working-class women differ throughout the world, thereby complicating efforts to improve their status. This chapter addresses such differences by comparing the views of two groups of women on women's status: those of women factory workers in two textile mills and those of women professionals in the Federation of Cuban

Women (FMC).[1] While Castro's dedication to communism precludes any mention of social class in Cuba, the economic status of factory and professional women differs, as do the resources available to them (e.g., time and leisure).

This chapter is organized in four sections. In the first, I describe the broad effects on women of the Cuban revolution of 1959. Then I discuss official policies on women in four areas: law, education, politics, and economy. Following this section, I describe the perceptions and priorities of a sample of women factory workers in Cuba and contrast these with the goals and strategies of the Federation of Cuban Women (FMC). In the concluding section, I examine how, in Cuba, the current economic crisis, the persistence of patriarchal ideology, and the FMC's lack of autonomy act as formidable barriers to women's equality with men.

The Cuban Revolution of 1959 and Its Aftermath

It is important to view Cuba from the perspective of other Third World societies. The status of women in pre-revolutionary Cuba was analogous to that of women in developing countries around the world today. Before 1959, the deprivation of Cuban women was part of the general poverty suffered by the society as a whole. Women, however, faced a potential triple subordination: (1) class subordination as peasants or as an exploited labor reserve for the preservation of colonial capitalism; (2) sexual subordination in a gender system where *machismo* and patriarchy were not only deeply entrenched in the culture but also reinforced by the Roman Catholic Church; and (3) color subordination in a system where racism was integral to the maintenance of the economic and political status quo (Dewart 1963).

Women first entered the industrial labor force in Cuba only with the abolishment of slavery in 1903 (Brundenius 1984). In that year, 70 percent of all employed women in Cuba were domestic servants. The majority of the remaining 30 percent worked as laborers in tobacco factories under substandard conditions. By 1919, although the percentage of women who worked as maids had decreased to 50 percent, 33 percent continued to work in the tobacco industry. These figures underscore the major handicaps the majority of Cuban women brought to the revolution; they had no formal education and training to prepare them for waged labor. Such preparation was considered unnecessary because all women were bound to their homes, children, and husbands (Brundenius 1984). The 1953 census showed that women comprised less than nine percent of the waged labor force, including 70,000 domestic servants. In rural Cuba, women made up only three percent of the paid labor force in agriculture, fishing, mining, construction and transport (Murray 1979). Of the 15 percent of employed women who might be classified as "professionals," 80 percent were elementary school teachers (Casal 1980).[2]

Chronic poverty in rural areas forced many women to migrate to the capital city of Havana where the survival choices were serving either as maids or as prostitutes. Prostitution, along with vice rings, drug syndicates, and gambling casinos, flourished in Havana during the last years of Batista's reign (1934-1944, 1952-1959). According to Mills (1960), in Havana alone, in 1957, there were over 270 licensed houses of prostitution, dozens of hotels renting rooms by the hour, and over 700 bars crowded with "hostesses" who were one step away from prostitution. Of the thousands of beggars on the streets of Havana, at least 25,000 were women (Cole 1980).

The traditional Cuban family, heavily influenced by Spanish heritage, was large, extended, and familistic (Nelson 1950). The husband/father was a patriarch and, when he could afford it, supported several mistresses in addition to his legal family (Randall 1974). With the exception of the poorest families, women were seldom wage earners. As a result, marriage was essential for a woman's economic survival, although courtship was idealized and romanticized. Nevertheless, marriages were explicitly arranged by the family, with economics rather than love between partners the crucial consideration. Young women were strictly chaperoned so that virginity at marriage was ensured and, upon marriage, a woman was expected to produce sons to inherit the family name.

The family maintained a strict division of labor by gender. Wives cooked all the meals, cleaned the house, supervised the children, and maintained the family status through contacts with and entertainment of relatives. Woman's work, thus, required little formal education (Bengelsdorf and Hageman 1979) and, according to the 1953 local census, at least one out of five women could neither read nor write; in rural areas, the figure was two out of five.

Housing and health were dismal for all but the rich. The homes of the majority of Cubans were *bohios*--huts with thatched roofs, dirt floors, and no running water or indoor plumbing. In the early 1950s, five out of every fifty children died before their first birthday. Most of the urban population paid rent which absorbed from a fifth to a third of their income.

Given these conditions, what were the most immediate consequences of the revolution? On March 6, 1959, all rents in Cuba were reduced by 50 percent and on March 17, all beaches were declared open to the public. The First Agrarian Reformation (during the summer of 1959) confiscated land that had been owned by Batista supporters, and private land ownership was fixed at a maximum of 1,000 acres. The American crime syndicates lost control, and thousands of prostitutes fled to New York City and Miami, along with gangsters and pimps. Alarmed by the realities of socialism, the upper and upper-middle classes also left the country (Fagen et al. 1968). Jolly (1964) reports that in the first three years after the revolution, over

250,000 Cubans, largely professionals and including approximately one-third of Cuba's physicians and 15 percent of its technical and professional workers, emigrated from the country.

The revolution also had profound consequences for women. According to the Central Report of the Second Congress of the Cuban Women's Federation (Second Congress 1975:93): "the triumph offered our women the opportunity to study and to work, it offered them economic security, thereby putting an end to oppression and hardship [and] it opened prospects of health care, of social security . . . For women, the Revolution meant the opportunity to attain human dignity." In practice, those people who suffered the most before the revolution--women, Blacks, and the poor--gained the most during its aftermath.

Twenty thousand maids initially enrolled in Schools for the Advancement of Domestic Servants in Havana, and ultimately, over 90,000 women were trained in these institutes. The Ana Betancourt School for Peasant Girls recruited 14,000 young women from the most remote areas of the rural countryside, taught them work skills, and raised their level of education to the sixth grade. Special schools, called "farms," were organized in different parts of the country to rehabilitate thousands of prostitutes. In addition to rehabilitation--for example, breaking drug habits and raising self-esteem-- women and young girls were educated and given job training.

In addition to groups that were organized to raise women's level of education and to train them in basic skills, others were established to raise their political consciousness. Among these groups was The Congress of Cuban Women for the Liberation of Latin America, founded in 1959. The Congress of Cuban Women was a product of the participation of 76 women in the International Federation of Democratic Women's Congress (held in Chile) on the rights of women and children. These women, headed by Vilma Espin, returned to Cuba with the initial goal of overcoming the exploitative effects of neocolonialism on women, largely through basic education and political studies (Randall 1981).

One year later, in August 1960, a women's organization was established which Fidel Castro named *La Federación de Mujeres Cubanas* (The Federation of Cuban Women, FMC), and which had over 70,000 members. The president, since the group's founding, is Vilma Espin, a guerilla in the revolution, a member of the Party's Central Committee, and the wife of Fidel Castro's brother Raul.

The FMC is structured hierarchically, with representatives at five levels (national, provincial, municipal, block, and delegation), and a governance system made up of 13 representatives from 14 provinces and 169 municipalities. As it is considered a mass organization (as are trade unions, student groups, and associations of farmers), membership in the FMC is automatic with a dues payment of US$0.75 every three months; in 1980, 77 percent of all women over age 14 (about 2.5 million) were dues-paying members (Boletin FMC 1980). The FMC is therefore largely self-supporting.

From its inception, the FMC has been dedicated to two goals: (1) "to raise consciousness through ideological education, so that new tasks could be performed" and (2) "to raise the ideological level through the tasks themselves" (Second Congress 1975:95). During its 33-year history, the implementation of these goals could be observed as three stages of development (Randall 1981).

First, from 1959 to 1963, the FMC attempted to draw women out of domestic isolation and to eradicate illiteracy. Toward this end, they organized day-care centers for the cildren of workers (Children's Circles); the Ana Betancourt School for Peasant Girls; training centers for Directors of Children's Circles; the Women's Improvement School for Domestic Workers; and First Aid courses (e.g., health, hygiene, and basic medication).

Once women had received basic education and their political consciousness had been raised, a campaign (1964-1974) to incorporate women into the active labor force was initiated. Finally, from 1975 to the present, the FMC has promoted women in elections, and has appointed women to leadership positions. Moreover, the FMC has launched campaigns to end sexism in the home, at work, and in the government.[3]

To summarize, Cuban women and men can now satisfy most of their basic needs--even though the majority of people in developing societies cannot. All Cubans are assured free education, basic housing, and free health care. These guarantees have contributed to high literacy rates among adults, relatively low infant mortality, and the elimination of malnutrition, polio, malaria, diphtheria, and other major diseases endemic to most developing countries. Moreover, in the 1976 Constitution, Cuban women were guaranteed legal equality, access to economic resources, and the right to control their own bodies. While participants at the three international conferences held during the United Nations Decade for Women (1976-1985) agreed that these rights are fundamental to the improvement of women's status worldwide (Tinker and Jaquette 1987), they remain elusive for most women.

The View from the Top: State and FMC Policies

Evidence from the international women's movement shows that in many societies some women are able to have a voice in the decisions that affect them while others are not: professional women actively formulate and implement policies in their own behalf through women's organizations; working-class women seldom have a voice in development plans and other programs with consequences for their lives (Tinker and Jaquette 1987). In addition to such class-based differences in power, the goals of women vary on the basis of ethnicity and race as well as class. For example, in the United States, the goals of the National Organization for Women (NOW) are oriented more toward the interests of middle-class than of working-class women. The need to address these differences in women's goals is gaining increased recognition. (See Antrobus 1989, for a unique and insightful article which extends this point internationally.)

This section discusses policies developed by the Cuban state and the FMC, theoretically to improve women's lives. In many cases, technically-skilled and professional women who were activists in the FMC played a role in shaping policies for women. Indeed, even Fidel Castro has credited the FMC with eliminating legal prostitution and reintegrating prostitutes into society, educating former domestics, helping rural women find jobs in factories and agriculture, and establishing day-care centers. Moreover, Castro (1980) has acknowledged the contributions of these women to the formulation of the Maternity Law and the Family Code. Leaders of the FMC have initiated and promoted most of the policies for women discussed below. In the sections which follow, I use quotes from FMC publications to illustrate the commitment of this organization to improving the lives of Cuban women.

Castro has explicitly labeled Cuba a communist society. Communist theory on women's subordination is based on Engels's *Origins of the Family, Private Property and the State* and Lenin's *On the Emancipation of Women.* These texts argue that women's oppression results from *economic* conditions that develop in a capitalist society. Cuba's post-revolutionary social policies and programs reflect this Marxist argument (Huberman and Sweezy 1969; Molyneux 1981). Assumptions inherent in Marxist theory, however, make its application problematic. For example, Marxist theory suggests that the inequality of women and the exploitation of men are both rooted in the economy. Thus, when private property is abolished, inequality will disappear, the family will be socialized, and men and women workers will share equal rights.

This argument is questionable, as a number of writers have pointed out (Eisenstein 1979; Hartmann 1979; Kuhn and Wolpe 1978). First, there is considerable evidence that women's subordination transcends economic boundaries. Second, no certain link has been established between women's productive work and their status relative to men. Third, this argument ignores the linkages between the economy and women's responsibility for the family and reproduction; calls for the collectivization of domestic labor and child care ignore the economic costs and cultural resistance associated with changes in the traditional gender division of labor.

Castro accepted Marxist theory and emphasized that the inequality of women would be solved by their entry into wage work. This view assumes that women's participation in the paid labor force improves their financial status and raises their consciousness. This view also precludes analyses of ideology and of economic and gender relations, thereby obscuring the mechanisms that perpetuate women's subordination even when they are involved in productive work. Finally, this view ignores the fact that state policies respond to crises in the economy and that these responses are not necessarily compatible with women's interests.

In the following subsections, I examine policies in four areas that have direct implications for women: law, education, politics, and economy. In each discussion, I highlight the major factors that constrain or enhance opportunities for Cuban women in different socioeconomic strata. My discussion focuses on a comparison between working-class and professional women.

Law

Cuban laws are more egalitarian than those in many other societies (including the United States). Nevertheless, a number of these laws, such as protective legislation, maternity laws, and the Family Code, include assumptions about women's roles that prevent them from achieving equality with men. These assumptions are similar to those inherent in certain economic policies. As Antrobus (1989:191) has forcefully written:

> far from reflecting a *failure* to take account of gender roles, these policies are actually based on a deeply gendered ideology which simultaneously minimizes the value of the tasks necessary for social reproduction and promotes a pattern of economic production based on the exploitation of the socioeconomic vulnerabilities of the female population.

Protective Legislation. Equality of women's rights in marriage, employment, salaries, and education is guaranteed in the 1976 Cuban constitution. Article 41 states: "Discrimination because of race, color, sex, or national origin is forbidden and will be punished by law." While gender is not specifically mentioned in Article 42, which deals with access to jobs, Article 43 is directed to women and mandates that the State provide them with jobs "*compatible with their physical constitution*" (emphasis added). On the basis of this mandate, the Ministry of Labor issued a resolution that explicitly restricted women from approximately 300 types of jobs due to "considerations of health" (Bengelsdorf 1985; Bengelsdorf and Hageman 1979). The jobs that were eliminated were deemed hazardous and unhealthy for pregnant women (such as jobs associated with heights or chemicals); night-shift work was also judged unsuitable for women. Therefore, women were restricted to specified jobs in textile factories and sugar mills. Thus, the

1976 Constitution, more liberal toward women than many such documents in the world, virtually categorized less physically demanding and unskilled jobs as "women's work" (Murray 1979).

Designing protective legislation is a complex problem but justifiable concerns appear to overlap with persisting gender-based assumptions. For example, a healthy woman who is not pregnant can do most jobs. Yet the legitimate concern to protect pregnant women often defines them, through labor codes, as weak and therefore unable to occupy productive roles.

Maternity Law. State policy on the family was intended to benefit women, but traditional norms permeate family law. For example, Cuba's 1974 "Maternity Law of the Working Woman" includes a number of unique benefits. It provides medical care to pregnant women, three months of paid maternity leave or one year of unpaid leave, remunerative leaves for a child's illness, and the right to return after leave to the same job at the same salary (Federation of Cuban Women 1980b). In practice, the law is more useful to professional women, who are more able to take one year's unpaid leave than are factory workers.

There is an intrinsic assumption about gender in these provisions: the *mother* is primarily responsible for child care. Men's wages tend to be higher than women's, and the cost to the employer of their withdrawal from work is greater than for women. Paternity leave is therefore not advocated. The maternity law also makes it more costly to hire women than men. Employers must pay the total cost of maternity and other family-related leaves. As Nazzari (1983:261) notes, "given the choice between hiring women who might become pregnant and hiring men, any enterprise required to show a profit would prefer to hire men." Indeed, a report to the Second Congress of the Federation of Cuban Women (1975) states that, "Managers sometimes refuse to employ female labor because this forces them to increase the number of substitutes with a consequent growth of the staff, which affects the evaluation of productivity."[4]

Family Code. Passed in 1975, the Family Code stipulates that "where both marriage partners are employed, husbands are required to share *equally* the responsibilities for tasks related to the household and to the rearing of children." Essentially the Code provision on the sharing of housework is an empty policy (Marieskind 1980). It establishes a policy but provides no mechanisms for implementation or any sanctions for violations. The Family Code thus constitutes a set of norms, rather than a law, designed to influence the marital division of labor (Bengelsdorf 1985).

As in many societies, those who are educated are often more likely to adopt egalitarian behaviors than their less-educated counterparts. The educated FMC women and the men they marry may thus establish a more equitable division of household labor in their marriages than working-class couples. Basically, the socialization of housework and child care proved too expensive for the government, and passage of the Family Code provided a solution to "women's problems" at no cost to the state (Nazzari 1983).

The Family Code of Cuba appears contrary to official communist policy: it holds parents rather than society responsible for the support of their children. It links child support directly to family income, thereby contradicting Castro's 1966 statement that a child's subsistence should be determined solely by the "needs of the child as a human being" (Nazzari 1983:258).

Theoretically, under communist policy children should not be an economic burden to individual parents because the state provides education, school meals and uniforms, health care, and low-cost food staples. Working-class women particularly benefit from these entitlements, because they have fewer material resources than professional women. Without such provisions, the Family Code compels them to remain preoccupied with family income (often controlled by the husband) and maternal responsibility.

Moreover, *individual women* must assume responsibility for enforcing the Family Code by taking their husbands to court for any of its violations. In short, no collective support is built into the system. It is unlikely that the FMC, or even the local CDR (Committee for the Defense of the Revolution) would provide group support to a woman whose complaint was her husband's failure to fulfill his Family Code obligations. It is even more unlikely that an individual woman would (or could) hire a private lawyer to prosecute her case. In a socialist country such as the People's Republic of China, members of local block organizations are responsible for speaking to a husband who is recalcitrant in his family obligations (Sokoloff 1982). In Cuba, on the other hand, the privacy of the family is upheld by State, legal system, and mass organizations (unless related to actual child abuse).

Education

Education is basic to the creation of a new Cuban socialist society, and gender equality has been advocated in educational policy. The State significantly improved women's educational opportunities through the basic Literacy Campaign of 1961 and subsequent educational programs. For example, data from a 1982 survey of women in Havana showed that only eight percent of those aged 15 to 29 left school at the primary level while 42 percent of those 30 years and older had completed only six years or less of school. Twelve percent of the daughters sampled in this study were attending a university, while less than two percent of their mothers had done so (Catasus et al. 1988). In 1984, women constituted more than half of Cuba's medical students and, in 1985, they comprised 70 percent of first-year law students (Evenson 1986).

There are, however, three factors that temper this record of progress. First, the Cuban educational system is theoretically a meritocracy, in which advancement is based on a student's ability rather than family position or resources. "Dropouts" usually become farm or factory laborers with scant hope for any change in their status.[5] Children, therefore, are pressured both to make excellent grades and to build a reputation for ideological commitment and motivation to serve the State. These dual pressures are considered the mother's responsibility, and tension arises from the contradiction between the professed social mobility available in Cuba and the reality by which family position, political power, and income facilitate entry into schools offering the best opportunities, as does gender.

For example, military schools (which recruit the most qualified teachers) enroll very few women students. According to Randall (1981), Cuba has approximately six scientific and technical vocational schools which have very high entrance requirements. The schools officially require applicants to have a grade-point average of 85 percent, but they often have so many qualified applicants that they select only those who have grade-point averages of 99 to 100 percent. Such a selection process has implications for the class composition of the population, in that it may create a technical elite and new class divisions. These implications are seldom discussed in Cuba.

Second, the media and other modes of socialization continue to portray conventional gender images, thereby perpetuating inequality between men and women. Motherhood is a central theme of official communist propaganda about women and the FMC, and mothers' brigades and mothers' days underscore the centrality of this role for women. Further, although women played an active role in guerilla struggles, the emblem of the FMC portrays a woman with a rifle in one arm and a baby in the other.

The journal of the FMC, *Mujeres*, is considered an important medium through which women can develop new ideas about themselves. Yet, fashion and beauty sections occupy an average of 20 percent of its pages; as Murray (1979:105) notes, the journal portrays "dresses which cannot be bought and which I never saw worn, modelled on pencil-thin, elegant white ladies." The journal also features interviews with women who have "succeeded," such as brain surgeons or engineers, and holds them up as role models for readers. The journal, however, includes no material advocating changes in men's roles. Masculinity in Cuba is embodied in the bearded guerilla/proletarian in a heroic stance; no poster exists which depicts a man with a gun in one arm and an infant in the other.

Third, although the leaders of the FMC are quite aware of the need to improve women's educational levels, their efforts to raise these levels have not been entirely successful. The primary objective of the Federation of Cuban Women is to improve women's cultural level [and] we have systematically continued our work in conjunction with the Ministry of Education to raise the cultural level of housewives, in the urban as well as the rural areas. [Nevertheless], there are still difficulties at the rank and file level: lack of proper preparation for the beginning of different courses; difficulties in the placement of teachers; delayed updating of the statistics on the educational level of housewives; lack of facilities for imparting the courses (Espin 1980:13).

Politics

Discussions of women and politics raise at least three issues: (1) the representation of women in the political structure, (2) the influence and autonomy of women's political organizations, and (3) these organizations' identification with feminist political objectives.

There is little that is novel about political representation in Cuba. Women have not achieved equal representation with men at high levels of political organization in any country in the world, socialist or capitalist. Within the Cuban Communist Party only 13.2 percent of party members were women in 1976, although by 1979, this proportion had increased to 18.9 percent (FMC 1980b). Similarly, only 22 percent of the members elected to the National Assembly in 1980 were women (Pedula and Smith 1985). Nevertheless, Espin (1980:24) argues that there is cause for optimism "because we have a large number of women who are well trained and are gaining experience that will get them promoted to positions of greater responsibility in forthcoming years."

The second issue raised by a discussion of women and politics is the influence and autonomy of women's organizations. In Cuba, the commitment of the male-dominated government and party to the FMC is based on both pragmatic and political considerations. Pragmatically, the demands and the effects of the revolution required (in fact, demanded) including women in the transformation process (for example, in the nation's defense, literacy and health care campaigns, and food production). Politically, Castro encouraged women to join the revolutionary effort to foster egalitarian relations between women and men in a genuine communist society. Women's participation in the process of change was vital; the FMC, therefore, provided an important means through which housebound, uneducated, and untrained women could be incorporated into the change process.

The objective of the FMC is neither consciousness raising, as understood by American feminists, nor personal change; rather, the objective of the FMC is to effect social change. Thus, the organization (which has a membership comprised of 58 percent housewives [Randall 1981]) does not directly address social relations among women or relations between husbands and wives, but it encourages women to emerge from their domestic isolation and become more active in public life.

Early policies formulated by the FMC during its first two stages of development (between 1959 and 1974) were not sufficient to engage many women in politics. The Federation's efforts were, in the words of Murray (1979:64), "more that of representing government policy to women than of representing women to the government." Consequently, in its third stage of development (1975 to the present) the FMC has organized neighborhood block meetings, through which it hopes to reach more women. This effort, however, has not been very successful:

> The raising of the ideological level of Federation members is an objective of capital importance. That is why throughout these years we have consistently worked for the political education of women . . . . A cold appraisal of the development of the ideological study groups will show that in many cases they do not live up to expectations . . . in the nation 16 percent of the organizations do not hold them and 35 percent of the Federation members do not attend (Espin 1980:14).

Espin (1980:11) suggests that the difficulties the block meetings have encountered are due to "lack of orientation and preparation, [and] faulty communication with the members" as well as meetings that are held irregularly and managed inefficiently.

Yet another reason that block meetings may not be popular is that they are organized as ideological study groups. Such study groups may be more appealing to activists in the FMC than to the greater number of factory workers in society, a point I return to below. The emphasis on ideology at the expense of practice may also discourage attendance.

In contrast to American feminist conceptions of women's political organizations, Cuba's FMC does not view women's groups as independent of other (usually male-dominated) political groups, nor does it give special prominence to the goal of women's equality. Similar to the Chinese Women's Federation, the FMC is primarily a social and educational organization, rooted in a traditional model of women's welfare that relies on women's non-wage, volunteer work. According to Sokoloff (1981), a major contradiction inherent in women's voluntary labor is that while such work brings women out of their isolated, husband-dominated homes, it is valuable work that is not remunerated. The problem, Sokoloff emphasizes, is that by not paying women for their labor (while paying men for theirs), society keeps women in a secondary position in society. Thus, while the FMC has undertaken vital activities in behalf of the emancipation of women, it has not challenged the structural barriers to women's equality with men.

The FMC, in short, neither possesses political autonomy nor transgresses conventional guidelines of socialist policy on women. It is responsible to the Political Bureau of the Party and dependent on it for direction. By promoting the myth that women are almost emancipated, by perpetuating the ideology of motherhood, by maintaining gender stereotypes in its training programs, and by encouraging women to work as volunteers rather than as paid employees, the FMC--however unintentionally--reinforces gender inequality. Despite these failings, the FMC (with Castro's support) has helped raise women's status in post-revolutionary Cuba to a level higher than that of most other women in developing countries (Sen and Grown 1987).

The third issue of concern raised by discussions of women and politics is the degree to which women's organizations identify with feminist objectives. Although the FMC has been instrumental in the advancement of women in Cuban society, its leaders do not consider it a feminist organization (Evenson 1986). To the contrary, the FMC leaders explicitly view themselves as "feminine," and symbolize their position with an elaborately coiffed and painted image of a woman's head on their official badge. This concept of women's emancipation as *feminine* rather than *feminist*, may be partially understood in an historical context. Sokoloff (1981) reminds us that at the time of the global women's movement in the 1960s, Cuba was seriously involved in its own revolution and isolated from much of the world by the United States blockade. The majority of Cuban women were therefore unable to benefit from the years of debate and struggle over issues that concerned Marxist and Socialist feminists in other countries, such as sexism and domestic labor. Rather, they have been taught that feminism is a capitalist, Western ideology--the most derogatory criticism possible.

Economy

The potential for women to achieve economic independence is perhaps the major change that has occurred in post-revolutionary Cuba. One of the earliest goals of the FMC was to incorporate women into production-- agricultural, industrial, or service. For the first two decades after the revolution, however, women were expected to volunteer their labor. While economic crises (such as the the 1969-1970 sugar harvest) drew women into the labor force as subsidiary workers, their work was not remunerated because they were still being educated and trained for paid labor. In fact, a major obstacle to the equal incorporation of women into waged work has been Cuba's persistent economic crises, evidenced in the government's struggle to surmount underdevelopment, repay its debts, and import sufficient capital goods to facilitate further industrialization (Fitzgerald 1978; Huberman and Sweezy 1969; Ritter 1974).[6]

It was obvious to the Cuban leadership as early as 1970 that economic survival would necessitate major changes, including some that targeted women in the labor force. Thus the Cuban leadership called for a renewed focus on the problem of employed women "working a second shift," that is, being solely responsible for housework and child care as well as earning an income (King 1977; Larguis and Dumoulin 1971). To ameliorate this problem, efforts to increase the quality and quantity of day-care centers (Children's Circles) increased.[7]

A shopping-bag plan (*plan jaba*) was also initiated which provided working women with priority service at local grocery stores (a beneficial plan which was, however, based on the assumption that *women* are responsible for all grocery shopping). Unfortunately, the solutions suggested in these efforts *enabled* women to combine home duties with paid employment, thereby making it more feasible for them to continue working a second shift. These measures, therefore, reinforced gender stereotypes rather than challenging the assumption that men have no responsibility for domestic labor.

Women's "second shift" also limits the time available to them for attending assemblies or meetings--activities that facilitate job advancement (Madrigal 1974). Factory workers, whose jobs and family responsibilities are more demanding than those of many FMC leaders, have less freedom to schedule political activities (a point I return to in the following section).

The Thirteenth Workers' Congress made a second and more fundamental change in 1973, by moving from the communist principle of "to each according to his need" to the socialist principle of "to each according to his work" (Nazzari 1983). This shift was defended as a "means of motivating those with labor skills, heavy responsibilities and tough or dangerous jobs" (Mesa-Lago 1981:150). Wage scales were established for specific jobs, and wages were linked to work quotas. The work quota system allowed wages to vary according to productivity, and it provided financial incentives to workers who produced beyond their quotas. In addition, employees who worked over-time were more likely to be compensated than earlier. In short, the State was demanding that industries produce *profits*; but this focus on profitability had profound consequences for women, including job segregation, income discrimination, and the threat of unemployment.

The female labor force, however, more than doubled in the period from 1970 to 1979 (Brundenius 1984). In the 1970s, nearly two-thirds of women workers were absorbed into the service sector (e.g., education and health). While private employment of domestic servants in the home was prohibited, women continued to work as servants in institutions such as hotels, schools, and hospitals. In 1975, women comprised 65 percent of workers in education, 62 percent in public health and welfare, 48 percent in administration, and 78 percent in the garment industry. Further, there was and continues to be a conspicuous lack of women in leadership and supervisory positions, even in areas where women workers are the majority. For example, in 1975 women constituted 78 percent of the work force but only 52 percent of the leadership in establishments producing ready-made articles (FMC 1975).

As a result of women's concentration in the service sector, their wages, on average, are lower than are men's. For example, in 1979 the lowest paid workers in Cuba were women who held cleaning jobs, for which they were paid approximately 75 pesos a month, and women who worked in day-care centers, earning a monthly average of 98 pesos (in 1979, one Cuban peso was approximately equivalent to one U.S. dollar). By contrast, in this same year occupations which tended to be male-dominated were rewarded with significantly higher salaries: physicians received approximately 600 pesos a month, university professors 500, cement-plant workers 250, and longshoremen 140 (Mesa-Lago 1981). The average military wage is also 17 percent higher than the civilian wage. Despite such gender differentials in wages, there are a number of women professionals in Cuba. The FMC, for example, claims that in 1979 over 30 percent of all women employed in Cuba were technicians, professionals, or managers (FMC 1980a).[8] If we accept this claim, then the wage difference *among* working women in Cuba may be as great as 10.0 to 1.0 (a difference much higher than the often quoted national ratio of 3.5 to 1.0).

The position of relatively unskilled women in the Cuban economy is clearly precarious. According to Espin (1980:21), "regretfully, we must admit that even graduates from polytechnical schools have difficulty finding jobs; sometimes because the necessary conditions do not exist at a given place for women to work there; at other times because of the negative influence of prejudices that still crop up in the use of unfair procedures that impede the incorporation of women." Because employment of all men is guaranteed in a society with a shortage of jobs, women are hired only as needed. Thus, although women's participation in the labor force has increased, this trend is unlikely to continue because their employment depends on the "requirements of the economic development of the nation" (Espin 1980:20). For example, a repercussion of these "requirements" was the recent contraction of the service sector and, accordingly, a decrease in the jobs available to lower-class women. These limitations and uncertainties inherent in women's position in the labor market require them to continue to depend on marriage and family for their economic security, thereby perpetuating the Cuban patriarchy.

As with many nations, a significant portion of capital that could have been spent on the development of social services in Cuba has been allocated to national defense. The emphasis on military expenditure is understandable. While Cuba is a small country, it is the first self-proclaimed communist society in the Western hemisphere. Consequently, because it is located only ninety miles from the Florida coast, it is a major political threat to the United States. From Castro's perspective, the need for Cuba to protect itself against American invasion has always been a chief concern. With the 1962 Bay of Pigs invasion (when Cuban exiles attempted to invade Cuba with President John F. Kennedy's support), and the United States attempts in the 1980s to destabilize Caribbean and Latin American political structures, Cuba has prepared to defend itself. This focus on militarization, however, strongly reinforces gender stereotypes and creates a climate in which women's issues are unlikely to be raised.

A View from Below: Factory Women's Perceptions

Institutional analyses of women in contemporary Cuba have seldom compared women's perceptions of their lives to the conditions in which they live. This last link is based on three assumptions. First, it is assumed that women's educational, occupational, and political experiences reflect egalitarian state policies; second, it is assumed that women perceive these policies to be beneficial; and third, it is assumed that Cuban women constitute a homogeneous category. This section discusses how women factory workers view their lives, highlights the differences between them and professional women, and supports my contention that at least two different women's interest groups exist in Cuban society, as well as in many developing countries.

The interview data summarized here were collected in 1984 from 61 women textile workers in two factories near Havana.[9] One factory produces school uniforms for children and the other, military uniforms. Although managers and supervisors are predominantly men, the labor force in the factories is female: seamstresses who work at machines set up in rows in one or two large rooms. The semi-structured interview schedule included many questions about jobs, marriage, family, and socialist policies, but respondents were encouraged to speak freely following questions and probes.[10] The interviews illuminated the way women's educational and economic status shaped their experiences. Factory women's views of work, family, and women's liberation differed from "the view from the top" as revealed in FMC policies and publications, as discussed below.

Jobs

The women reported that work permeated their lives: paid work, housework, and "care" work (a term commonly used to describe the combination of labor and love that went into the care of husband, children, and relatives). While the women considered care work, followed by housework, their primary responsibility, the fact that they must organize this work around the time constraints of their paid jobs is a frequent source of dissatisfaction.

In the women's view, working for wages is a *family* responsibility; operating a sewing machine in a factory was neither interesting nor a community responsibility in their estimation. The money a woman earns is used for subsistence, but it was hoped that her pay, in combination with her husband's wages, would improve the family's standard of living. Thus, while women must work, they look to the day when they can work fewer hours or quit their jobs. Their paid labor was necessary but their families were more important. Jobs were temporary but the family was permanent.

While the women considered sewing jobs "easy work," in contrast to construction or cane-field work, more than one-third (36%) reported that they would probably be unable to continue in their jobs for more than five years. Their work environment, which included constant noise, monotonous routines, pressures to produce, long periods of sitting and bending over machines, and detailed work, exposed them to health hazards.

Undoubtedly, these physical and social aspects of their work influenced the women's view of their jobs. Yet they expressed conflicting ideas about housework and jobs. They did not see their jobs as an escape from the family, because the major reason they work is for the benefit of the family. Nor did they view the family as a haven from the work world. Both job and family constitute work worlds for these women who frequently expressed frustration over the time constraints posed by their two jobs. The belief that women should respond to family needs as they arise conflicted with their attempts to juggle their triple responsibilities of housework, care work, and paid work.

To rationalize such conflicts, the women adopted a world view that defined women's lives as lives of work. Women's work is done at different times, in different locations, and with different degrees of personal attachment, and home is as much a work place as is the factory. Only husbands and children are allowed to equate home with rest and retreat. When asked about leisure or "play," the women referred to their children's activities or their husband's visiting bars or meeting other men on the streets. Holidays were family times and, while enjoyable, necessarily involved hard work on the part of a woman who had to organize them.

Another way that women tried to make sense of their multiple responsibilities was to stress the way each job complemented, rather than contradicted, the other. They considered the varying social relations of their work lives to be interconnected, rather than encapsulated in different arenas (the official government position). Family work is highly valued and defended strongly, and factory work is work *for* the family, providing money for food, clothing, and household needs. Several women drew analogies between sewing work in the factory and housework. In each of their multiple jobs, women seek freedom from some other type of work. They are, however, realistic about the constraints of their lives, and do not romanticize their circumstances. While they dream of quitting their jobs, most could offer few examples of women who had been able to leave the factory and find economic security in the family.

Differences. Publications of the FMC emphasize that jobs are vehicles of upward mobility, promise financial independence, and provide opportunities for improved status and political recognition. Occupational liberation (in the view of the FMC) is equated with women's access to, and advancement in, previously male-dominated professions. The factory women, in contrast, did not see their paid work as promising promotion, mobility, or economic independence. In their view, liberation was tantamount to a release from wage labor.

Women's Liberation

The women were not interested in discussing politics, perhaps because they were either born after, or were very young at the time of, the Revolution. They thus have little memory of personal liberties, and are inured to a communist state which socialized them from childhood to hate capitalism. Youth are not exposed to, much less taught, critical thinking about political issues, and most of what the women see on television, hear on the radio, and read in the newspapers has been carefully chosen and edited by the government.[11] They therefore have learned the rules and penalties for communicating any public information considered helpful to "yankee imperialism."

Women's liberation, in contrast, sparked the women's interest, and they expressed strong and negative opinions about American feminism and contrasted women's liberation with their own ideas of gender. Women's equality was not their goal, even though the majority have more education, make a greater economic contribution to their families, and have more freedom to choose contraception and abortion, than did their mothers. The mildest critics viewed U.S.-style feminism as a waste of time, a questioning of the institution of marriage, relations between men and women, and the values of the family. More vociferous critics attacked the movement, while at the same time offering bitter, but resigned, reports of their husbands' extra-marital relations. They identified the United States women's movement with sexual liberation (as part of the general liberation of women), which they believed gave men license to have sex freely, thereby threatening the stability of marriage. Consequently, they objected to sexual freedom being taught to their children, either in the school or in the home.[12]

The women considered the Federation of Cuban Women (FMC) as one among a number of state organizations (e.g., trade unions and youth groups). In their view, the FMC is a benevolent, voluntary organization (social and educational) which does good and important work but which is marginal to their daily lives. All of the women were dues-paying members of the FMC, and several noted that it is impossible to get a job without a FMC membership card. Nevertheless, fewer than one-third attended FMC meetings, because they did not have the time, meetings were held after work when they had domestic obligations, and their husbands were unable to care for the children because they too had to attend meetings. In my view, however, the basic reason for the women's lack of attendance was their disinterest; women were more interested in meeting friends and discussing personal issues than in sitting in study groups discussing political issues.

More than one-half of the women felt pressured by people outside their circle of acquaintances to attend FMC meetings. In their view, they were more or less "guests" at these meetings, and they felt that well-educated women ran the organization. In response to the suggestion that if more women attended this problem might be obviated, they argued that this solution ignored the obstacles they faced in getting to meetings. They indicated that if they could set the agenda, it would focus on solutions to everyday problems that they and their families face: for example, conditions in the work place, insufficient and low-paying jobs, the dearth of low-cost day care centers, and lack of housing. They also emphasized that these problems concern men as well as women.

These women did not envy professional women, such as doctors, who they believed had neither personal nor family lives. They did not identify with such women because they felt that as factory workers they had no opportunity to move up the job ladder. They have always worked to help support the family, and they have seldom been able to move out of, or advance in, their current occupations. Moreover, they pointed out that the media's emphasis on women in non-traditional occupations implies that work as a sewing-machine operator is of lesser value. They also stressed that their idea of liberation means release from wage work and freedom to focus on the family. Toward that goal, they placed their hopes for improved jobs and wages for their *husbands* rather than for themselves.

According to the women, policies that emphasize jobs for women pose two threats to their position in the labor market. First, as uneducated women, they are concerned that if more educated women enter the labor force, job opportunities for themselves and/or their husbands may decrease. Second, the parallel idea of financial independence from husbands was disturbing to them because it meant the possibility of having to support their children and other family members alone. They were not comforted by the examples they have been shown of liberated Russian women doing heavy work as farm laborers, garbage collectors, bricklayers, and steel workers.

Any discussion of women's liberation and job equality exposed the women's fears of changing gender roles and their empathy with the problems that working-class men face. First, the women believed that they had more in common with blue-collar working men than they did with professional women, who they identified with the women's movement. They know the hardships that men in their families face, they have struggled with their husbands for better lives, and they realize that many men are restricted to jobs that require hard work with few rewards. Second, they feared that a women's movement could worsen, rather than improve, existing relations between women and men, by exacerbating traditional antagonisms between the sexes.[13]

Although they acknowledged these antagonisms, the women avoided the subject of conflict with men, expressing contradictory views of men which ranged from sympathy to suspicion. For example, a number of the women associated sexism with the problems that *men* face. Invoking the centrality of man's place in the Cuban family, they claimed that a man who makes little money is caught between the ideology of masculinity (*machismo*) and his frequent inability to live up to it. They then used this dilemma to explain such male problems as drinking, lack of job or family commitment, and sexual infidelity. Attempts to combat sexism in the name of women's liberation, they argued, would only make things worse between men and women. Thus, one of their solutions to men's *pecados* (sins) was to rely as much on families as on husbands.

The women frequently invoked stereotypical gender norms. They believe it is natural for men to be protectors/defenders and women to be caretakers/supporters, calling up the image of men as soldiers as evidence for this view. Certainly, persistent media attention to the threat of war in Cuba provides strong legitimation for traditional gender roles. In the context of their lives, however, the women expressed (often with humor) contrary images of men: they are helpless and need their attention; they are easily led astray to alcohol, gambling, and sex; and they have fragile egos.

Their suspicions about men's nature were revealed even more clearly during discussions about enforcing gender equality through legislation. For example, women pointed out that under the Family Code, a woman can divorce her husband if he does not help *equally* with the home and children, but she would then have to assume *total* responsibility for these duties. They feared, therefore, that divorce might reverse existing marital obligations. Currently, husbands are obligated to support their wives and children, but the women believed that the law could be used to obligate them to support husbands who are out of work or whose incomes are lower than their own. They consequently speculated that some husbands might never go to work. Believing that gender equality would eliminate their current rights, the women endorsed protective legislation. Further, they rejected the suggestion that housework and child care might be collectivized because men might then feel they had no obligation to marry.

Differences. Those who speak and write for the FMC on the subject of women's liberation frequently assume that all women are potentially like themselves, and they emphasize the opportunities available to all women in Cuba. Their goals, which are reflected in FMC policy, are to free women from economic dependence on the family and ensure them positions equal to men in the economy and polity. The factory women, in contrast, did not believe the movement represented them or their goals and priorities. They were concerned about changes in the organization of the family, not because they are opposed to women's rights, but because they feared men might be irresponsible in the absence of external restraints that control their behavior.

Family

The suggestion that many feminists believe the family is the locus of women's oppression, prompted the women to respond that such a belief confirmed their negative opinion of the women's movement. It was clear that their definition of the family diverged significantly from the white, middle-class ideal of the nuclear family in which the marital relationship is central.[14]

In the women's view, the family is made up of a large network of kin, male and female, who support and help each other even if they are geographically scattered. While brothers, uncles, aunts, cousins, nephews, nieces, and grandparents are all considered part of the close family, the tie between the mother and daughter is the strongest, followed by that between sisters.[15]

Women are the glue in this network. They communicate with each other about individual problems or crises, attempt to devise solutions, and delegate responsibilities to other family members for providing support and practical assistance. While women do most of the networking, they insist that men are the center of family activities, indicating that men's centrality is self-evident in terms of their importance in the family.

The family is integral to the women's value system, and is the major source of their identity, aspirations, help in times of need, and their reason for living. They believe family work or care work humanizes their labor, and is a form of human activity that expresses love and affirms their identity as women. The women stressed, however, that the family is not necessarily conflict free, but they were reluctant to discuss the personal costs of reciprocity in the extended family. What little they did say, suggested that they believe these costs are natural, a necessary and expected part of life.

Another, but equally important, subject for the women was their children. The interviews showed that children give women their primary sense of control over their lives. They viewed mothering as a special type of care work, which was consistently affirmed by children, husbands, families, and the State. While they seldom verbalized high expectations for themselves, they were emphatic that they wanted better futures for their children, and they praised educational reforms that make it possible for children to achieve professional careers. They questioned Cuba's educational meritocracy, and spoke to ways of motivating children to try harder and study more. Acutely aware of the competition among students, they frequently wished that fathers would pressure children to excel.

The women did not romanticize motherhood. Several acknowledged that it was difficult to be a very good mother (such as the model mother in magazines) when they return home from work exhausted. Their competitiveness, however, was apparent when they evaluated each other's child-rearing skills, by sharing and comparing success stories. The majority of the women valued families with large numbers of children, but they know maintaining such groups requires a great deal of money. They thus were critical of women who had more children than they could care for. Given their comments about economic obligations and the importance of males in the family, we expected the women to prefer investing in their sons', rather than their daughters', educations. This was not the case, however; they frequently encouraged their daughters to be ambitious. But at the same time, they encouraged them to develop feminine qualities that would make them marriageable.

Differences. The FMC leaders focus on gender equality in *marriage* rather than on the responsibilities of care work in the family. This position is reflected in the Family Code, which is directed at marital relations and the nuclear family. The factory women, in contrast, defined family in terms of kinship and networks of support, emphasizing the influence of women in families, and the rewards--tangible support and personal fulfillment--that derive from extended families.

The issues raised by the factory women extend beyond the Cuban context, and highlight the dangers of homogenizing women. The intersection of gender with class, race, ethnicity, and nationality shapes women's lives in very different ways, and is implicated in their interests and goals.[16] Moreover, assumptions about the relationship between women and the *family* must be further specified to obtain an accurate picture of social reality.

Many women who experience multiple disadvantages by virtue of their race, class, nationality and gender find members of their social networks to be their major source of strength for resisting subordination--who may provide them their *only* source of power (however unequal to men's) to cope with a variety of male-dominated systems (Kibria 1990). Feminists (whether in Cuba's FMC or the United States NOW) must be sensitive to what could be interpreted as "anti-family" tactics. For example, the factory women viewed proposed changes in gender relations (outlined in the Family Code) as serious threats to their economic and social survival. In sum, "feminism needs to offer women more than the abolition of the only place in society which is theirs" (Ramazanoglu 1989:183).

Discussion and Conclusions

Cuba has not yet instituted the kinds of structural changes that would facilitate women's liberation without threatening the family. At the same time, significant barriers prevent Cuban women from achieving equality with men.   These barriers include the country's economic situation, the organization of the FMC, and Cuba's traditional gender ideology.

Economic situations which called for maximum productivity made the revolutionary goal of radical change in class and job equality obsolete. Resources were targeted for military and industrial development, leading to increased budget cuts and rationing of food, gasoline, electricity, and other necessities (Whitefield 1990).   The service sector, which offers women employment opportunities and domestic assistance, is allocated a small proportion of the Cuban national budget, thereby contributing to women's inequality in the economy and perpetuating the patriarchal family.   Women with few alternatives in the selection of jobs or marriage (those with limited job skills) are hit the hardest.

The economic situation in Cuba is moving in directions antithetical to women's equality, and the dedication to a socialist ideology (equality of all people) is being severely undermined.   Castro is trying to improve the economy by revitalizing Cuba's image as a sophisticated playground of the Caribbean.   Cuba is now acclaimed to have more gambling casinos than Las Vegas, and foreign investors (primarily from Spain) own a majority of the beach hotels; these are off limits to the Cuban people, a sacrifice Castro asks them to make in exchange for the promise of better times.   Scarcities are increasing with rationing and all food is strictly allocated; a gas station is wryly defined as a place to get air for bicycle tires.   Cubans, however, are beginning to express their dismay.   Whitefield (1990) quotes a twenty-four-year old former tour guide who said, "Those who are integrated in the revolution and in the party are fine . . . They get better jobs and privileges . . . I just don't want to put up with all the [Communist] party stuff . . . I want to lead my own life and not go to all the meetings."

In 1991, more than 1,000 Cubans (mostly young men) risked death to flee by raft from Cuba to Florida, and increasing numbers of support groups have been organized by mothers grieving for their children lost at sea (Tallahassee Democrat 1991b).   Powerful Cuban-Americans have announced the formation of a blue-ribbon commission to develop a plan for the peaceful replacement of Fidel Castro, and for Cuba's rapid transition to democracy and a free-market system (Tallahassee Democrat 1991a).   A split from Russia also appears imminent with the recent dissolution of the Soviet Union and its movement toward democratization and privatization.[17]

A turn toward capitalism, however, does not bode well for women.   The rejection of Communist ideology in the early 1990s by former socialist states was accompanied by a renunciation of gender equality.   Commenting on the basis of her attendance at the World Institute for Development Economics Research meetings in Helsinki, Risman (1991:13) wrote:

The goal of women's equality is seen as one more mistaken communist notion. . . . This provides an ideological rationalization for saving money on the 'creches' (day care centers) which are now being closed in East Germany, Romania, and the Soviet Union. Women's unemployment is considered 'easy' unemployment to accept because women's primary attachments are/should be in the home.

The definition of women's roles by the government, rather than by women, and the absence of an autonomous women's organization, limited the emergence of a feminist consciousness among Cuban women.[18] Women's subordination is obscured by the FMC's stress on the legalized opportunities available to women and by public endorsement of women who have advanced in previously male-dominated professions. There are at least two categories of women workers: technically-skilled and professional women who are actively involved in the FMC and believe that they have already been emancipated; and less-skilled and less-educated women, who are bound to the family, and believe that there is no need for women's liberation.

The power of *machismo* is deeply ingrained in Cuban culture and remains an unquestioned source of women's subordination. Both professional and working-class women believe that Castro and other government leaders sincerely have "women's best interest at heart." Yet, even when Cuban men are concerned, they do not (and perhaps cannot) understand women's situation and the gender division of labor. One reason is that Cuba failed to redefine *men's* roles when women's roles were redefined. While the Family Code prescribes men's acceptance of equal responsibility for housework and child care, it provides no incentives for it.

There are no paternity leaves or "shopping bag plans" for husbands and fathers and no communist awards for husbands whose wives take jobs. There are no educational campaigns to train boys in housework or child care nor any inducements to lead them into traditionally female occupations. The media continue to accentuate male-female differences along customary lines. Given persistent Cuban ideologies of romantic love, selfless motherhood, and male-headed families--all camouflages for the exploitation of women's labor-- the move toward capitalism (and its correlates of individual competition, [consumerism], and class-structured privatization) ensures the continued subordination of women. Moreover, the homophobia inherent in *machismo* precludes men from being willing to do women's tasks or to enter such women's occupations as child care or nursing.[19]

There may be so many economic and ideological obstacles to changing *men's* attitudes and behaviors in Cuba that it may be politically impractical. The Cuban case offers a number of lessons for other developing countries. Periods of rapid change under a popular leader (such as immediately after the revolution in Cuba) are the most auspicious times for pursuing gender equality and the deconstruction of the patriarchal family system. We can only speculate that this did not occur in early post-revolutionary Cuba because it was considered more politically expedient to reward men as revolutionary heroes than to threaten them with changes in the existing gender order (Sokoloff 1981); most of these men would have been hostile to losing control over women at the end of a revolution that promised to *improve* each individual's condition. Men's position relative to women is ideologically a natural right, and men expected their position to be strengthened rather than weakened. Moreover, many men who had lived in relative poverty prior to the revolution would have felt deprived had they been denied the right to take care of a wife and family with dignity.

The Cuban Family Code thus can be interpreted as a product of the ideological and economic exigencies of post-revolutionary Cuba. By guaranteeing women and children the economic support necessary for survival, the law binds husbands to their family responsibilities, thereby assuring their support during recessions when jobs are insufficient and women are sent back to the home. Women's economic dependency, in short, is solidified and the patriarchal family is sustained.

To conclude, women's equality is a complex issue. The process of achieving equality involves changes in institutions that are essential to social order in both socialist and capitalist societies. Calls for change are often framed by a false dichotomy in which either the government *or* women take responsibility (and the blame if unsuccessful).

Change cannot, however, simply come from the top down, as the findings for Cuba show. Cuba, more than many other societies, has implemented policies that reveal the enormous economic and social costs of women's care work. The persistence of the traditional family is not primarily the fault of the State. On the contrary, the State has devised policies, such as for education, employment for women, free abortion, birth control, and day care, that are potentially threatening to gendered family roles. Nevertheless, subordination by gender persists, while subordination by race apparently does not. The question for feminists is why it is possible for a socialist regime to change race relations, but not gender relations? I would argue that in Cuba, the answer can be found in its economic dependence on existing gender arrangements and the traditional family (see also, Antrobus 1989:192, on the "super-exploitation" of women).

Change also cannot occur simply from the bottom up. Women are not a homogeneous group, and even if unity among them were possible, they lack adequate material resources and political power to create societal change. Women's liberation calls for *both* state policies and an autonomous women's movement. Regardless of economic and political exigencies, it is necessary to translate "women's work" to "people's work" in every institution. Making women's equality a separate and distinct priority would be a more revolutionary goal than any yet conceived by societal leaders.

Notes

I thank Alfred Pedula and Lois Smith (Department of History, University of South Maine) for their generous encouragement of my research on Cuban women and their helpful comments on earlier drafts of this chapter.

1.   The views of factory workers regarding women's position were obtained during interviews conducted for a research project directed by the author in 1984. In the course of the research I also talked with numerous professional women associated with the FMC, and I collected a variety of their official publications. The views of professional women are a product of these conversations and publications.

2.   For historical accounts of women's employment in Cuba, see Cole (1980), Murray (1979), Purcell (1973), Randall (1974), Rowbotham (1974), and Sutherland (1969).

3.   The agenda of the 1984 Fourth Congress of the FMC focused, as in the past, on problems such as keeping day-care centers and schools open on Saturdays (a work day) and on the rule that only women relatives can provide 24-hour care to a hospitalized person (Bengelsdorf 1985).   In essence, children and health care continue to be women's responsibilities.

4.   According to Cuban economists, "for every three women who joined the work force, a fourth must be employed in institutions supplying supportive services" (Nazzari 1983:257).

5.   Cuba maintains adult education schools in which workers can enroll in various programs that range from technical to academic. Thus, although further education is possible, it is difficult to combine with full-time employment (Pedula and Smith 1985).

6.   Cuba's problems, outlined in a special issue of [*Journal of*] *World Development* in 1987, include the following: in 1985, 42 percent of Cuba's hard currency earnings came from the re-exportation of Soviet petroleum. The extreme drop in world oil prices cost Cuba over $200 million per year in lost earnings. In addition, the reduced 1986 sugar harvest, damaged by Hurricane Kate, caused the level of sugar prices to fall. The 1986-1990 trade and aid agreement between the Soviet Union and Cuba increased the direct aid package to Cuba by approximately US$3 billion, a fifty percent increase over the previous five-year period (Zimbalist 1987).

7.   While the quality of day care in Cuba is excellent, the number of day-care centers is insufficient (Kleiner 1974). In 1980, there were only 832 day-care centers caring for about eight percent of children age six or under. Though initially free, in 1970 the government started charging US$25 a month per child for day-care services (Pedula and Smith 1985).

8.   It is difficult to obtain data on the number of Cuban women who are "professionals," because in the Cuban census the occupational category for women includes both "professionals and technicians." This category is

defined as workers "involved at high and medium level in all spheres of science, technology, education, research, medicine, culture and art" (Catasus et al. 1988:120). Applying this definition in their 1982 survey of Cuban women, Catasus et al. (demographers at the University of Havana) report that 47.2 percent of employed women sampled in the Havana province were "professionals and technicians"; 38 percent were "office and service workers"; and around 10 percent were factory and other "non-agricultural workers."

9.   The researchers were interested in current (not retrospective) family dynamics and therefore sampled women who were currently married (not necessarily to first spouse), living with their husbands, with at least one child in each household. Of the approximately 400 women employees in the two factories, around 40 percent were currently married, 30 percent divorced, 20 percent single, and 10 percent in consensual unions. In comparison, the 1982 sample of women in the province of Havana by Castasus et al. (1988) found the following distribution of conjugal status: 46.2 percent married, 19.4 percent divorced, 23.6 percent single, 7.9 percent consensual union, and 2.9 percent widowed.

The sample was a systematic random selection from lists provided by the factories. Of the 80 women identified, 61 could be located and agreed to be interviewed in their homes. The length of these interviews averaged between one and one-half to two hours. The age range of the sample was 25 to 42 years, their average educational level was less than high school, and their monthly salary range was 86 to 120 pesos.

10.   An English translation of the interview schedule is available from the author on request. The woman interviewer informed each subject that this study on the life experiences and attitudes of factory working women would be used to provide social scientists in the United States with information to understand the lives of average women in Cuba today. The interviewer emphasized that the subjects' answers would be anonymous and that the confidential nature of their answers would be respected. This explanation included several reassurances that no one in their place of work would have access to their answers.

11.   The broadcasts by Radio Marti have circumvented government censorship. Jorge Mas Canosa, Cuban exile living in Miami and chair of the Cuban American National Foundation, is the driving force behind U.S.-supported Radio Marti and TV Marti.

12.   In 1977, The National Working Group on Sex Education (GNTES) was founded as part of the National Assembly of the People's Power Permanent Commission on Children. The GNTES was charged with setting national sex education priorities and developing corresponding programs. It is not clear whether or when GNTES-designed curricula entered school programs, but it appears obvious from Cuban publications that parents, teachers, and health officials disagreed with GNTES about what should be taught about sexuality and in what grades.   One consequence of this

disagreement is that many Cuban teenagers today "remain ignorant of the most basic reproductive knowledge" (Smith 1988:6).

13. The Cuban government and The Federation of Cuban Women (FMC) constantly propagandize (in glowing terms) the post-revolutionary, companionable, conjugal family. However understated in the media, the interviews raised questions about the ideology of marital happiness and stability. Castasus et al. (1988) also report that "more than 25 percent of the women interviewed, irrespective of educational level, had been married or entered into a consensual union two or more times" (1988:79). They also present statistics showing that, in Havana province, one out of every five women is divorced or separated (1988:40). According to Evenson's (1986:313) statistics, the divorce rate in Cuba, now over 30 percent, has tripled since the Revolution.

14. The prevailing impression from the women interviewed is that marital quality is relatively less important than family cohesiveness, and the women appear to have quite limited expectations of their husbands. The official survey by Catasus et al. (1988) includes some data on marital problems that support my research. According to their study, the most frequently mentioned marital problems in the Havana and Buenavista provinces were the husband's failure to take part in child care and housework (over 70 percent of the women reported such problems). In rural Yateras, the husband's infidelity was the most reported difficulty by women (50 percent), followed by lack of help with housework (40 percent) and husbands' frequent drinking (26 percent). Women also reported experiencing problems with the household division of labor, and a majority in all three provinces reported that most of the burden of household work was theirs alone (82 percent in Havana and 96 percent in Yateras). Certainly this is not a picture of the ideal, egalitarian, socialist family.

15. The "family" can also include godparents and close friends.

16. My research focused primarily on women who live and work near the large city of Havana. For an insightful account of women's struggles for equality in rural Cuba, see Stubbs (1987). Stubbs interviewed women in two rich tobacco-growing provinces: Pinar del Rio (western Cuba) and Sancti Spiritus (central Cuba). Traditionally, tobacco was a small-farm crop produced by a large, unpaid family labor force, and peasant women did the bulk of unpaid labor. Women gained greater equality with the introduction of CPAs (agricultural production cooperatives) in the late 1970s. The CPAs are farmed and managed collectively and their profits are roughly divided into three shares: the State, maintenance and future production needs, and to *individual* members (women as well as men) proportionate to their labor contribution. Because the well being of the cooperative depends directly on collective economic success, women's participation is recognized *explicitly* as integral and important.

17. As I finish this chapter (in late April 1992) dire predictions for Cuba's economic and political future are appearing in the news (see Tamayo 1992). Cuba's future may well center on the continuing United States trade boycott. Exiled Cuban leaders (who claim United States patronage) support the boycott, arguing that it may foment a revolt against Castro's presidency. Diaz (in Tamayo 1992), a disillusioned ex-Castro supporter now living in Berlin, however, warns that only if the United States government lifts the boycott is there a possibility of a peaceful resolution for Cuba because Castro is unlikely to make concessions and reconcile with the exiles.

18. At the Third Conference of the Women's Continental Front Against Intervention, held in Havana in October 1988, Vilma Espin defined the FMC as "an autonomous organization, separate from the Cuban government, but [which] works closely with the government to improve conditions for women" (Ross 1989:10). The continuing struggle in Nicaragua for an autonomous women's association is analogous to the competing priorities of Cuban women. The state coalition worries that feminism will weaken the Nicaraguan family, and women activists argue for autonomy (Light, 1991).

19. A number of Cubans, including Castro, joked publicly about shipping their "perverts" to America in the 1980 "Mariel exodus" (when Castro allowed over 125,000 Cubans to board boats for Florida from the port of Mariel).

References

Antrobus, Peggy
    1989 The Empowerment of Women. In: *The Women and International Development Annual*, Volume I, edited by Rita S. Gallin, Marilyn Aronoff, and Anne Ferguson. Pp. 189-208. Boulder: Westview Press.

Bengelsdorf, Carollee and Alice Hageman
    1979 Emerging from Underdevelopment: Women and Work in Cuba. In: *Capitalist Patriarchy and the Case for Socialist Feminism*, edited by Zillah R. Eisenstein. Pp. 271-295. New York: Monthly Review Press.

Brundenius, Claes
    1984 *Revolutionary Cuba: The Challenge of Economic Growth with Equity*. Boulder: Westview Press.

Castro, Fidel
    1980 Central Report. *Boletin FMC*. Havana: News Bulletin Published by the Federation of Cuban Women.

Catasus, S., A. Farnos, F. Gonzalez, R. Groove, R. Hernandez, and B. Morejon
   1988   *Cuban Women: Changing Roles and Population Trends*. Geneva: International Labour Organization.

Cole, Johnnetta B.
   1980   Women in Cuba: The Revolution Within the Revolution. In: *Comparative Perspectives of Third World Women*, edited by Beverly Lindsay. Pp. 162-178. New York: Praeger.

Eisenstein, Zillah (ed.)
   1979   *Capitalist Patriarchy and the Case for Socialist Feminist Revolution*. New York: Monthly Review Press.

Espin, Vilma
   1980   Central Report. *Boletin FMC*. Havana: News Bulletin Published by The Federation of Cuban Women.

Fagen, Richard R.
   1968   *Cubans in Exile: Disaffection and the Revolution*. Stanford: University of California Press.

Federation of Cuban Women (FMC)
   1975   *Second Congress Cuban Women's Federation*. Havana: Editorial Orbe.

   1980a *Boletin FMC*. Havana: Federation of Cuban Women.

   1980b *Cuban Women 1975-1979*. Havana: Editorial Orbe.

Fitzgerald, Frank T.
   1978   A Critique of the "Sovietization of Cuba" Thesis. *Science and Society* XLLL (Spring):1-32.

Gallin, Rita S., Marilyn Aronoff, and Anne Ferguson (eds.)
   1989   Introduction. In: *The Women and International Development Annual*, Volume I. Pp. 1-22. Boulder: Westview Press.

Hartman, Heidi
   1979   The Unhappy Marriage of Marxism and Feminism. *Capital and Class* 8(Summer):1-33.

Huberman, Leo and Paul Sweezy
   1970   *Socialism in Cuba*. New York: Monthly Review Press.

Jolly, Richard
  1964   Education. In: *Cuba: The Economic and Social Revolution*, edited by Dudley Sears. Pp. 32-51. Chapel Hill: University of North Carolina Press.

Kibria, Nazl
  1990   Power, Patriarchy, and Gender Conflict in the Vietnamese Immigrant Community. *Gender & Society* 4:9-24.

King, Marjorie
  1977   Cuba's Attach on Women's Second Shift 1974-1976. *Latin American Perspectives* 4:106-119.

Kuhn, Annette and Ann-Marie Wolpe (eds.)
  1978   *Feminism and Materialism*. London: Routledge and Kegan Paul.

Larguis, I. and J. Dumoulin
  1971   Towards a Science of Women's Liberation. *Casa de las Americas* (March-June), La Habana, Cuba. Reprinted in English as *Red Rag* Pamphlet No. 1.

Leiner, Marvin
  1974   *Children are the Revolution: Day Care in Cuba*. New York: Penguin.

Light, Julie
  1991   Nicaragua: Autonomous Feminism. *Ms. Magazine* 2(1):17.

Madrigal, Stasia
  1974   The Feminists of Cuba. *Off Our Backs*. May:7-11.

Marieskind, H.I.
  1980   Protective Legislation. In: *Women in the Health System*, edited by Inter-American Commission of Women. Pp. 173-176. St. Louis: C.V. Mosby.

Mesa-Lago, Carmelo
  1981   *The Economy of Socialist Cuba: A Two Decade Appraisal*. Albuquerque: University of New Mexico Press.

Mills, C. Wright
  1960   *Listen Yankee: The Revolution in Cuba*. New York: Ballantine.

Molyneux, Maxine
   1981   Socialist Societies Old and New: Progress Towards Women's
          Emancipation. *Feminist Review* (Summer):1-34.

Murray, Nicola
   1979   Socialism and Feminism: Women and the Cuban Revolution.
          Feminist Review 3:99-108.

Nazzari, Muriel
   1983   The "Women Question" in Cuba: An Analysis of Material
          Constraints on its Solution. *Signs* 9:246-263.

Nelson, Lowry
   1950   *Rural Cuba*. Minneapolis: University of Minnesota Press.

Pedula, Alfred and Lois M. Smith
   1985   Women in Socialist Cuba, 1959-1984. In: *Cuba: Twenty-Five Years
          of Revolution, 1959-1984*, edited by Sandor Halebsky and John M.
          Kirk. Pp. 79-92. New York: Praeger.

Purcell, Susan Kaufman
   1973   Modernizing Women for a Modern Society: The Cuban Case. In:
          Female and Male in Latin America, edited by Ann Pescatello. Pp.
          181-195. Pittsburgh: University of Pittsburgh Press.

Ramazanoglu, Caroline
   1989   *Feminism and the Contradictions of Oppression*.   New York:
          Routledge.

Randall, Margaret
   1974   *Cuban Women Now*. Toronto: The Women's Press.

   1981   *Cuban Women Twenty Years Later*. New York: Smyrna Press.

Risman, Barbara J.
   1991   Gender and Perestroika. *SWS Network News* 8:3,13.

Ritter, Archibald R.M.
   1974   *The Economic Development of Revolutionary Cuba*. New York:
          Praeger.

Ross, Loretta
1989   Bridging a Short Gap to the Caribbean. *National NOW Times* (January):10.

Rowbotham, Sheila
1974   *Women, Resistance and Revolution: A History of Women and Evolution in the Modern World*. New York: Vintage.

Sen, G. and C. Grown
1987   *Development, Crises, and Alternative Visions: Third World Women's Perspectives*. New York: Monthly Review Press.

Smith, Lois M.
1988   Teenage Pregnancy and Sex Education in Cuba. Paper presented at the Latin American Studies Association Congress, New Orleans, March 17-19.

Sokoloff, Natalie
1981   Cuban Women: Strengths and Weaknesses of the Cuban Revolution for Women. Paper presented at the American Political Science Association annual meeting. New York City, September 1981.

Stubbs, Jean
1987   Gender Issues in Contemporary Cuban Tobacco Farming. *World Development* 15(1):41-65.

Sutherland, Elizabeth
1969   *The Youngest Revolution*. New York: Dial Press.

Tallahassee Democrat
1991a   Exiles Say Cuban Leaders Plan for Post-Castro Era. Tallahassee, FL, May 18, 1991.

1991b   Rafters Risk Death, Jail Time by Fleeing Cuba. Tallahassee, FL, June 16, 1991.

Tinker, Irene and Jane Jaquette
1987   UN Decade for Women: Its Impact and Legacy. *World Development* 15(3):419-427.

Whitefield, Mimi
1990   In Havana, Moods are Darkening. *Miami Herald*, December 7, 1990.

Zimbalist, Andrew
   1987   Editor's Introduction: Cuba's Socialist Economy Toward the 1990s.
           World Development 15(1):1-4.

6

Women and Industrialization in the Caribbean: A Comparison of Puerto Rican and Dominican Women Workers

Helen I. Safa

Export-led development strategies have become increasingly popular in Latin America and the Caribbean in the past decade, especially in the manufacturing sector. Although the Border Industrialization Program in Mexico is the best known and most important in terms of exports to the United States, other countries, sometimes spurred by the neo-liberal policies of the International Monetary Fund, have also turned to export as a way of earning foreign currency and alleviating the current debt crisis.

In the smaller countries of Central America and the Caribbean, exports have long been the primary development strategy, ever since their incorporation into the world economy in colonial times. Starting in the 1960s, however, in addition to traditional agricultural exports such as sugar, coffee and bananas, there was an increase in manufacturing, following the "industrialization by invitation" strategy initiated by Puerto Rico a decade earlier. Import substitution industrialization, which was designed in the postwar period to stimulate domestic industry in the rest of Latin America, never achieved great success in the Caribbean, due to the lack of capital and technology in these countries (even more acute than in the larger countries). The small size of these countries, combined with their low purchasing power, also limited the possibilities of developing a viable internal market, which is critical for import substitution. To gain access to foreign markets, capital, and technology, Caribbean countries are forced to sell through multinational corporations.

In recent years, spurred by the debt crisis and growing unemployment, the competition among Latin American and Caribbean countries for foreign investment in export manufacturing has been intense. Governments attempt to encourage foreign investment by lifting trade barriers and by offering tax holidays, subsidized credit, export subsidies, and freedom from import duties on raw materials and machinery needed for production. Most countries also allow unrestricted profit repatriation. Special export processing zones are constructed at public expense for export manufacturing plants, complete with water, electricity, and roads. Thus the state has played a major role in fostering export manufacturing, often aided by the United States Agency for International Development, which has recently made this a key development strategy throughout Latin America (Joekes with Moayedi 1987:5).

United States government support for export manufacturing is reflected in items 806.30 and 807 of the United States Tariff Codes, introduced in the early sixties to reduce duties on imports with U.S. components assembled or processed abroad. These items aided the competitive position of American industry by limiting United States tariffs to the "value added" upon goods assembled abroad, thus substantially reducing labor costs. Item 807 in particular provided the basis for the *maquiladora* plants under the Mexican Border Industrialization Program, as well as stimulated the growth of assembly plants in the Caribbean, where manufacturing exports grew rapidly during the 1960s and 1970s (Deere et al. 1990:143-144).

The support by the United States government for export manufacturing was enhanced by the 1983 enactment of President Reagan's Caribbean Basin Initiative (CBI). The CBI enables qualified Caribbean Basin countries to acquire one-way duty-free access to United States markets for certain exports for a twelve-year period. This expands the market for export growth, and obviates the need to develop the internal market required under import substitution. The market for export manufacturing is entirely external, and therefore demands the maximum reduction of production costs, principally wages, in order to compete effectively on the international level. In fact, the availability of cheap labor appears to be the prime determining factor for investment; hence, most of the jobs generated through export manufacturing are for women, who previously represented a small percentage of the industrial labor force under import substitution.

Lim (1990:105) estimates that in the mid-1980s there were approximately 1.5 million women directly employed in export manufacturing in developing countries, between a third and a half of them in wholly or partly foreign-owned enterprises, including not only multinationals from the United States and other industrialized countries, but also firms from other newly industrializing countries such as South Korea or Hong Kong. Most of these women are employed in Asia, but an increasing percentage are in Latin America and the Caribbean.

This chapter examines the impact of paid employment in export manufacturing on the status of women in two Caribbean countries, Puerto Rico and the Dominican Republic.[1] Although it has never been publicly stated, Puerto Rico's Operation Bootstrap has served as a model for export-oriented industrial development under the CBI, as well as earlier strategies of "industrialization by invitation" (Pantojas-Garcia 1985). Thus, Puerto Rico can offer important lessons for the rest of the Caribbean on the limitations of this model. The Dominican Republic, on the other hand, is a classic case of recently initiated export manufacturing, with a total of 24 free trade zones in various regions of the country in March 1992. Employment in free trade zones almost quadrupled between 1985 and 1988, when it reached a total of 85,000 persons (Abreu et al. 1989:141), and by March 1992 it had risen to nearly 135,000 workers in a total of 385 firms (Consejo Nacional de Zonas Francas 1992). This sharp increase is directly attributable to currency devaluations mandated by the International Monetary Fund, which lowered the cost of labor and other expenses in the Dominican Republic to one of the lowest levels in the Caribbean. About three-fourths of these jobs are held by women, most of whom are still employed in the three original free trade zones created before 1980.

Export processing is an important source of foreign exchange for the Dominican Republic, and in 1987 generated US$97.1 million or 13.5 percent of total exports (Abreu et al. 1989:135-37). If it had not been for export processing, tourism, and the remittances of Dominican migrants in the United States and Puerto Rico, the Dominican economy would have collapsed entirely because of the deterioration in the balance of payments during the first half of the 1980s. Clearly export manufacturing is a key component of Dominican development strategy, and it now constitutes a principal source of women's industrial employment.

In this chapter, I focus on the garment industry, which has been the area of greatest growth in export manufacturing in the Caribbean. Between 1983 and 1986, textiles and apparel imports into the United States from the region grew by an average annual 28 percent, increasing to 39 percent in 1987, and accounting for approximately one-fourth of all imports (Deere et al. 1990:167). Although textiles and garments have been excluded from the CBI, due to opposition from United States labor, they continue to benefit from special import quotas assigned by the United States to certain Caribbean countries through the Guaranteed Access Levels program, sometimes referred to as 807A. Most of the growth in garment exports from the region is under item 807, however, with exports from the Dominican Republic, Haiti, and Jamaica increasing by more than 20 percent annually during the 1980s (Deere et al. 1990:167).

The Puerto Rican data were collected in a survey conducted in 1980 among 157 women workers in three branch plants of the same United States garment manufacturer, all of which were located in the western part of the island. While the interviews were done by a research assistant, I also interviewed plant managers and collected secondary information, and in 1986 followed up with in-depth interviews with a sub-sample of 15 women. For the Dominican Republic, I was fortunate to be able to utilize survey data collected by the Centro de Investigación para la Acción Femenina (CIPAF), a private Dominican women's research center, which in 1981 conducted a survey of 529 women workers in both domestic industries and in the three major export processing zones then operating in the country. In this chapter, I have analyzed only the data on the 231 women workers in export processing zones. In 1986, together with a research assistant, I conducted similar in-depth interviews with a sub-sample of 18 Dominican women, all working in the garment industry in La Romana, one of the largest and the oldest export processing zones, established in 1969 by Gulf and Western, a principal sugar producer in the Dominican Republic. This chapter focuses largely on the results of the sample survey, but the insights gained from the in-depth interviews enabled me to go beyond the survey data and obtain a better understanding of the impact of paid employment on the lives of these women workers, as I outline below.

Gender Subordination and Industrialization

There is now an intense debate in policy as well as academic circles regarding the benefits of export manufacturing for women workers (Tiano 1986). Some argue (e.g., Rosen 1982; Lim 1990) that export manufacturing "integrates women into development" by providing them with badly needed jobs, while others (e.g., Fernández Kelly 1983; Ong 1987; Ward 1990) maintain that this form of industrialization only intensifies women's exploitation because the jobs are unskilled, poorly paid, and offer no possibility of upward mobility. In reality, these positions are not mutually exclusive, because women, like members of other marginal groups, may be integrated into exploitative jobs. Thus, I wish to go beyond this debate and explain what permits women to be taken advantage of as a cheap and vulnerable labor force. The essential question then becomes: What makes women more vulnerable as workers than men? Why have they become the preferred labor force for export manufacturing?

Clearly there are historical precedents for the use of women in labor-intensive industries such as export manufacturing. Historical studies show that women have always constituted a source of cheap labor for industrial capitalism, since the early days of the Industrial Revolution in England, France, and other western European countries (Tilly and Scott 1978). In the United States as well, there was a constant search for cheap labor, with industries moving from the employment of the daughters of farm families, to immigrant women, to overseas production through export manufacturing as the cost of domestic labor became too high (Safa 1981). But what made women cheaper to employ than men?

The answer lies in the sexual division of labor brought about by industrial capitalism. With the movement of production outside the home into the factory, the family ceased to function as a productive unit and became dependent on wages earned outside the home. Although production became increasingly public, reproduction remained within the private sphere of the family, though many reproductive functions such as education were also taken over by the larger society. Men became the primary breadwinners and women, because of their child-rearing responsibilities, were relegated largely to the domestic sphere. In this way, the new sexual division of labor forced most women to become dependent on men as wage earners, and the family lost much of its economic autonomy.

Marxist feminists have emphasized that the separation of women's productive and reproductive roles resulting from industrial capitalism is a primary source of women's subordination. Paid employment is seen as one way of breaking down women's isolation and dependence on men; it is expected to give women greater economic autonomy, to increase their authority in the household, and to develop their class consciousness as workers. There are many obstacles to achieving such goals, however, including the segregation of women into poorly paid, unstable jobs (such as export manufacturing), their double burden of paid employment and domestic labor, and a gender ideology that continues to portray women as "supplementary" workers even when they are fully employed (Hartman 1981).

In short, women's dual productive/reproductive role weakens the effects of paid employment on their status. Women are a more vulnerable labor force than men because they are still primarily defined in terms of their domestic role, and therefore not given full legitimacy as workers. This has led feminist scholars like Barrett (1980:211) to argue that the family is "the central site of the oppression of women." According to Barrett, gender ideology is formed principally within the family through a woman's dependence on a male wage and is reflected at other levels of society such as the workplace and the state.

I argue, however, that there are various levels of women's subordination-- within the family, within the workplace, and within the state--and that these different levels need to be kept analytically separate. It is true that the social construction of gender takes place largely within the family and is reflected at other levels of society. However, this does not eliminate the labor market or the state as independent sources of women's subordination, as I will show. In short, I do not dismiss the family as a source of women's oppression, but I think its importance needs to be examined in relationship to these other two areas.

The data also demonstrate that paid employment has an impact on gender ideology, which is neither as static nor uniform as Barrett depicts. Her model of a nuclear family with a principal male wage earner and dependent housewife does not apply to the sample of Puerto Rican and Dominican households studied here, where women are making a major contribution to the household economy. As we shall see, their economic contribution has had a major impact on gender ideology in the family, but it has not affected women's status as subsidiary workers in the workplace and in the eyes of the state. In the following pages, I examine the status of Puerto Rican and Dominican women workers in the workplace, at home, and at the level of the national state.

Wages and Working Conditions

Between 1970 and 1980, the female industrial labor force in developing countries increased by 56 percent (ILO 1985:7), and this trend continued in the 1980s, particularly in countries with large export processing zones. Standing (1989) attributes this increase in female employment to the growth of export-led industrialization, labor market deregulation, and the search for cheap labor, all of which were intensified by greater international competition and the debt crisis which many countries faced in the 1980s.

The ILO (1985:39) reports that wages for women workers in multinational industrial enterprises in developing countries typically range from a minimum of five to 25 percent of wages paid for similar jobs to workers in their Western industrialized home countries. These wages are usually at or above the legal minimum wage, and are higher than women's wages in domestic industries and alternative low-skill occupations, such as farming, domestic service, and most service-sector jobs. Still, these wages are 25 to 50 percent lower than those of comparable male workers, and are usually not sufficient to support a family (ILO 1985:42-43).

Low wages in export manufacturing reflect the common misconception that women's wages are only a supplement to the family income and therefore need not be adequate to support their dependents. This tends to confirm Barrett's argument that men are seen as primary wage earners, which legitimates the payment of lower wages to women. It is reinforced by the fact that most women workers in export manufacturing worldwide are young and single and it is assumed that they are only responsible for their own expenses and may even be supported by their families. The data from Puerto Rico and the Dominican Republic, however, show that even young, single women are making a major contribution to the household income. This is especially true for a single woman who lives at home and who may be one of several contributors to the household income. For example, in our sample of Puerto Rican women workers in the garment industry, a woman's salary never represents less than 40 percent of the total household income, while many women living alone or with their children are the sole source of support for their families (Safa 1985:103).[2]

Management prefers to hire young women because they are supposed to be more efficient, have lower rates of absenteeism, and cost less in terms of maternity benefits. In line with traditional gender ideology, some managers also believe that married women belong in the home. This belief helps to explain the overwhelming predominance of young, single women in export manufacturing, where 85 percent of women workers worldwide are under the age of 25 (ILO 1985:31). Both in Puerto Rico and the Dominican Republic, however, in a departure from the global pattern, the majority of women workers in export manufacturing are married, while there is also a considerable percentage of female heads of household, particularly in the Dominican Republic.[3] In fact, employers in the Dominican Republic indicate a preference for women with children because they feel their need to work ensures greater job commitment (Joekes 1987:59). Their economic need is shown by the fact that in the CIPAF study of women workers in the three principal free trade zones, 38 percent of the women workers claim that they are the principal breadwinner for the family. It is clear that these women are not dependent on a male wage in the way that Barrett suggests. Nevertheless, the preference for women with children has not led employers to improve their wages, which have actually been reduced through devaluation. With the exchange rates prevailing in August, 1986, the monthly average wage for these women was approximately US$90 (Joekes 1987:55).

Wages are much higher in Puerto Rico than in other areas, and in our sample most women earned between US$120 and US$129 weekly in 1980, or more than five times as much as in the Dominican Republic. Most women are paid on a piecework basis, and can increase their wage considerably with more experience and greater productivity. In Puerto Rico, despite a concerted effort to diversify industrial employment, the garment industry is still the largest industrial source of employment on the island, representing one-fourth of all manufacturing employment. The average hourly wage of US$4.28 an hour in 1988 was the lowest industrial wage on the island, but still much higher than neighboring Caribbean countries in which average hourly wages in this year fluctuated between US$.55 and US$2.10. This competition from other areas has led to a severe decline in industrial employment in Puerto Rico, including the garment industry, where employment fell 26 percent between 1976 and 1983 (Priestland and Jones 1985:6). Competition from other areas has increased with the CBI, stimulating Puerto Rico to establish a twin plant syndrome, similar to that along the Mexican border.[4] One of the plants studied in Puerto Rico was conducting the labor-intensive phase of its operations in the Dominican Republic.

Competition from other areas also helps account for the high unemployment rates in Puerto Rico, despite continuing outmigration to the United States. Unemployment rates for men are higher than for women, and in 1980 stood at 16.5 percent and 14.5 percent, respectively. Ninety percent of the Puerto Rican sample say it is easier for women to find jobs than for men, again emphasizing that these women no longer look to men as primary wage earners. This reflects the shift from an agrarian to an industrial economy since 1940, with occupational changes tending to favor female employment over male. More than half the new jobs created between 1960 and 1980 went to women, and in 1980 their participation in the manufacturing sector was approximately equal (Dept. of Labor and Human Resources 1981:2-3). By 1980, labor force participation rates for women had increased to 29.1 percent, while those for men declined from 70.1 percent in 1950 to 54.4 percent in 1980. Some men withdrew from the labor force, while others migrated to the United States in search of employment.

Export manufacturing tends to seek out areas of labor surplus because high unemployment (for men as well as women) often forces women into paid employment. In the Dominican Republic, for example, open unemployment in 1980 stood at 19 percent, and was still higher for women (25%) than for men (16.5%), many of whom are still employed in the agricultural sector. There were signs, however, that, as in Puerto Rico, women were taking on increasing responsibility for the maintenance of their families; male labor force participation rates have been declining since 1960, while female rates have increased dramatically over the same period, to 37.5 percent among women aged 15 years or more in 1980.[5] Standing (1989) notes a trend toward falling male participation rates and rising female participation rates in both developing and developed countries in the 1980s, and attributes this "global feminization" to the greater vulnerability of women workers and to the changes in the international economy noted earlier.

Increases in the female participation rate in the Dominican Republic have been greater than in Puerto Rico, where transfer payments such as welfare and food stamps reduce the need for women to work. No such transfer payments exist in the Dominican Republic, and the severe economic crisis in the Dominican Republic since 1980 has reinforced the need to incorporate additional wage earners into the family for survival. The crisis was brought on by declining terms of trade and rates of investment, resulting in sluggish growth in GDP, which averaged only 2.2 percent between 1983 and 1987 (Deere et al. 1990:19). Due to the severe external debt and public sector deficits, the Dominican government appealed to the International Monetary Fund, which imposed an austerity program resulting in devaluation, a decline in real earnings, growing unemployment, and rampant inflation.

Open unemployment stood at 28 percent of the economically active population in 1987, while inflation soared to 44.4 percent in 1988 (Deere et al. 1990:20-21). Under pressure from industrialists in the export processing zones, the Dominican government granted them access to the parallel market, thereby enabling them to buy Dominican currency at a far more favorable rate.[6] As a result, operating costs, especially labor costs, were drastically lowered. Despite increases in the minimum wage, the real wage in the Dominican Republic in July 1987 was estimated to be only 70 percent of that earned in January 1980 (Ceara 1987:26). This new exchange rate policy is the main reason for the rapid growth there of export manufacturing since 1985. As one Dominican government official proudly told me: "We have the lowest wages in the Caribbean--even lower than Haiti!"

Why don't workers protest? An abundance of surplus unskilled labor, ready to take even these low-paying jobs, and the constant threat of companies to relocate elsewhere, weakens the possibility of labor solidarity among women workers in export manufacturing. There is little investment in machinery or physical plant, so these labor-intensive firms can move to a new location at minimal cost. Labor turnover is very high, due both to the footloose nature of these plants, and to some questionable labor practices. In the Dominican Republic, one-third of the sample working in free trade zones had been employed by the same plant for less than a year (Reyes 1987:43), while in Puerto Rico a third had been working for more than ten years.[7] Workers are forced to serve an apprenticeship, which can last as long as three months, during which they receive only half the regular wage and can be discharged for any reason. Many workers cannot withstand the intense competition of piecework and the pressure of high production quotas. The normal work week is 44 hours, but many plants require employees to work overtime, whether they wish to or not, thereby placing a particular strain on women with young children. There is usually no public transportation to the free trade zones, which generally lack proper eating facilities, medical services, or child care services. Discontent is expressed in absenteeism and eventual withdrawal, rather than through unions, which do not operate in the export processing zones of the Dominican Republic, although they are not prohibited by law (Joekes 1987:46). Workers are fired and blacklisted if any union activity is detected among them.

Turnover in export manufacturing has also been attributed to the nature of the labor force recruited. Since the majority of women workers in export manufacturing are young and single, it is assumed that many of these women are only working for a few years until they marry and/or have children, thereby reinforcing a traditional sexual division of labor and dependence on a male wage. Most of the single women we interviewed in the Dominican Republic and Puerto Rico, however, plan to continue working after they marry and/or have children, which again suggests that gender ideology is changing. In fact, in the Puerto Rican sample, a higher percentage of single women than married women or female heads of household feel that married women with children should work, probably reflecting changes in attitude due to their age differences. Given the high rates of unemployment and cost of living in both countries, younger women especially realize they cannot depend solely on a male wage to support a family.

In Puerto Rico, where all the plants studied are unionized, working conditions are considerably better, with shorter work weeks, comprehensive medical insurance, paid vacations, and other fringe benefits provided both by the government and the union contract. Nevertheless, workers still lack public transport and child care facilities, though the majority of women workers see the latter as a need and would be willing to pay for it. The relative stability of employment helps to explain the high proportion of long-term employees, many of whom have worked in the same plant for twenty to thirty years, although there is no increase in salary with seniority. The greatest problem facing these women is the possible loss of employment due to production cutbacks and possible plant closings. In fact, one plant did close down in the process of the fieldwork, but because of union regulations, workers were given the opportunity to relocate to another branch plant of the same firm in a nearby town. All of the plants have been plagued with production cutbacks, which has brought about periodic loss of employment for 85 percent of the Puerto Rican women in the sample. Because of the many years they have been working in the garment industry, the older workers do not feel capable of starting a new job and are not likely to be hired over younger workers. Thus, the lack of job alternatives also restricts labor unrest among women workers in export manufacturing.

In the Dominican Republic, the job alternatives open to women are even more limited. In 1983, 30.8 percent of Dominican women were still employed in domestic service (Duarte et al. 1989:113), while others tried to eke out a living in the informal economy as self-employed vendors or artisans. In fact, many Dominican factory workers try to supplement their meager incomes with a *sam*, or rotating credit association, and other informal economic activities. Job advancement is also limited because there are relatively few technical or supervisory personnel, most of whom are men and often foreigners (ILO 1985:56).

Thus, many factors contribute to the lack of class consciousness and worker solidarity in these new industrial plants, including the youth and constant turnover among workers, their recent entry into industrial employment, low wages, high unemployment, lack of job alternatives, the fear of plant closures, and restrictive labor legislation which prohibits unions, strikes, and other forms of protest. All of these are class-related factors which could apply as well to men. In fact, we have seen that these women are entering the labor force in increasing numbers in part because of the difficulties men face in finding a decent job. Still, women suffer from certain gender-specific disadvantages in the labor market which are rooted in their position in the household. Barrett (1980:157) is correct in maintaining that women's primary role in the family prevents them from achieving full legitimacy as workers and increases the possibility of their exploitation in the workplace. Women's increasing importance as wage earners has not yet been recognized, and management, unions, and the state regard them as subsidiary workers. Nevertheless, the women themselves recognize the importance of their paid employment, which has had a significant impact on household authority patterns, as we shall see in the next section.

The Family, Life Cycle, and Household Composition

While Barrett underlines the importance of the family in understanding women's subordination, she fails to take into account all the structural as well as ideological factors that shape the impact of paid employment on gender roles in the family. In particular, the impact is likely to vary considerably for single women, married women, and female heads of household. These households are very different in size and composition, thereby affecting the sexual division of labor and authority patterns. At the same time, different stages in the life cycle also affect women's attitudes toward work and their identification as workers.

For example, hiring young, single women is less disruptive of traditional authority patterns because, as a daughter, a woman worker does not directly challenge the male role of economic provider in the same way a wife may (see also Lamphere 1986:127). A daughter continues to defer to her father, even if he is not working, especially if he owns the house in which the family lives. Most of the young, single women in the Puerto Rican sample are members of large rural households, in which there are usually two and often three to five persons working. The effects of this multiple wage-earning strategy can be seen in the relatively high family incomes among these single women, where over 40 percent of the households have annual incomes over US$14,000. These relatively high incomes, however, represent a particular stage in the family's life cycle; a maximum number of wage earners are contributing to the family income, but the earnings of the children will be lost as they marry and set up households of their own. No households reported income from children no longer living at home.

These large rural Puerto Rican households tend to maintain strong patriarchal traditions and to follow a strict sexual division of labor, which is supported by the extended family setting. Men are not expected to participate in housework or childcare as long as there are other women around to carry out these chores. Mothers often take over household responsibilities (such as cooking and cleaning) for their working daughters. In this way, daughters are relieved of the double burden of paid employment and household responsibilities which wives face, and as a result they feel less conscious of the need to challenge traditional gender ideology.

Tightly knit networks of kin and neighbors, who help each other out with tasks such as child care, house building, and shopping, are also maintained in these rural Puerto Rican households. Nearly all of the younger women in the sample have relatives living nearby, and over 60 percent have relatives working in the same factory, with whom they often travel to work. Though there is a strong sense of sharing and solidarity, it is not so much with fellow workers as it is with female kin and neighbors, who constitute the most important reference group for these young women.

There is little evidence of class consciousness among these young, single Puerto Rican women. They have not been working very long and are generally satisfied with their jobs. Though they are aware of problems on the job and in the larger society, such as inflation and the movement of industry to other areas, they do not identify with these issues. If they lost this job, most of these young women would look for another job rather than stay home because they need the money. Younger women are quite confident that they can find another job if they should be laid off, even in a better paying pharmaceutical or electronics firm. Nearly 80 percent have a high-school diploma, which gives them an advantage over older, less educated women. Most of them plan to continue working after marriage, and they are already saving to buy or build their own homes (still a tradition in the rural area). They are concerned with getting ahead, finding a husband, and having a family, all matters which do not challenge the existing gender ideology or system of class inequality.

Older Puerto Rican women are less optimistic and some are also more isolated and alienated than their younger counterparts. This is particularly true of female heads of household, who tend to live in the city in small households of one to three persons. They have fewer kin living nearby and tend to socialize infrequently, even with neighbors or fellow workers with whom they may have been working for many years. Small family size limits the number of wage earners per family, and many of the female heads of household depend entirely on their own salary for a living. Not surprisingly, over half of these households have the lowest incomes of US$5,000 to US$8,000 annually.

In contrast, older married Puerto Rican women whose husbands also contribute to the family often enjoy annual incomes as high as US$12,000 to over US$14,000. Despite the lack of male employment in the area, some of these men make over US$175 a week, and may be employed as managers or other lower level professionals. Most men, however, earn between US$100 and US$175 a week working in a factory, for the government, or in their own business such as carpentry or driving *públicos* (cabs that follow standard routes and take several passengers). Very few husbands are unemployed, and over half have been employed at the same job for the last five years, suggesting most of these men have stable jobs. Still, married women generally contribute from 40 to 60 percent of the household income.

Older Puerto Rican women are more likely than the younger, rural women to question management's authority and to argue for their rights. This helps explain why management prefers young workers, who are not considered as "troublesome." Many of the older workers have worked in the plant for twenty to thirty years and, in contrast to younger women, have little opportunity for obtaining another job outside the garment industry. They are very concerned with job stability and feel extremely threatened by production slow-downs and possible closure, as happened with one plant. This is particularly true of female heads of household, whose entire livelihood often depends upon their continued employment and who may even be cut off from union pensions if they are laid off before age 62. While this could tend to make them more docile, it appears that long-term paid employment has contributed to a sense of self-worth and independence among these older women, while urbanization and isolation from kin has weakened the patriarchal tradition still prevalent in the rural area. Thus, older women may identify more strongly with the workplace than younger women, but they lack the cohesion necessary to develop a sense of collective action and to promote class solidarity.

Paid employment has had a greater impact on the sexual division of labor in the households of married women than in those of single women. Married women tend to live in nuclear families, and they cannot count on the assistance of other household members as much as single women can. The husband is forced to help out more with household chores, although primary responsibility still rests with the wife. Age also makes a difference, with a slightly higher percentage of young married women saying their husbands help out, reflecting generational changes in gender roles.

Authority patterns have shown a more decisive shift than the sexual division of labor. In the Puerto Rican sample, 57.2 percent of the married women said that they shared important household decisions with their husbands, compared to the 31.4 percent who said their husbands are the major decision-makers, with older women being somewhat more conservative. Because both are working, earnings are usually pooled for household expenses and husbands no longer have exclusive budgetary control, as was common when the man was the sole breadwinner (Safa 1974:44). Most importantly, most Puerto Rican men now expect their wives to work and no longer consider it a threat to their authority. In fact, none of the divorced or separated women, most of whom are over 45, blamed the breakdown of their marriages on their working outside the home. Marital breakdown was generally blamed on the man's personal behavior, such as drinking, seeing other women, or jealousy. Most men were employed at the time of the breakdown, suggesting that unemployment and the inability of the man to carry out his role as economic provider was also not a major problem. According to the women, their husbands were not threatened by their working. It appears that paid employment, while not precipitating marital breakdown, at least enables women to leave an unsatisfactory marriage by providing them with alternative sources of income.

In the Dominican Republic, the industrialization program is much more recent than in Puerto Rico, and nearly half the women workers in the CIPAF sample have been employed less than two years. These women are also much younger than the Puerto Rican sample: 68.4 percent of the Dominican women in the sample are under 30 years of age compared to 43.9 percent of the Puerto Rican women. Nevertheless, 51 percent of the Dominican women workers are married and 27 percent are female heads of household. Two-thirds of the Dominican women who identified themselves as married lived in consensual unions, which are far more prevalent than in Puerto Rico, where almost all of the women in the sample who identified themselves as married had been wed in a church or civil ceremony. Fertility levels are also higher, with almost half of the Dominican women with children having three or more children (Catanzaro 1986), compared to 12.7 percent of the Puerto Rican respondents.[8]   In part, this is due to intensive family planning programs, which have been more widespread in Puerto Rico than in the Dominican Republic. Almost 78 percent of the Puerto Rican respondents used some method of contraception, of whom more than half had been sterilized, compared to only 27.6 percent of Dominican respondents.

In spite of rapid educational advances in both countries, general educational levels are higher in Puerto Rico than in the Dominican Republic, where in 1981 15 percent of women had finished high school, compared with 39 percent in Puerto Rico in 1980 (Duarte et al. 1989:64; Presser and Kishor 1991:60). Nevertheless, the educational levels of the women workers in the two samples are roughly comparable and in both cases 39 percent of the sample have completed high school. The higher percentage of high school graduates in our Dominican sample compared to the national average demonstrates that Dominican women workers in export processing are drawn from the better educated segment. In comparing them to the Puerto Rican sample, however, it also must be remembered that most of the women in the Dominican sample are much younger, and younger women generally have higher educational levels. Many Dominican women workers continue to study at night or on weekends as they work.

As in Puerto Rico, life cycle has a profound impact on the way in which women regard their earnings and their contribution to the household economy. While 37.7 percent of Dominican women workers consider themselves the principal economic provider, the figure is lower for single and married women, and much higher (75%) for female heads of households, most of whom are divorced. Among married women, 57.4 percent consider their husbands to be the principal economic provider and the person chiefly responsible for basic items such as food and housing. The majority of single and married women maintain, however, that their families could not survive without their wages, suggesting that their wages are not supplementary but are making an essential contribution to the family income.

When this study was conducted in 1981, the unemployment rate among the husbands of these Dominican workers was lower than the national average (11 percent vs. 17.7 percent), and a number of them held fairly good jobs in factories or other skilled occupations. The importance of men's wages in the household economy of Dominican women workers may help explain the persistence of strong patriarchal authority patterns. Eighty percent of the married women in the Dominican sample consider their husbands to be the heads of the household, and the men tend to dominate financial decisions such as making major purchases or paying the bills. Nevertheless, couples are beginning to share decisions on matters such as the number of children to have and the children's education, while the majority of married women make their own decisions on matters such as the use of contraceptives and what organizations to join.

Dominican women in consensual unions have a greater tendency to make their own decisions regarding finances and childrearing than women who are legally married, suggesting that the former may be less subordinate to men and less dependent on them economically (see also Brown 1975).[9] In contrast, when women were asked their opinions about women's rights (such as sharing household tasks, the right to work outside the home, and to have equal access to education and equal opportunity in the workplace), women in consensual unions generally favored less equality for women than women who were legally married; the majority of women, however, were in favor of more egalitarian relationships. This difference may be partially explained by the higher educational level of legally married women, 49 percent of whom have completed high school in contrast to 23 percent of women in consensual unions. Higher educational level and legal marriage may be associated with a higher socioeconomic class, suggesting a difference in class background between the two groups of women. The greater receptivity of women in consensual unions to patriarchal norms, however, also suggests that these women may want the relative economic security and high status that is supposed to accompany legal marriage. Their receptivity suggests that while women in consensual unions may enjoy greater autonomy than those in a conjugal relationships, they also must carry a greater burden of responsibility for maintaining the family than women who are legally married. To oblige a man to assume this responsibility, a woman cannot directly challenge his role as head of the household and thus she is forced to support the maintenance of patriarchal authority patterns. This strong indication of the persistence of traditional gender ideology reflects the constraints women face in raising a family on their own.

The extreme poverty which most Dominican female heads of household suffer helps explain the continued dependence upon men as providers. Even in Puerto Rico, female heads of household are generally poorer than single or married women because they are largely dependent on their low wages for survival. In the Puerto Rican sample, most female heads of household are older than married women and living alone or with other adults. They are thus able to manage on their low wage, particularly if they own their own home. Half of the female heads of household in the Puerto Rican sample receive some assistance from the government, mostly in the form of food stamps, and some have older children or other relatives contributing to the household; over half, however, have no other source of income other than their salary. Clearly this sample of employed female heads of household differs from the growing number of Puerto Rican female heads dependent on welfare for their support, which increased from 18 to 24 percent from 1970 to 1980 (Colón et al. 1988:26).

As noted above, Dominican female heads of household receive no government assistance and many in the sample have young children to support, making their situation far more precarious. In 1980, employed female heads of household in the urban areas of the Dominican Republic earned only slightly more than half as much as male heads from their principal occupation (Baez 1985:57). Female-headed households often result from unstable consensual unions, and these women may have to support children from more than one union. Therefore, it is not surprising that they would prefer to have men share this responsibility.

These data do not prove that paid employment is the only factor explaining the change in gender ideology that has taken place in some Dominican and Puerto Rican households, particularly because a comparative sample of non-working women was not undertaken.[10] Gender ideology is affected by other factors such as age, household composition, the life cycle, rural vs. urban residence, level of education, and length of employment. It appears that paid employment has a greater impact on wives than on daughters because wives play a critical role in the household division of labor. It also appears that changes in gender ideology have been more extensive in Puerto Rico than in the Dominican Republic, where most married women still regard husbands as the principal economic providers and heads of household. Undoubtedly, many other factors need to be taken into account to explain the wider acceptance of female paid employment and more egalitarian authority patterns in Puerto Rican than in Dominican working-class households, including migration and greater exposure to the women's movement in the United States, level of education, and the virtually total transformation from an agrarian to an urban industrial society, all of which have had less impact in the Dominican Republic. High and prolonged male unemployment has probably weakened men's roles as economic providers to a greater degree in Puerto Rico than in the Dominican Republic, where it has only recently been made more acute by the economic crisis.[11] But in both areas, we can begin to see the erosion of patriarchal authority patterns as women become essential contributors to the household economy.

Role of the State

The final factor to be taken into account in examining the impact of paid employment on the status of women workers in export manufacturing is the role of the state. For countries to remain competitive in the international market, governments must assure export manufacturers a cheap and reliable labor force and may institute restrictive legislation prohibiting unions, strikes, and other forms of labor unrest. Governments fear that labor unrest and higher wages will induce export manufacturing industries to move elsewhere, as happened in Jamaica under the Manley government (Bolles 1983) and in Puerto Rico with the extension of the federal minimum wage law to the island. Nevertheless, the ILO (1985:62) claims that "there appears to be no correlation between restrictive labour legislation or unionization and attractiveness for foreign investment." The ILO maintains that there are great differences in unionization rates by country and by industry and that multinational enterprises (not only those employing mainly women) are more likely to be unionized than national enterprises.

The CIPAF data from the Dominican Republic contradict the ILO assertions regarding the level of unionization in multinationals and national enterprises. There are no labor unions in the export processing zones of the Dominican Republic, although 70 percent of the women interviewed in the CIPAF survey indicated they were in favor of unionization. Unions are not legally prohibited in the free trade zones and, in fact, workers' right to organize is supposedly required under the United States General System of Preferences and the Caribbean Basin Initiative, both of which have been extended to the Dominican Republic (Joekes 1987:46). In the CIPAF study, comparative data were drawn from women working in national manufacturing industries, and it was found that one-fourth of these women are unionized compared to none in the free trade zones. In addition, among women working in national manufacturing industries, wages were generally higher than in the free trade zones, and daily working hours were shorter (Ricourt 1986:55). Part of the wage differential may be explained by the fact that 65 percent of the women in national industries had received salary raises compared to 46 percent in the free trade zones, who have generally been working for less time (Ricourt 1986:55-56).

Nevertheless, wages in the export processing zones fall well below the mean level of women's earnings in the Dominican Republic and, because they are tied to the minimum wage, they are unlikely to be raised without government support (Joekes 1987:71). As noted above, labor costs have actually been lowered by the government granting industrialists in the export processing zones access to the parallel market, which gives them a far better exchange value for the dollar. Although wages were raised after devaluation of the Dominican peso, the actual average real wage in manufacturing industries was reduced 17 percent between 1981 and 1984 (Joekes 1987:54-55). At the same time, worker productivity in the Dominican Republic is estimated at 70 percent of United States levels, which is higher than in almost all Caribbean and Central American countries (Joekes 1987:47-48); therefore, employers could clearly afford to pay higher wages.

Several studies have noted that the discipline in the Dominican export manufacturing plants is brutal, with women not being allowed to talk to anyone or to go to the bathroom and with some women being forced to stand for hours (e.g., Corten and Duarte 1986; Catanzaro 1986; Ricourt 1986; Reyes 1987). The Dominican respondents also reported that women workers were sexually harassed or given privileges in exchange for sexual favors to supervisors or managers. Workers have lost their jobs for attempting to organize unions or other pro-labor activity, and they have been blacklisted by other firms in the zone as well. Women who have tried to take complaints of mistreatment or unjust dismissal to the government Labor Office have generally been rejected in favor of management. It is not surprising, then, that in the CIPAF survey, less than 20 percent of the women had ever presented complaints to the Labor Office (Catanzaro 1986).

State services for workers are painfully inadequate. There is no public transportation to the zones, forcing women to use private minibuses which are costly, hazardous, and distant from many of their residences. Some women are forced to take two busses, so the trip can last over an hour. Public child care is also lacking and housing is very expensive, leading many women to leave their children with relatives in the rural area. The lack of state health services is a major cause of women's absenteeism and reduced productivity; some industrialists are now consequently offering health facilities to workers. State health services are very slow, there is an appalling lack of personnel and supplies, and services are not extended to workers' families, causing secondary absenteeism among women with children (Joekes 1987:49-50).

In Puerto Rico, working conditions in unionized plants are much better. The majority of the Puerto Rican respondents feel that unions have brought much improvement, including fringe benefits such as medical insurance, vacation, and retirement pay. The most important concerns of workers, however, are higher wages and more job stability, and unions in Puerto Rico have been rather ineffective in promoting either. Their leadership realizes that industry has been leaving the island because there is low-wage competition elsewhere, including in the Dominican Republic, where the firm studied already has a twin plant which does the initial processing. Therefore, they try to offer workers compensation in the form of fringe benefits rather than higher wages. Unions are having increasing difficulty offering attractive contracts, however, because the Puerto Rican government already offers an array of worker benefits, including medical care, unemployment insurance, and social security. Union membership in the manufacturing sector has declined from 30 percent in 1970 to just seven percent in 1988, due both to the problems outlined above and to their neglect of women workers (Santiago Rivera 1989:94). In the plants studied, the International Ladies Garment Workers Union (ILGWU) never called meetings of the general membership, except to inform them of new terms agreed upon between the union leadership and management.

State transfer programs, all of which are supported by the Federal government, while ostensibly a subsidy to workers, actually enable marginal industries (such as garment manufacturing) to continue paying low wages and to weather fluctuations in demand by temporarily laying off workers. For example, workers can claim unemployment insurance for production slow-downs that do not enable them to work a full 40-hour week. The food stamp program, which covers about half of the population, enables Puerto Ricans to buy food at cheap prices. About one-fourth of the households in the Puerto Rican sample received food stamps--chiefly the large, rural households or female-headed households. Transfer payments thus have become a device for keeping low-wage, labor-intensive industries on the island. Plant managers complain that these transfer payments have reduced the work ethic of the Puerto Rican worker, causing absenteeism and withdrawal from the labor force. Nevertheless, nearly 90 percent of the Puerto Rican respondents indicated that they expected to stay on the job indefinitely and 85 percent indicated they would look for another job if they were laid off, indicating a strong work commitment. In addition, over half of the respondents (especially female heads of household) were never absent from work during the past year, even for illness or pregnancy. These data suggest a strong work ethic among Puerto Rican women workers, despite the opinion of some of their employers.

Puerto Rico is not able to adopt the harsh, coercive anti-labor measures of the Dominican Republic because its workers are better organized and have more options, principally transfer payments and migration. Jobs have tended to keep more women than men on the island (Monk 1981), and only about one-fifth of our sample has worked in the United States, while over 60 percent of the husbands of married women have migrated for a year or more. These workers also bring back principles of labor organization learned in the United States and are likely to be more knowledgeable about worker rights. Although Dominican migration to the United States has increased considerably during the past two decades, it still has not reached the proportions of Puerto Rico.

The state policies discussed here do not apply exclusively to women but to workers generally, demonstrating a strong class bias in favor of management, especially in the Dominican Republic. Class subordination, however, is closely linked to gender subordination, particularly in the case of state policies concerning export processing, an industry in which the majority of workers are women. For example, the lack of support services such as child care and adequate public transportation results in a special burden for women workers who have heavy domestic responsibilities. Yet the head of the ILGWU in Puerto Rico, when informed about the overwhelming desire for child care among women workers, the majority of whom were even prepared to pay for this service, rejected the notion by saying it was management's problem. Clearly the union is afraid to make any additional demands on management for fear the plants will leave the island for cheaper production sites elsewhere.

Both coercion in the Dominican Republic and co-optation in Puerto Rico have produced a relatively docile labor force. The major threat to Puerto Rican workers is the fear that plants will move elsewhere, and unions and the government seem unable to stop the exodus. In the Dominican Republic, export manufacturing plants have therefore experienced a considerable attrition rate, with one-third of the plants leaving between 1970 and 1982 (Joekes 1987:69). The continued influx of new plants and the growing importance of export manufacturing as a development strategy suggest, however, that the government will do little to deter foreign investment in the near future. We can expect to see only minimal improvement in wages, working conditions, or state services. It could be argued that the government has little choice, given its staggering debt and poor terms of trade. Nevertheless, workers are being exploited in the process, and the fact that most are women may contribute to the state's apparent indifference to their plight.

Conclusions

While export manufacturing has served to integrate women into development by offering them a new source of industrial employment, its impact on their status in the family and in the larger society is contradictory. On the one hand, by taking advantage of women's inferior position in the labor market, export manufacturing may reinforce their subordination through poorly paid, dead-end jobs. On the other hand, women's increased ability to contribute to the family income may challenge traditional patriarchal authority patterns and lead to more egalitarian family structures. This is particularly true where, as in Puerto Rico and the Dominican Republic, women have become critical contributors to the household economy.

Changes in gender ideology are not simply a question of whether or not women are employed, they are also a consequence of women's contribution to the household economy.[12] The data that I have presented on Puerto Rican and Dominican women workers point to several factors that condition the contribution women make to the household economy: wages, working conditions, length of time employed and other job-related factors; structure of the household economy, in particular, the status of men's employment; the life cycle of the women employed (a determining factor in the degree of dependence on men's wages); alternative income sources for women (including not only jobs, but transfer payments and the possibility of migration); and the role of the state and unions in supporting women's demands in particular and workers' rights in general. In each of these areas, Puerto Rican women workers generally fare better than their Dominican counterparts, suggesting that they are in a better position to make a substantial contribution to the household economy and therefore should have more leverage in family decisions.

The data confirm this hypothesis. It appears that with the increased incorporation of Puerto Rican women into paid employment, there has been a fundamental change in authority patterns and the sexual division of labor in the household. Even in the Dominican Republic, the absolute authority of men in the household is being increasingly challenged, although men are still considered the head of the household. In place of the patriarchy of the past, a more egalitarian pattern is emerging in which women and men share responsibility for the maintenance of the household as well as for decision-making and some housekeeping tasks. This pattern is the result of a gradual process of negotiation, in which women use their earnings--and the family's increased dependence on them--to bargain for more authority and a more equal division of responsibility within the household (see also, Roldán 1985:275).

Among female-headed households, paid employment is often critical to the family's survival, and income levels are very low. This is particularly true in the Dominican Republic, where women do not have recourse to transfer payments as in Puerto Rico. The data suggest, however, that these female heads of household feel even more vulnerable than do other women workers and have not lost their ideological dependence on a male provider. In fact, we have seen that women in consensual unions in the Dominican Republic remain committed to patriarchal norms, at least at the ideological level. It seems that women prefer to bargain for more authority and respect in the household than to live alone with their children and fend for themselves. The question is: Why?

The evidence presented suggests that women, even if they are working and major contributors to the household economy, prefer a stable conjugal relationship, though they are aware that it subjects them to male dominance. As Stolcke (1984:292) notes, there are material as well as ideological pressures that continue to reinforce the nuclear family among the working class. The extreme poverty of female-headed households makes all women realize how difficult it is to get along without a male provider. Women may be disillusioned with men as providers, but they are also aware of the severe disadvantages they face in the labor market. Women's ideological commitment to the family is more difficult to explain. As Stolcke (1984:286) notes, the family provides women with a social identity as wives and mothers which proletarianization as wage workers has not diminished. This is evident among the women workers studied here, who continue to identify primarily as wives and mothers, despite their increasing importance as wage earners. In fact, most of these women now consider paid employment part of their domestic role because they are working to contribute to the family's survival rather than to increase their own self-esteem or personal autonomy.

Thus, the family provides women with a social identity at the same time that it is a source of their subordination. Barrett fails to recognize the benefits the family provides for women, and stresses only its negative aspects. It may be that the social role of wife and mother is more highly valued and less alienated in Latin American culture than in the English middle-class families upon which Barrett's theory is based. Class differences are also apparent because middle-class women can obtain greater gratification from their employment than can the working-class women studied here. It seems to me that these Dominican and Puerto Rican women are aware of the contradictory nature of the family. But they are attempting to resolve this contradiction by trying to establish a more egalitarian relationship with their husbands, while retaining the family as a source of emotional and material support and social identity.

At least the women studied here have been more successful in negotiating change at the household level than in the public world of work. It is clear from the data presented that in the Dominican Republic, women workers are subject to extraordinary exploitation by management, and they receive little or no support from the government in their efforts to achieve better wages and working conditions. Puerto Rican women workers are much better off, but they too are limited by a paternalistic union which refuses to recognize many of their needs and by a government very dependent on foreign investment. Here the fault lies more with the lack of support women workers receive from government, political parties, and unions than with the women themselves. At present these women workers have no adequate vehicles to express their grievances nor to transform their sense of exploitation (which is very real) into greater class consciousness. Until women workers are given the same legitimacy as men, and not regarded as subsidiary or supplementary, they will be more vulnerable as a source of cheap labor.

Women's increasing importance as wage earners should enable them to achieve greater recognition and higher levels of class consciousness as workers in their struggle with unions, management, and the state. It appears from the data presented that these institutions have proven more resistant to change than has the family, and they are still governed by a traditional gender ideology which the women themselves have begun to abandon. Dominican and Puerto Rican women workers have effected considerable change at the household level, one domain over which they still have some control. Their exploitation and vulnerability at the extra-household level may explain their reluctance to abandon the family and their continued primary identification as wives and mothers.

Notes

1.   I wish to acknowledge the financial support of the National Institute of Mental Health for collection of the Puerto Rican survey data, and the Wenner Gren Foundation for collection and analysis of the in-depth interviews in both Puerto Rico and the Dominican Republic. Several institutions and individuals assisted me in this endeavor. Foremost thanks go to Magaly Pineda, Director, and to the other staff members of CIPAF, who supplied me with the data they had collected on Dominican women workers. I am grateful to Francis Pou, who assisted me in conducting the in-depth interviews in the Dominican Republic, and to Lorraine Catanzaro, Quintina Reyes and Milagros Ricourt, whose analysis of the survey data in their M.A. theses greatly facilitated my own study. Susan Joekes's data on export manufacturing provided me with valuable insights. I also wish to thank Carmen Perez, who conducted the survey on the Puerto Rican women in 1980, and Clifford Depin and his staff of the Puerto Rican office of the International Ladies Garment Workers Union, who facilitated access to the factories and data from their own files. Finally, my appreciation goes to

Lourdes Benería, Carmen Diana Deere and June Nash, for their critique of an earlier draft, and to María del Carmen Baerga for her editorial comments on the Spanish draft of this paper, many of which have been incorporated here.

An earlier version of this chapter appeared in Stichter and Parpart (1990). I appreciate their permission to publish a revised version here. A Spanish version will also be published by Editorial Universitaria in Puerto Rico in a book on the garment industry edited by María del Carmen Baerga.

2.   This percentage represents the total salary of the women compared to total family income and not her actual contribution to the household, which was unfortunately not asked. Among single women especially this contribution may be less, since they tend to reserve a portion for their personal expenses. Another indication in the survey of the extent to which single women are contributing to the household is the number of expenses such as food, housing, and utilities in which they share, although they are rarely the sole contributor as in the case of some married women or female heads of household. The in-depth interviews also indicate single women contribute less.

3.   I use the term "female head of household" to denote women who are separated, divorced, widowed, or single mothers, that is, all women who have no stable conjugal partner. In Puerto Rico, the majority of female heads of household are older and live apart, though younger unmarried mothers may live with their parents.

4.   In twin plants, the final and more skilled stages of the manufacturing operations are carried out in Puerto Rico, with the initial stages in cheaper wage areas such as the Dominican Republic, Haiti, and other Caribbean islands. In January 1989, Puerto Rico had a total of 60 twin plants, 29 of which were located in the Dominican Republic (Deere et al. 1990:171).

5.   The figures given are derived from national surveys conducted by the National Office of Statistics and the National Planning Office in 1980, which are considered more reliable than the census. The census excludes from the economically active population persons willing to work but not seeking employment at the time, and this results in lower female labor force participation rates. For example, the 1981 census reported a female labor participation rate of 27 percent (Duarte et al. 1989:105,112).

6.   Prior to this measure, producers in the free trade zones were required to handle their foreign exchange transactions through the official market, in which the peso was priced at a par with the US dollar, which had the effect of inflating the dollar costs of their operations (Joekes 1987:38).

7.   The Puerto Rican sample is not representative of the female labor force in the island's garment industry; it deliberately over-represented women who had been garment workers for more than ten years in order to more fully assess the impact of long-term employment on women's status. We selected a sample of about 20 percent of the women who had worked for less

than ten years, compared to 25 percent for those working more than ten years.

8. Given the youth of the Dominican sample, the number of children may reach even higher levels. In both countries, there has been a rapid decline in fertility since 1950, but in Puerto Rico the fertility rate is even lower, at 2.8 births per woman in 1980, compared to 4.2 in the Dominican Republic (Presser and Kishor 1991:61; Duarte et al. 1989:22).

9. The apparent autonomy of women in consensual unions may be due to the fact that many of them have children from previous unions; the current partner has little financial responsibility or authority over them. A man's authority is also diminished when he moves into a woman's house.

10. Another study comparing married and divorced Puerto Rican women also found a more egalitarian relationship among married women, who share household decisions with their husbands and who have achieved a more flexible division of household tasks (Muñoz Vasquez 1979).

11. I am indebted to Emilio Pantojas-Garcia for this insight.

12. I do not wish to suggest that women's contribution to the household economy in Puerto Rico or in the Dominican Republic starts with industrialization. In Puerto Rico, for example, the census figures show that female participation rates were higher in 1930 and 1940 (before the beginning of Operation Bootstrap) than they were after, due largely to the large-scale incorporation of women into the home needlework and tobacco industry (Picó de Hernández 1979:27). But export processing industrialization led to the massive incorporation of women outside the home, often with stable, long-term employment and better salaries, tending to place women workers on a more equal footing with men.

References

Abreu, Alfonso, Manuel Cocco, Carlos Despradel, Eduardo García Michael, Arturo Peguero
  1989   Las Zonas Francas Industriales: El Exito de una Política Económica   Santo Domingo: Centro de Orientación Económica.

Baez, C.
  1985   *La Subordinación Social de la Mujer Dominicana en Cifras.* Santo Domingo: Dirección   General   de   Promoción   de   la Mujer/INSTRAW.

Barrett, Michele
  1980   *Women's Oppression Today.* London: Verso Editions.

Bolles, Lynn
  1983 Kitchens Hit by Priorities: Employed Working-Class Jamaican Women Confront the IMF. In: *Women, Men and the International Division of Labor,* edited by J. Nash and M. P. Fernandez Kelly. Pp. 138-160. Albany: State University of New York Press.

Brown, Susan
  1975 Love Unites Them and Hunger Separates Them: Poor Women in the Dominican Republic. In: *Toward an Anthropology of Women,* edited by R. Reiter. Pp. 322-332. New York: Monthly Review Press.

Catanzaro, Lorraine
  1986 Women, Work and Consciousness: Export Processing in the Dominican Republic. Unpublished Masters Thesis, Center for Latin American Studies, University of Florida.

Ceara, Miguel
  1987 Situación Socioeconómica Actual y su Repercusión en la Situación de la Madre y el Niño. Santo Domingo: Instituto Tecnológico de Santo Domingo (INTEC) and United Nations Childrens Fund (UNICEF).

Colón, Alice, Marya Muñoz, Neftali García, Y Idsa Alegría
  1988 Trayectoria de la Participación Laboral de las Mujeres en Puerto Rico de los Años 1950 a 1985. In: *Crisis, Sociedad y Mujer: Estudio Comparativo entre Países de América (1950-1985).* Habana: Federación de Mujeres Cubanas.

Corten, Andre and Isis Duarte
  1986 Proceso de Proletarización de Mujeres: Las Trabajadoras de Industrias de Ensamblaje en la República Dominicana. In: *Trabajadores Urbanos: Ensayos sobre Fuerza Laboral en República Dominicana,* edited by I. Duarte with A. Corten and F. Pou. Pp. 213-262. Santo Domingo: Editora Universitaria, Universidad Autónoma de Santo Domingo.

Dauhajre, Andrés, E. Riley, R. Mena, and J.A. Guerrero
  1989 *Impacto Económico de las Zonas Francas Industriales de Exportación en la República Dominicana.* Santo Domingo: Fundación Economía y Desarrollo, Inc.

Deere, Carmen Diana, Peggy Antrobus, Lynn Bolles, Edwin Melendez, Peter
Phillips, Marcia Rivèra, Helen Safa
1990   *In the Shadows of the Sun: Caribbean Development Alternatives
and U.S. Policy*. Boulder: Westview Press.

Dept. of Labor and Human Resources (Departamento del Trabajo y
Recursos Humanos), Estado Libre Asociado de Puerto Rico
1981   *La Participación de la Mujer en la Fuerza Laboral*.   Informe
Especial E-27.

Duarte, Isis, Clara Baez, Carmen J. Gómez, and Marina Aríza
1989   Población y Condición de la Mujer en República Dominicana.
Santo Domingo: Instituto de Estudios de Población y Desarrollo.
Estudio No. 6.

Fernández-Kelly, María Patricia
1983   *For We Are Sold, I and My People: Women and Industry in
Mexico's Frontier*. Albany: State University of New York Press.

Hartman, Heidi
1981   The Family as the Locus of Gender, Class and Political Struggle:
The Example of Housework. *Signs* 6(3):366-394.

ILO (International Labor Organization/United Nations Centre on
Transnational Corporations)
1985 ˙ *Women Workers in Multinational Enterprises in Developing
Countries*. Geneva: ILO.

Joekes, Susan
1987   *Employment in Industrial Free Trade Zones in the Dominican
Republic*. Washington: International Center for Research on
Women. Prepared for USAID/Dominican Republic.

Joekes, Susan with Roxana Moayedi
1987   *Women and Export Manufacturing: A Review of the Issues and
AID Policy*. Washington: International Center for Research on
Women. Prepared for the Office of Women in Development,
USAID.

Lamphere, Louise
1986   From Working Daughters to Working Mothers: Production and
Reproduction in an Industrial Community. *American Ethnologist*
13(1):118-130.

Lim, Linda
   1990   Women's Work in Export Factories: The Politics of a Cause. In:
           Persistent Inequalities: Women and World Development, edited by
           Irene Tinker. Pp. 101-119. New York: Oxford University Press.

Monk, Janice
   1981   Social Change and Sexual Differences in Puerto Rican Rural
           Migration. In: *Papers in Latin American Geography in Honor of
           Lucia C. Harrison*, edited by O. Horst. Pp. 28-43. Muncie:
           Conference of Latin Americanist Geographers.

Muñoz Vasquez, Marya
   1979   The Effects of Role Expectations on the Marital Status of Urban
           Puerto Rican Women. In: *The Puerto Rican Woman:
           Perspectives on Culture, History and Society*, edited by E. Acosta-
           Belén. Pp. 75-84. New York: Praeger Publishers.

Ong, Aihwa
   1987   *Spirits of Resistance and Capitalist Discipline: Factory Women in
           Malaysia*. Albany: State University of New York Press.

Pantojas-Garcia, Emilio
   1985   The U.S. Caribbean Basin Initiative and the Puerto Rican
           Experience: Some Parallels and Lessons.   *Latin American
           Perspectives* 12(4):105-128.

Picó de Hernández, Isabel
   1979   The History of Women's Struggle for Equality in Puerto Rico. In:
           The Puerto Rican Woman, edited by E. Acosta-Belén. Pp. 25-37.
           New York: Praeger Publishers.

Presser, Harriet B. and Sunita Kishor
   1991   Economic Development and Occupational Sex Segregation in
           Puerto Rico: 1950-1980. *Population and Development Review*
           17(1):53-85.

Priestland, Carl H. and Smiley Jones
   1980   *Problems Facing the Local Apparel Industry of Puerto Rico*. A
           Study for the Puerto Rican Needle Trades Association and the
           Economic Development Administration. San Juan: Economic
           Development Administration.

Reyes, Quintina
   1987   *Comparative Study of Dominican Women Workers in Domestic and
           Free Trade Zone Industries*. Unpublished Masters Thesis, Center
           for Latin American Studies, University of Florida.

Ricourt, Milagros
   1986   *Free Trade Zones, Development and Female Labor Force in the
           Dominican Republic*. Unpublished Masters Thesis, Center for
           Latin American Studies, University of Florida.

Roldán, Martha
   1985   Industrial Outworking, Struggles for the Reproduction of
           Working-Class Families and Gender Subordination. In: *Beyond
           Employment: Household, Gender and Subsistence*, edited by N.
           Redclift and E. Mingione. Pp. 248-285. New York: Basil
           Blackwell Inc.

Rosen, Bernard
   1982   *The Industrial Connection: Achievement and the Family in
           Developing Societies*. New York: Aldine Publishing.

Safa, Helen I.
   1974   *The Urban Poor of Puerto Rico: A Study in Development and
           Inequality*. New York: Holt, Rinehart and Winston.

   1981   Runaway Shops and Female Employment: The Search for Cheap
           Labor. *Signs* 7(2):418-433.

   1985   Female Employment in the Puerto Rican Working Class. In:
           Women and Change in Latin America, edited by J. Nash and H.
           Safa. Pp. 84-104. South Hadley: Bergin and Garvey Publishers.

Santiago Rivera, Carlos
   1989   Industrial Reconversion and Economic Restructuring: The
           Challenge for the Puerto Rican Labor Movement. *Radical
           America* 23(1):91-98.

Standing, Guy
   1989   Global Feminization through Flexible Labor. *World Development*
           17(7):1077-1096.

Stichter, Sharon and Jane L. Parpart (editors)
  1992   *Women, Employment and the Family and the International Division of Labour.* Philadelphia: Temple University Press.

Stolcke, Verena
  1984   The Exploitation of Family Morality: Labor Systems and Family Structure on Sao Paulo Coffee Plantations, 1850-1979. In: *Kinship Ideology and Practice in Latin America*, edited by R.T. Smith. Pp. 264-296. Greensboro: University of North Carolina Press.

Tiano, Susan
  1986   Women and Industrial Development in Latin America. *Latin American Research Review* XXI(3):157-170.

Tilly, Louise and Joan W. Scott
  1978   *Women, Work and Family.* New York: Holt, Rinehart and Winston.

Ward, Kathryn (editor)
  1990   *Women Workers and Global Restructuring.* Ithaca: Industrial and Labor Relations Press.

About the Contributors

PAMELA A. DEVOE has been engaged in research involving migrants and change since the early 1970s. As an Asian specialist she became interested in the influx of Southeast Asian refugees with whom she has carried out research since 1980. Active in the American Anthropological Association and its subgroups involving migrants, refugees, and other displaced persons, she is also contributing editor for the Committee on Refugee Issues and a member of its executive board.

MARGARET E. GALEY, formerly professional staff member, Committee on Foreign Affairs, United States House of Representatives, is currently project director, Women, Politics, and the United Nations, Elliott School of International Affairs, George Washington University.

CHRISTINA H. GLADWIN is an anthropologist-agricultural economist with a 1978 Ph.D. from the Food Research Institute, Stanford University. Her experience in development issues and international agriculture derives from living and studying in Cape Coast, Ghana (1967-69), Puebla, Mexico (1973-74), and Totonicapan, Guatemala (1977-79). Since 1980, she has studied family farms in Florida and taught in the Food and Resource Economics Department, University of Florida.

MARIE WITHERS OSMOND, Associate Professor of Sociology at Florida State University, has research interests in the family in comparative perspective, social inequality (race, class, and gender), and institutional linkages with families. Her most recent publications include chapters in *The Handbook of Marriage and the Family* and the *Sourcebook of Family Theories and Methods*, and articles in the *Journal of Marriage and the Family, Journal of Family Issues,* and *Journal of Alternative Lifestyles.* Currently she is writing a monograph on gender and family analysis.

HELEN I. SAFA is the author of *The Urban Poor of Puerto Rico*, co-author of *In the Shadows of the Sun: Caribbean Development Alternatives and U.S. Policy*, co-editor of *Women and Change in Latin America*, and author of numerous articles on women and development, particularly in Latin America. Her work on migration, urbanization, ethnicity, and development has appeared in a variety of books and scholarly journals. Dr. Safa is currently Professor of Anthropology and Latin American Studies at the University of Florida, where she was formerly Director of the Center for Latin American Studies. Past president of the Latin American Studies Association, she has also served on the selection committees of the Fulbright program and the Inter-American Foundation.

BROOKE GRUNDFEST SCHOEPF is an economic and medical anthropologist who received her Ph.D. from Columbia University in 1969. She has taught and conducted research in eight African countries since 1974 and has published more than 50 works on development and health issues.

Index